# Drug Testing At Work

# A Guide For Employers

Beverly A. Potter, Ph. D.

J. Sebastian Orfali, M.A.

Ronin Publishig, Inc.

Post Office Box 522, Berkeley, CA 94701

www.roninpub.com

Published by
**Ronin Publishing, Inc.**
Post Office Box 522
Berkeley, CA 94701
www.roninpub.com

*Drug Testing At Work*
*A Guide For Employers*
ISBN: 1-57951-007-8
Copyright® 1998 by Beverly A. Potter

NOTE: Substantial portions of material in this book were published under the title, *Drug Testing At Work: A Guide For Employers And Employees,* and was copyright ® 1990, 1995, by Beverly Potter & Sebastian Orfali.

Printed in the United States of America

9 8 7 6 5 4 3 2 1


Cover design: Judy July, Generic Typography
Design & layout: Beverly Potter

Printed by Bertelsmann Industry Services, Inc.
Distributed by Publishers Group West

# Acknowledgements

We are grateful to the many people who helped us in research-ing, writing, editing and producing this book, and to the companies who gave us information about their services and products.

A special thanks to the following people for giving us help and material:
Mark Hart of Hewlett-Packard, David Smith, M.D.,of the Haight Ashbury Free Medical Clinic; Barbara Lang Rutkowski, Ed. D., and Arthur D. Rutkowski, J.D., of the newsletter, *Employment Law Up-date;* William Adams, Esq., of Orrick, Herrington, and Sutcliffe; John True, Esq., of the Employment Law Center; Daphne Macklin of the American Civil Liberties Union, Peter Strom of the State of Califor-nia Department of Personnel Administration; Kathy Deines of PharmChem Laboratories, and Sydney Perry of the State of Califor-nia Department of Personnel Administration Policy Development Office.

We appreciate the following organizations for informtion re-garding their products and services:
Hewlett-Packard Company, Inc., Roche Diagnostic Systems, a Division of Hoffman-LaRoche Inc., PharmChem Laboratories, Inc., Rutkowski and Associates, Inc., The American Civil Liberties Union, and the Haight Ashbury Free Medical Clinic, Inc.

NOTE TO READER:

Substance abuse prevention and drug/alcohol testing programs bring risk of legal liability if conducted improperly or in violation of Federal, State or local laws. Compliance with Federal laws does not necessarily mean that an employer is in compliance with State and local requirements. Employers' obligation for maintaining a drug-free workplace and employees' rights are continually evolving.

The material herein is presented for reference and informational purposes only, not as legal advice. The authors and publisher advise readers to consult an attorney specific legal advice.

# Table Of Contents

# The Authors

*Beverly A. Potter, Ph.D.,* earned her doctorate in counseling psychology from Stanford University and her masters in vocational rehabilitation counseling from San Francisco State.

Dr. Potter has had a wide range of experience with law enforcement, the criminal justice system, corporations, associations and colleges. She has trained police officers in "crisis intervention" and has been "on the beat". She has seen the problems of substance abuse first hand. As a researcher, she lived on a heroin treatment ward as a "participant observer" and she worked with inmates in the San Francisco County Jail.

Dr. Potter is a specialist in management psychology and has provided training for Hewlett-Packard, GTE, SUN, Becton-Dickinson, IRS, Stanford Medical School, Stanford University Staff Development, Design Management Institute, Department of Energy and others. She is the author of several books including *From Conflict to Cooperation: How To Mediate A Dispute, Overcoming Job Burnout: How To Renew Enthusiasm For Work, Turning Around: Keys To Motivation And Productivity, Brain Boosters: Foods And Drugs That Make You Smarter, The Worrywart's Companion: Twenty-One Ways To Soothe Yourself And Worry Smart, Finding A Path With A Heart: How To go From Burnout To Bliss,* and *The Way Of The Ronin: Riding The Ways Of Change At Work.*

*J. Sebastian Orfali, M.A.,* earned his masters degree in philosophy from the University of New Mexico. As publisher of And/Or Press and Ronin Publishing, he published over 150 books about controlled substances, health, technology and current issues, including *The Cocaine Handbook, Controlled Substanced: A Chemical And Legal Guide To The Federal Drug Laws, The Holistic Health Handbook, Secrets Of Life Extension, The Psychedelic Encyclopedia.* He is the author of *Brain Boosters: Foods And Drugs That Make You Smarter.*

# Foreword

When in presenting his administration's National Drug Control Strategy, President Bush stated that the Federal government has a responsibility to take an active role in comprehensive drug-free workplace policies. He encouraged both public and private sector employers to train supervisors on how to identify employees who use drugs, including drug testing where appropriate, and to educate employees about the established plan.

*Drug Testing At Work* is a comprehensive guide to accomplishing both objectives. The book begins with a social history of drugs including alcohol and their impact on the workplace. It correctly emphasizes that legal drugs such as alcohol and nicotine cost industry more money than do highly publicized illicit drugs such as cocaine.

A comprehensive review of drug testing methodology is presented, followed by a discussion of the legal issues of drug testing including employer liability and the right to privacy. This is a particularly important section for employers who are rushing to implement low cost programs which do not include adequate input from all sectors of the complicated workplace environment.

The section on guidelines for employers including deciding on a drug program and establishing a drug testing policy provides a framework for making such decisions. I was also happy to see a strong component on setting up employee assistance programs and preventing drug use without testing.

In this era of drug testing and discipline it should be emphasized that demand reduction prevention and employee assistance are vital elements to a comprehensive strategy aimed at reducing substance abuse in the workplace. This excellent book provides such a comprehensive view and will be of benefit to both employers and employees.

David E. Smith, M.D.
Founder and Medical Director
Haight Ashbury Free Clinic, Inc.
Research Director of Merritt Peralta Institute
Associate Clinical Professor of Occupational Medicine
    and Clinical Toxicology

At the turn of the Century Americans consumed cocaine in a variety of elixirs, tonics, medicines and just plain soda pop commonly available at the grocery store. Pictured here is an advertisement for Coca Cola™ from 1887, a time when the beverage contained cocaine.

# CHAPTER 1

# Drug Usage Past And Present

As far as we know humans have always used mood altering substances. Opium was used in Greece and Cyprus for rituals as early as 2000 B.C. Ololiuqui, a Central American flower which produces psychoactive effects similar to LSD, was used by the ancient Aztecs. Witches supposedly rubbed their bodies with hallucinogenic ointments in the Middle Ages. Historians believe that George Washington used hemp to relieve tooth and gum pain. President Ulysses Grant used cocaine while writing his memoirs. Sigmund Freud, along with many turn-of-the-century intellectuals, advocated cocaine usage for a time.

After the Civil War, doctors prescribed opium-based remedies for common maladies such as headache and skin rashes. Narcotic potions, such as "Mrs. Winslow's Soothing Syrup" and "Hooper's Anodyne, the Infant's Friend", were commonly used by Victorian ladies to calm their babies. At the turn of the century, heroin and morphine derivatives were sold legally in drugstores and by mail-order catalogues.

## Cocaine

The Peruvian Indians in the Andes have been using coca leaves for over 5,000 years, and their mild stimulation and appetite-depressing effect has been an important part of their culture. Coca was central in the Inca Indian's culture where they used the leaves as money.

When cocaine, the drug, became commercially available in a pure form in 1884, its many useful qualities were hailed worldwide by doctors. Because it worked simultaneously as a painkiller and vasoconstrictor, cocaine became a popular anesthetic for procedures, such as eye and throat surgery, in which clearing away blood was difficult. It anesthetizes the body, but keeps the mind sharp; so doctors prescribed it for the terminally ill. Cocaine was used in cough medicines, hemorrhoid balms, nasal sprays and wine. Vin Mariani, the popular coca wine, bore the endorsements of President William McKinley, Thomas Edison, and Pope Leo XIII. And, of course, cocaine was once the major ingredient in Coca-Cola®. In 1884 Freud wrote, "Absolutely no craving for further use of cocaine appears after the first or repeated, taking of the drug."

Attitudes changed and by the end of the Twentith Century crack cocaine dominated the Nation's illicit drug problem. The number of users peaked at 5.7 million in 1985 then declined and stabilized at 1.75 million in 1996. Nevertheless, supplies are abundant in nearly every city and it is estimated that around 650,000 Americans try cocaine for the first time each year. While most cocaine users in the late 1990s are older, inner-city crack addicts, there are indications of a new groups of users: teenagers smoking crack with marijuana in "blunts" which are cigars emptied of tobacco and refilled with marijuana, often in combination with another drug.

## Opiates

In the late Nineteenth Century, an estimated one in 400 Americans used opiates regularly. Parke-Davis Pharmaceuticals manufactured many products containing cocaine, including cigarettes, cheroots, coca skin salve, and face powder. By 1900, America had developed a population of opiate and cocaine addicts estimated at 250,000. Deaths, sickness, and crime caused by drugs became commonplace. By the turn of the Century public opinion began to change violently.

Despite the opposition of U.S. drug companies, many states passed laws regulating cocaine and opiates. In 1909, the import of opium was banned. In 1914, the Harrison Narcotics Act made numerous drugs illegal under Federal law. By the 1920s, cocaine, heroin, and morphine use had declined dramatically.

Once widely regarded as harmless cure-alls, cocaine and opium became America's most feared and loathed drugs and quickly went underground. Most Americans in the years after World War I indulged in bootleg gin. However, some jazz-band musicians and avant-garde actors and artists still used cocaine.

In recent years, heroin has come out of the closet once again. There has been an increasing trend in first time heroin use since 1992, with an estimated 141,000 new heroin users in 1995. The estimated numbers of people who used heroin in the previous month increased from 68,000 in 1993 to 216,000 in 1996. A large portion of these recent new users were smoking, snorting, or sniffing heroin, and most were under age 26. The increase in use and the change in delivery of the drug—from injection into the blood stream to smoking and snorting result from the greatly increased purity of heroin that is readily available in every city in the Nation.

# Marijuana

Mexican immigrants, who came north looking for jobs in the 1920s and 1930s brought marijuana with them. During prohibition, the popularity of marijuana grew. *Reefer Madness*, a 1936 film, warned that smoking the "killer weed" would lead to insanity, and hell. In December of 1937, the Marijuana Tax Act made the plant illegal. *Cocaine Fiends and Reefer Madness: The History of Drugs in the Movies* by Michael Starks is an excellent chronicle of social attitudes about drugs as revealed in films.

Drugs stayed on the fringe of society throughout the fifties. Beat Generation artists began enhancing their perceptions with pot, and later with more mind-bending hallucinogens. LSD's hallucinogenic qualities were discovered by Albert Hofmann, a chemist who accidentially dosed himself with it in 1943. In the early 1960s, Harvard professor Timothy Leary experimented with the religious and psychological use of LSD with selected graduate students. After he was fired by Harvard, he became a counter-cultural hero of the baby boom generation, remembered for the phrase, "Turn on, tune in, and drop out." When young people found out that marijuana didn't drive you wild and mad, the government lost what little credibility it had. This generation knew little about drugs or their dangers, and was ready to explore the psychological-enhancing properties of experimental substances.

In an age of youth rebellion, the fact that parents were shocked by drugs was all the more reason for young people to take them. Hollywood and Broadway, ever-sensitive to changing mores, romanticized the drug culture with pot-smoking anti-heroes in *Easy Rider* (1969) and "let-it-all-hang-out" hippies in *Hair* (1968). "Marijuana had a meaning beyond just getting high. It was a source of shared identity among people who had a common point of view, notably that their parents were stupid, the government was immoral, and the war in Vietnam was wrong." Despite the war on drugs, marijuana continues to be used by over 10 million Americans, including doctors, lawyers, other white collar professionals, blue collar workers, rap artists, slackers, cyberpunks, ravers, and many others.

In the late 1990s marijuana was the most prevalent and most readily available illegal drug in the United States with approximately three-quarters (77 percent) of current illegal drug users using marijuana or hashish. During the same time frame came the introduction of medical marijuana and the several successful voters initiatives legalizing marijuana for medical use.

## Stimulants

Methamphetamine use steadily increased for several years and began leveling off in the late 1990s. While most methamphetamine comes from large-scale Mexican operations, local labs remain common. Ritalin, (methylphenidate) a prescription stimulant, is commonly abused by heroin users. MDMA or "ecstasy" (methylenedioxymethamphetamine) is frequently used by young adults and adolescents at clubs, raves and rock concerts.

## Depressants

Use of GHB (gamma hydroxybutrate) has become wide spread in the club scene. A mixture of GHB, ketamine, and alcohol—called "Special K-lude" because its effects are similar to those of Quaalude (methaqualone) emerged in New York City.

## Hallucinogens

PCP (phenecyclidine) is often used in combination with other drugs. A frequently reported combination is joints or blunts containing marijuana dipped into PCP. Rates of using PCP have remained relatively low, whereas LSD (lysergic acid diethylamide) use increased throughout the 1990s.

## History Repeats

The dark side of drugs emerged when San Francisco's Haight-Ashbury, which spawned "Flower Power," became a seedy slum of strung-out addicts. Heroin sent urban crime soaring as addicts turned to crime to sustain their habits. In spite of bad LSD trips, social drug use had become so deeply entrenched that it continued to permeate all levels of society, particularly the youth culture. Although still illegal, some drugs became socially acceptable in many quarters. Marijuana was smoked as openly as tobacco while police looked the other way. On the other hand, man-made chemicals like phenylcyclidine, better known as "angel dust" or PCP, reportedly drove users into violent frenzies, making the myth of wild-eyed drug fiends—which had been scoffed at by college students of the 1960s—a horrifying reality.

The mid-1970s marked the second coming of cocaine, the perfect drug for the "Me Generation." "The new morality of young Americans is success, the high-performance ethic," says university professor Ralph Whitehead. "Pot bred passivity. On alcohol you can't perform. You smell. People can tell when you've been drinking. But cocaine fits the new value system. It feeds it and confounds it. Young adults walk a tight line between high performance and self-indulgence, and cocaine puts the two together."

In show business and in chic society of the 1970s, dinner guests were offered crisp white lines of cocaine along with their demi-tasse. Fashionable silver spoons worn as jewelry began to adorn the hip and rich. Coke became a workplace pick-me-up, like coffee. Said Dr. Wesley Westman, Chief of the Alcohol and Drug Dependency Center at the Veteran's Administration Hospital in Miami, "Cocaine is the drug of choice by people who are into the American Dream. I love my job, I am successful—except that they don't and they're not."

Cocaine use increased dramatically as the availability increased and the price went down during the 1980s. During this decade there was a tremendous increase in the use of crack, a form of freebase cocaine. David Smith, the Director of the Haight-Ashbury Free Clinic, said that crack is "like a McDonald's hamburger. If you had to go through all the problems preparing the hamburger, you might not eat it. If you had to get a freebase kit and convert the cocaine yourself, you might not smoke it. This is cocaine that's ready to smoke. It's already prepared in freebase form."

Crack is actually more expensive than powdered coke, but is sold in amounts that make it more available to poor people. For example, in San Francisco, smokeable cocaine sold for about $30 by the tenth of a gram in the late 1980s and early 1990s. Cocaine powder, which cost between $100 and $120 a gram, was cheaper. Crack users paid $300 for a gram, but only $30 at a time. After crack came "ice," a smokeable form of methamphetamine or speed, which was introduced in 1989 in Hawaii and spread to the West Coast. The dangers of ice surpass those of crack because the high is longer lasting and it is easier and cheaper to manufacture. During the 1990s the use of methamphetamine in all forms rose dramatically because of the relative ease of chemical synthesis, resulting in low cost and availability.

The National Household Study of Drug Abuse in 1996 reported that the prevalence of inhalants, hallucinogens like LSD and PCP, and psychotherapeutics such as tranquilizers, sedatives, analgesics, or stimulants used for non-medical purposes remained stable at around 1 percent. LSD is inexpensive, with dosage units costing as little as twenty-cents wholesale. This orderless drug, which is often carried on blotting paper, can even be purchased via mail-order.

By the late 1990s illicit drug use had dropped by 50% from the historic high levels in 1979, when they reached their peak of 25 million or 14.1 percent of the population. By 1996 only 13 million Americans or 6.1 percent of the household population were current users.

# Changing Heroin Use

Heroin use remains a serious problem in the United States. There are approximately 320,000 occasional heroin users and 810,000 chronic users in the United States. Emergency room visits caused by heroin use, for example, rose form 38,000 in 1988 to 63,000 in 1993—an increase of 65 percent. This increase is believed to be a result of the increased purity of the heroin available on the street. The Drug Enforcement Administration (DEA) reports that purity of an ounce of heroin rose from 34 percent in 1990 to 66 percent in 1993. The greater purity of heroin probably results in more overdoses and, in turn, more hospital visits.

Increasingly people are snorting and smoking heroin, rather than injecting it. Dr. Wiebel and Dr. Cone of NIDA believe that this change over has been caused by the increase in purity making it easier for people to get high using these less efficient routes of administration. Also, many people, fearing exposure to AIDs, have switched from injecting heroin to smoking and snorting. NIDA researchers fear that the popularity of smoking and snorting heroin is particularly dangerous because it makes it easier for people to start the habit, since the revulsion for needles is removed.

# Therapeutic And Recreational Use

Psychoactive drugs are often self-prescribed to relieve pain or stress, achieve psychological insight, or to get "high." Many drugs that began in a therapeutic context evolved into recreational drugs. Nitrous oxide, for example, was an anesthetic that became widely used recreationally. Quaaludes (methaqualone), another therapeutic drug, were popular as a recreational drug in the late 1970s. Drug use for therapeutic and religious purposes goes back historically to the use of peyote, and, more recently, to their use by philosophers such as Aldous Huxley, who used mescaline as a drug for insight. Later LSD and MDMA were used for philosophical and spiritual insight.

MDMA, methylenedioxymethamphetamine, is related to both amphetamines and mescaline. It began to be used in the 1970s as a therapeutic drug, and tests on human subjects began in the early 1990s in the United States. MDMA, commonly called "Ecstasy," is another psychotherapeutic substance that became a popular recreational drug. Users claim it has the power to make people more trusting, to banish jealousy, and to break down barriers separating lover from lover, parent from child, therapist from patient. Yet, unlike LSD, it does not induce hallucinations and users are able to distinguish between reality and fantasy. Bruce Eisner's book, *Ecstasy: The MDMA Story*, chronicles the history, use and dangers of MDMA.

By the early 1990s, psychiatric drugs such as Prozac gained a lot of attention for their ability to fundamentally alter long-standing patterns of depression. *Listening to Prozac* by Dr. Peter Kramer chronicles the use of Prozac for personal development.

# Public Outcry

According to a report by Charles Schuster, Director of the National Institute on Drug and Alcohol Abuse, during the 1980s people had been backing away from almost all drugs. Long feared as the "gateway drug," marijuana declined in use among younger people in the 1980s. In 1978, according to government surveys, 10 percent of all high-school seniors smoked marijuana everyday, whereas by the late 1980s, the percentage dropped to about 5 percent. However, by the 1990s, use of "designer drugs" surged among young people.

During the mid-1980s, there was a new toughness on drugs, reflected in the sharp increase in public support for treating even possession of small amounts of marijuana as a crime. A Gallup/Newsweek poll conducted by telephone found that most Americans favored testing all workers for drug use, emphasized the need for treatment, and saw education as the key area of government action. Another Gallup poll, this time of employee opinions, found that 97 percent agree that workplace drug testing is appropriate under certain circumstances and 85 percent believed that urine testing may deter illicit drug use. Testing for the right reasons has the support of most employees.

The anti-drug crusade of the 1980s reflected public opinion that the sale and use of narcotics was one of the most serious problems facing the United States, and that it was of compelling National urgency. When faced with higher taxes to build more prisons, an overwhelming majority of taxpayers said they would pay a hundred dollars a year more in taxes in order to give stiffer sentences. According to a Time/CBS poll, 16 percent said people convicted of selling cocaine or crack for the first time should be sentenced to 30 days in jail; 22 percent favored a year in jail; and 42 percent recommended more than a year in jail for first-time cocaine sellers.

Widely publicized instances of drug abuse among talented and superbly conditioned athletes, including the deaths of University of Maryland basketball star Len Bias and Cleveland Browns' football player Don Rogers, created a demand that young people's sports models police their own ranks and submit to urine tests when required. People started to feel that it was reasonable to expect strict compliance with the anti-drug laws from professionals responsible for the safety of other people, such as airline pilots, air-traffic controllers, surgeons, and police officers.

During the 1970s, when marijuana became regarded as a "soft drug," like alcohol and tobacco, more people began using it. President Carter called for the decriminalization of marijuana in 1977.

Some states, not wanting to imprison members of the younger generation, decriminalized. Eventually, 11 states decriminalized, and Alaska legalized marijuana. Twenty-nine other states made possession of small amounts of marijuana a misdemeanor. Some 20 million to 30 million people or more were smoking marijuana by 1980. In the early 1990s, after an onslaught of anti-marijuana publicity, voters in Alaska voted to repeal legalization. Things flip-flopped again when voter initiatives to legalize medical marijuana won California and Arizona at the turn of the Century.

# War On Drugs

In 1979 drug use among Americans hit an all time high of more than 25 million people. In response President Reagan declared a "war on drugs" and created a network of 12 Organized Crime Drug Enforcement Task Forces across the country. The battle was on. In response to lobbying by parents, revision of the 1878 Posse Comitatus Act, which prohibited the military from entering civilian affairs, made it possible for the military to play a limited role in the war on drugs. The Reagan Administration's strategy, a five-pronged program that attacked the problem from every important angle, sounded like a winner, at least in theory. It took into consideration the fact that any war on drugs must pursue both law enforcement and education programs to be successful. Executive Order No. 12564 (1986) made it a condition of employment for all Federal employees to refrain from using drugs. This order required every Federal agency to develop a comprehensive Drug-Free Workplace Program.

In the words of Dr. Carlton Turner, the Reagan's chief adviser on drug policy, its goal was "to take the customers away from the dealers as well as to take the dealers away from the customers." The money spent on the war on drugs rose dramatically in the middle 1980s, reaching 15 billion dollars by the late 1990s.

In spite of law-enforcement attempts to eradicate it, over 2,000 tons of high-quality American-grown marijuana is reported to be available for sale each year. In the United States, marijuana is the largest cash crop after corn, according to the National Organization for Reform of Marijuana Laws (NORML).

With each new administration comes a renewed commitment to the "drug war". Clinton promised to move aggressively to prevent abuse, especially among the Nation's youth. Since taking office the Clinton Administration increased funding for drug control activities by 32 percent, from $12.2 billion in 1993 to $16 billion in 1998. As part of the overall Clinton strategy, the Department of Health and Human Services (HHS) increased resources dedicated to preventing youth substance abuse. For 1998, HHS allocated $116 million for new youth-focused initiatives from its new higher budget of $2.5 billion, an increase of 6 over its 1997 budget. The HHS awarded $15 million in State Incentive Grants for Community-Based Action to Governor's offices in five States to support statewide planning for coordinated substance abuse prevention services. In 1993, the Supreme Court placed some limits to the use of asset forfeiture laws—widely heralded as a panacea in the Reagan/Bush "War on Drugs" era. The tide appeared to be turning from a military and police model of drug enforcement to a medical and recovery model of public health options for solving the country's drug problem.

A 1994 American Management Survey indicated that 87.2 percent of companies tested employees for drug, an increase of over 300 percent since 1987. 91 percent of organizations with more than 1,000 employees and 81 percent of smaller companies were testing for drugs. Further, they found that the test-positive rate, which had fallen steadily since 1989, leveled in 1993 at 2.5 percent. The AMA attributes the lower positive rate to the increased numbers of people being tested (most of whom are drug-free), rather than to drug testing being a deterrent. Reports based upon government surveys released in 1998 indicated that overall use of drugs in the United States has fallen by half in the last 15 years of the Century. The total number of current illicit drug users, as defined by having used an illicit drug at least once in the past month, has remained flat since 1992. In 1996, an estimated 13 million Americans, which is 6.1 percent of the population over 12 years old, were current illicit drug users—half of the 1997 peak level of 25.4 million current users. The SmithKline Beecham Drug Testing Index showed that for the eleventh consecutive year, the over all "positive" rate in the workplace declined to its lowest lever ever from 5.8 percent in 1996 to 5.0 percent in 1997, a decrease of 14 percent.

Barry McCaffrey, Director of the Office of National Drug Control Policy under the Clinton Administration, unveiled the 1998 National Drug Control Strategy which is a ten-year plan to reduce illegal drug use and availability by 50 percent (to 3.1 percent of the household population) by 2007. The Strategy focuses on "prevention, treatment, research, law enforcement, protection of the borders and international cooperation."

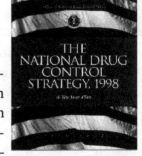

# War on Alcohol

According to the National Institute on Alcohol Abuse and Alcoholism, about 12 million people are addicted to alcohol. Alcoholism causes absenteeism, high medical bills and reduced work quality. Estimates by Research Triangle Institute in North Carolina put the annual cost to the U.S. economy of alcohol and drug use on the job at $117 billion in the 1990s.

The Omnibus Transportation Act, aimed directly at reducing alcohol, brought an additional 2 million people under regulation. New alcohol testing rules require extensive use of breath analysis. Larger employers were required to implement alcohol testing by January 1, 1995, smaller employers by January 1, 1996.

Dealing with alcohol is tricky because the American Disabilities Act (ADA), which has severe penalties, classifies alcoholism as a disability. This means that how an employer interacts with a person who has been in an alcohol treatment problem is highly regulated.

# CHAPTER 2

# Social Cost Of Drug Abuse

Estimates of the costs of drug use in the U.S. vary widely. In 1980 the Research Triangle Institute of North Carolina calculated the toll to the Nation at $47 billion as a result of lost productivity and related deaths, crime, and medical treatment. By the late 1990s that figure had climbed to nearly $70 billion. The literature contains references to the cost of drug abuse to American industry but most of these are estimates, extrapolations, and projections.

There is a common belief that drug use always results in reduced performance and lessened cognitive and intellectual abilities. There is the assumption that a dysfunctional work or life history is caused by use or preference for a drug, and that those who use drugs will soon malfunction like the drug abusers seen in treatment programs. Some drugs, however, seem to improve performance on tests of conceptual ability, rapid visuomotor, scanning, tracking, and set-shifting, abstracting abilities, and other kinds of intellectual and verbal functioning.

Laurence Miller of Fair Oaks Hospital in Summit, New Jersey, researched the presence of neuropsychological impairment in chronic users of CNS depressants, including alcohol, opiates, and cocaine. He found that neither total lifetime consumption nor current frequency of drinking was related to cognitive performance. Rather, "there was a significant association between current quantity of alcohol consumed per drinking occasion and impairment on neuropsychological tasks. Most seriously affected were the processes of abstraction, adaptive abilities, and concept formation." Curiously enough, and contrary to common assumptions, the neuropsychological studies of marijuana users have generally failed to document any permanent impairment in cognitive functioning as a result of marijuana use alone.

## The Marijuana Question

The "marijuana question" continues to be the object of a lot of interest especially with the emergence of so called "medical" marijuana. Carlin and Trupin compared daily marijuana smokers who officially denied their use with a control group of abstainers. The marijuana smokers performed significantly faster than the nonsmokers on tests of rapid vasomotor, scanning, tracking, and set-shifting. On the other hand, publications from the Department of Health and Human Services (HHS) report that experienced pilots in a flight simulator were impaired for at least 24 hours after a dose, long after the subjective "high" had worn off. Certainly research is needed because what functional impairments occurs with prolonged use is not known. Unlike other drugs of abuse which can be detected for short periods of time and then wash out of the body, metabolites of THC, the active ingredient in marijuana, accumulated in the body, and can be detected for weeks, after use.

Grant's research group studied heavy use of marijuana and found that better performance on certain tasks actually correlated with heavy use, replicating the findings of Carlin and Trupin. Bruhn and Maage compared four groups of subjects on an variety of intellectual and cognitive tests. The groups were non-drug users, marijuana and hallucinogen users, hallucinogen and amphetamine users, and marijuana, hallucinogen, amphetamine, and heroin users. Their results showed that use of these drugs had no significant effect on neurocognitive functioning, alone or in combination. However, Bruhn and Maage's results were disputed by Helen Jones in *The Marijuana Question,* where she presented a great deal of data indicating mental impairment from regular marijuana consumption. What this research highlights is that the social costs of marijuana use are complex and difficult to assess.

*"In terms of sheer numbers our worst problem drugs are the legal recreational drugs, alcohol and tobacco. Out of a total population of 240 million Americans, more than 100 million use alcohol, and 10 to 13 million are probably addicted to it. Roughly 56 million American are addicted to tobacco. Almost all users are addicts.*

*"Among illegal drugs, marijuana is still the most popular. According to the U.S. government, 20 million Americans smoke marijuana occasionally. My own studies, based on government data, suggest that the number of marijuana users—people who smoke at least once a year —is probably between 35 and 40 million. Of these perhaps three million smoke it everyday, which is one definition (among many) of an addict. But my guess is that no more than 1.5 million are compulsive users— smokers who would suffer great discomfort if forced to suddenly stop using the drug. So I suspect that roughly one in every 20 pot users is totally addicted, while roughly 1 in 10 alcohol users is.*

*"Somewhere between 12 and 15 million Americans probably use cocaine at least once a year. Of those, perhaps 500,000 to 750,000 use it every day. Another 3 to 5 million may use heroin at least once a year, and about 300,000 to 500,000 are addicts. Finally, a couple of million Americans are addicted to valium and other more obscure drugs that aren't much talked about."*

Arnold S. Trebach
Professor of Justice, American University

# Drugs And Crime

It is clear that crime is directly fueled by drug abuse. "I believe the crime problem in America today is the drug problem," declared New York City Police Commissioner Ward. Numerous studies have confirm the relationship between committing a crime and using drugs, especially "hard" drugs. The lessons of Prohibition, however, make it clear that prohibitive drug laws may in fact *contribute* to crime, since there are high profits to be made by illicit drug-traffickers.

A 1996 study by the National Center on Addiction and Substance Abuse (CASA) revealed that from 1980 to 1996 the number of prisoners who have been implicated in crime involving drug and alcohol abuse more than tripled. The drug-law violators account for 30 percent of the increase in State prison population and 68 percent of the increase in the Federal prison population.

The use of alcohol and other drugs has long been suspected as a risk factor for homicide victimization. Alcohol use can lead to an increased risk of being killed. Usage increases the likelihood that the users will engage in risk-taking and provocative behavior. Alcohol, being a CNS depressant, may release inhibitory control mechanisms, and thereby permit expression of aggressive or violent behavior. Also, being "drunk" makes people easier targets for robberies and other types of crimes.

Richard A. Goodman studied the blood-alcohol levels in homicide victims who were killed in Los Angeles, and found that alcohol consumption was common. Wolfgang found that alcohol use prior to the homicide had been reported for 50 percent of the victims in Pennsylvania, and that in nearly 44 percent of all homicides, alcohol use had been reported for both the victim and the offender. Voss and Hepburn reported a history of alcohol use for 54 percent of all homicides in Chicago. The results clearly indicate that an increased use of alcohol is associated with more homicides. Most of the results reported are very modest, because information about alcohol use is not routinely collected during police investigations, and can only be indirectly inferred from autopsy reports.

"We've always been a drug-ridden society. There were probably as many psychoactive drugs in use 100 years ago, but there was no crime associated with drugs. Most of the crime associated with drugs has to do with their enormously inflated price, which is a direct consequence of their illegalization, so that people have to get the money to afford them, which often involves committing crimes. But the pharmacological effects of many drugs are against violence. That's certainly true with heroin and probably with marijuana."

Dr. Andrew Weil
*From Chocolate to Morphine*

"It's a sad commentary on our times that the `Not as bad as alcohol and tobacco' test has become so relevant. For one thing, it shows that two extremely dangerous drugs have become the standard of acceptability. Yet it is hard to imagine anything much worse than alcohol and tobacco. These two drugs account for 30 percent of all premature deaths—some 525,000—in the United States annually. That's almost as many as the 650,000 Americans who have died in combat in **all** the wars that we have ever fought, including the American Revolution. Each year, 325,000 Americans die from the effects of smoking, but only 29,557 Americans died fighting in World War II.

"But it isn't just the loss of life that takes a toll. The economic loss to society due to alcohol—including health care costs, accidents, and work loss—runs $120 billion annually. For tobacco the figure is $65 billion a year."

*The War On Drugs*
*Fighting To Lose The Coming Revolution*

Drug abuse kills 14,000 Americans each year. Alcohol contributes to as many as 200,000 deaths annually in the United States. Tobacco contributes to another 250,000. There are no comparable figures on the long-term lethal effects of cocaine abuse, but some comparative data does exist on "crisis deaths." The NIDA (National Institute on Drug Abuse) maintains a Drug Abuse Warning Network (DAWN), which collects information on drug overdoses from emergency rooms and medical examiners in 26 metropolitan areas. The data are sketchy, but they do give some indication of the relative dangers of the various drugs. In 1984, cocaine was implicated in 604 deaths, and was third on the list behind heroin and morphine, which caused 1,072 deaths, and alcohol use in combination with other drugs, which led to 1,131 deaths. In the 1990s drug-related deaths increased 42 percent between 1990 and 1995 to 14,218 deaths. Accidents, crime, domestic violence, illness, lost opportunity, and reduced productivity are the direct consequences of substance abuse. Drug and alcohol use by children often leads to other forms of unhealthy, unproductive behavior such as delinquency and premature, unsafe sex. Drug abuse and trafficking hurt families, businesses, and neighborhoods. It impedes education and clogs the criminal-justice, health and social-service systems.

## Addiction

Once viewed as a moral or character defect, addiction now is considered a "disability" under the American Disabilities Act (ADA) with complex behavioral and medical condition with personal, social and biological underpinnings, as well as a chronic, relapsing disease. Research shows that some individuals are at greater risk than others of developing drug-related problems and that addiction invariably alters brain chemistry. Drug-seeking and use alters thinking pattern and, in essence, retrains the brain. With heavy, frequent drug use, the change in cerebral function can be profound, and interventions to date—although effective in modifying behavior—have not demonstrated the capacity to fully restore brain chemistry. Person of any background can become addicted to drugs. Approximately 45 percent of Americans know someone with a substance-abuse problem, nearly 20 percent state that drug abuse has been a cause of trouble in their families.

# Hospitalizations and Deaths

The alarming rate at which the number of cocaine deaths increased in the late 1980s stabilized in the mid-1990s. Between 1980 and 1985, the number of deaths reported to DAWN involving cocaine increased by 324 percent with the introduction of crack cocaine. Yet, as late as 1986 cocaine deaths were still relatively infrequent. By the late 1980s the number of deaths attributed to cocaine rose to 1,582 according to a NIDA report.

From 1990 to 1996, estimates of drug-related visits to hospital emergency rooms increased. 531,600 drug-related visits occurred in 1995, up slightly from 1994. More than half of these were due to drug overdoses. There were nearly 143,000 cocaine-related visits, with increases in people 35 years old and older. Heroin-related visits increased by 19 per cent from 1994, and marijuana-related visits increased by 17 percent. Methamphetamine-related visits decreased by 34 percent from the first to second half of 1995. HHS statistics report 14,000 drug-abuse related deaths a year. A study conducted in 1997 by DAWN found that the number of emergency room visits due to drugs declined 6 percent to 487,600 in 1996 from 517,800 in 1995.

The health cost of drug abuse was estimated by one National Center for Health Statistics study at $59.7 billion in 1983, but the medical bill for alcohol abuse was $116.7 billion. "There is no question that alcoholism in terms of social costs remains our number-one problem. We can't lose sight of that because of our emphasis on drugs," said the NIDA's Schuster.

A similar paradox exists with marijuana. Mark Kleiman, past Director of Policy Management Analysis at the Criminal Division of the Justice Department, said, "Marijuana is certainly not a purely benign drug, at least for the 2 or 3 million Americans who smoke five joints a day. But it's hard to prove that Saturday-night marijuana use does much damage. The scientific evidence is just not that impressive. Assume the worst about the evidence linking it to lung cancer, and the danger is still small compared with that of tobacco smoking. The studies linking marijuana to drops in IQ just don't hold up. Evidence that it weakens the immune system is interesting but inconclusive."

Dr. Phillip W. Landfield of Wake Forest University in Winston-Salem, North Carolina, said in a report to the Associated Press in 1986 that animal research indicated that THC might affect the structure of the brain in the same way as memory loss. He said that THC, the psychoactive ingredient in marijuana, might act like a steroid hormone, reducing the density of the brain cells in the hippocampus of the brain by 20 percent. The decreased number of cells is similar to that seen in aging animals in this part of the brain, he said. There is speculation that a drug-induced loss of brain cells of 20 to 30 percent, combined with a similar loss due to normal aging, might cause conditions similar to Parkinson's disease at an early age.

On the other hand, physiological psychologists Bruhn and Maage in 1975, and Grant and his group in 1978, failed to find evidence of any significant neuropsychological impairment as a result of persistent amphetamine abuse or marijuana use. Marijuana use was not found to be associated with any impairment in mental capability. However, *The Marijuana Question* by Helen Jones and Paul Lovinger, describes hundreds of studies of marijuana and presents the most convincing data available about the hazards of marijuana use.

Some medical doctors speculate that the repeated use of cocaine, even in small doses, can eventually trigger seizures like the one suspected of killing basketball star Len Bias. Government scientists reported that a "kindling" process gradually leaves the brain more vulnerable to cocaine toxic effects, probably by altering neurological systems that govern emotion and the body's motor functions.

The "kindling" phenomenon, according to Dr. Robert Post of the Health and Human Services Department, occurs because cocaine is a "dirty drug" that combines stimulant properties with local anesthetic properties. This could explain some of cocaine's exceedingly unpredictable behavioral effects, such as panic attacks. Dr. David

Smith, Director of the Haight-Ashbury Free Clinic, warns, "Smoking a dangerous drug is even more hazardous. A heart can be perfectly healthy and still stop working, because the electrical rhythm is disturbed by smoking cocaine. The healthiest person in the world can die of a cocaine overdose."

Dr. Andrew Weil comments, "The government continues to subsidize tobacco addiction, and cigarettes are the worst form of drug abuse in this culture, the greatest public-health problem that we have, and the most flagrant example of drug pushing, since most of it is pushed on teenagers, who are lured by advertising into thinking it's cool to smoke. If you want to talk about death penalties for drug pushers, start with the executives of tobacco companies. I think there is no illegal drug that comes near alcohol in dangerousness. All you have to do is ask law enforcement agencies about the association of alcohol and violent crime."

Designer drugs are chemical variations on Federally controlled synthetic drugs that mimic the effects of classic narcotics, stimulants, and hallucinogens and pose severe health hazards. By slightly altering the molecular structures, black-market chemists create new, untested legal drugs. The term "designer drugs" also refers to new street drugs, such as crack, which are concentrated forms of already existing drugs, uniquely marketed for a target income group. As the variety of designer drugs began to flourish on the black market, there was a sudden rise in overdose deaths and neurodengenerative diseases with Parkinson-like symptoms. Two of the most obvious risks are clear. First, many of the designer drugs are new drugs whose potency and selective action are unknown. Second, because they are produced illicitly by phantom chemists practicing questionable quality control, many of the substances are contaminated by impurities and dangerously toxic by-products.

Many of the synthetic narcotics are not detected by routine chemical analysis. So they are attractive to parolees, prison populations, and the growing number of white-collar workers who are fearful of mandatory drug testing. According to the National Institute of

Mental Health (NIMH), many heroin users are beginning to show symptoms of Parkinson's disease. In attempts to manufacture MPTP, a heroin synthetic analog known as "China White," underground chemists sometimes contaminate batches with MPTP, a by-product which was created by a faulty chemical procedure. MPTP has been linked with symptoms of Parkinson's Disease.

Lethal mistakes can be made during the simple process of mixing the active ingredient with a common cut or dilator. Because the fentanyl derivatives, used as a substitute for heroin, are so potent, the actual dose may be as little as a microgram—less that a grain of salt. Dealers along the way attempt to dilute the product, a technique requiring skill and sophistication, which most street dealers don't have.

Illicit synthetic narcotics have spread dramatically. The drugs can be disguised to look like whatever organic heroin is currently being sold on the street, or sold as cocaine or methamphetamine to unsuspecting users. They are made to look, taste, and feel like the real thing. The dangers have skyrocketed for both addicts, recreational users and first-time experimenters.

# CHAPTER 3

# Drug Use On The Job

Drug use on the job isn't new. Nonetheless alcohol, the most commonly abused drug, has only recently been recognized as a problem. It is estimated that 10 percent of the workforce is alcoholic, and that nearly half of all industrial injuries can be linked to alcohol abuse. But other drugs, as they become more available, also become more of a problem. The Federal Drug Enforcement Administration estimates that, within any given month, seven million people abuse prescription drugs, such as stimulants and sedatives. Increasingly, workers are bringing prescribed drugs into the workplace.

A study of drug abuse in the general population conducted by the New York State Narcotic Addiction Control Commission in 1971 found that drug use among employed persons parallels drug-use patterns in the overall population. The rate of regular use of certain drugs such as marijuana, sedatives, and heroin was only slightly higher than in the general population. At the time of the study, cocaine was not even included as a separate category because its use was so low. By the mid-1990s, however, drug and alcohol use was far greater among unemployed than those employed, and cocaine was one of the drugs most frequently used on the job. While still high, there was a decline in percentages of people using drugs and alcohol on the job, probably as a result of the drug testing programs. In 1996, for example, only 5.8 percent of employees tested positive for drug, down from 13 percent in 1995, and fewer than at any time since 1996.

# Alcohol Use At Work

The most serious drug abused at work is alcohol. The National Institute on Drug Abuse (NIDA) household survey conducted in the mid-1990s revealed that 7.5 percent of Americans employed full-time reported drinking five or more drinks per occasion on five or more days in the previous month which was classified as "heavy drinking". This is a frightening figure because statistics reported in *Occupational Medicine* indicated that up to 40 percent of industrial fatalities and 47 percent of industrial injuries are linked to alcohol consumption. The Substance Abuse and Mental Health Services Administration (SAMHSA) report in their statistics sourcebook that in the early 1990s that the cost of alcohol and other drug use to American business was estimated at over $80 billion in lost productivity, with 86 percent of the cost attributed to drinking problems alone. More recent estimates are not available.

> *"Ironically, the common use of alcohol as a mainstay of the workplace was the ground in which the first roots of job-based alcohol rehab programs took hold. Throughout much of the first half of the nineteenth century, workers in practically all occupations drank on the job, frequently at the employer's expense, and often during specific times set aside for imbibing. In the Southern United States, for example, men often took off from work for 'eleveners,' a whiskey and brandy version of the coffee break. In England, dockworkers during this period, and on into the twentieth century, typically had at least four or five drinking breaks with 'practically no restrictions in the workers' access to liquor during the hours of labor.' These practices were even more evident in eighteenth century England. In London during this century it was commonplace for workers in many trades to be di-*

*rectly dependent upon tavern keepers, since taverns were the employment agencies of that period. In one extreme instance, men who worked on coal-carrying ships were almost required to drink specific amounts each day; the cost of the assigned amount was taken from their wages — whether it was drunk or not. Other employers sold drinks in the workplace and frequently charged the cost of these against wages."*

Harrison Trice & Mona Schonbrunn

Absenteeism among problem drinkers is substantially higher than for other employees. In fact, non-alcoholic members of alcoholic families take ten times as much sick leave compared to family members of non-alcoholic families.

# Cocaine At Work

American workers in the 1980s rediscovered the use of cocaine as a stimulant to improve performance. The temptation to use stimulants while working can be seen among athletes performing for endurance, and musicians, actors, speakers, people on TV, and TV personalities who have to lose their inhibitions and project charisma. Cocaine is used much as caffeine is, except that cocaine is euphoric and, at first, engenders conviviality and a feeling of omnipotence that you can succeed at anything.

Probably the greatest surge in the use of drugs in recent history was during World War II and the Vietnam War, when many major military operatives had a chain of distribution of stimulant drugs, which included cocaine, dexedrine, or methedrine. These gave the ordinary soldier a feeling of invincibility, and enabled him to go out into battle. Ironically, cocaine appeals to those who would never think of using alcohol on the job, because it gives a sense of enhanced intellectual capabilities and doesn't interfere with motor functioning.

# Decline In Productivity

The cost of employee drug abuse takes many forms, and can sometimes be substantial. It has been estimated that dysfunctional drug-abusing employees lose three times as much time from the job as do other employees. In addition to absenteeism, other evidences of dysfunctional employee drug abuse are lessened productivity, safety problems, theft, and increased turnover. Also, drug use often seems to spread after it is introduced into a work unit.

The cost to society of alcohol and drug abuse in both financial and social terms is devastating. More than 100 million people are currently employed in the U.S. Between 5 and 10 percent of the workforce suffers from alcoholism. Estimates of the nature and extent of drug abuse among American workers are more difficult to pinpoint, because general unawareness of the signs and symptoms allow many drug users to filter undetected through most personnel procedures. It is estimated that 3 to 7 percent of the employed population use some form of illicit drugs on the job, ranging from marijuana to heroin, on a daily basis. Marijuana appears to be the principal substance used, and accounts for 90 percent of current users.

The use of alcohol and drugs in the work site sometimes presents a clear danger, especially when heavy equipment or other potentially hazardous tools are involved. But alcohol and drug consumption off the job can also impair work performance, since alcohol and many drugs remain active in the body for differing periods of time. The danger to the public safety is clearly evident when drugs are used by pilots, air-traffic controllers, bus, taxi, and train drivers, nuclear-plant operators, and military personnel. Employees with a drinking or drug problem are absent 16 times more than the average employee, have an accident rate that is 4 times greater, use a third more sickness benefits, and have five times more compensation claims while on the job; 40 percent of industrial fatalities and 74 percent of industrial injuries can be traced to alcohol abuse.

While drugs may make a worker feel more productive, stoned assembly-line workers and coked-up executives or typists are not necessarily working well, especially over the long term. Drug-related work impairment shows up as a reduction in work quality, capacity, or creativity. The amount of tolerable impairment depends on the work task and on whether situations might arise that require peak performance. A commercial airline pilot's impairment due to a hangover, for example, may not be apparent during routine flight condition, but may be disastrous if the aircraft has an equipment malfunction.

Drug-related work impairment can also result when chronic use of alcohol, marijuana, or cocaine causes brain dysfunction persisting beyond the period of intoxication. Drug use away from work can result in family discord or personal problems that preoccupy the employee's mental activity while at work.

Researchers Parker, Parker, Brody, and Schoenberg did a study on a representative sample of 1,367 employed men and women in Detroit. The subjects responded to questions about their drinking practices, and then completed cognitive tests that measured abstraction abilities. Abstraction, tested while respondents were sober, decreased significantly as the reported quantity of alcohol consumed per drinking occasion increased. Additionally, the study investigated consumption during the previous 24 hours, and found that the impact of recent drinking on cognitive processes lasted longer than 24 hours.

Unfortunately, the drug testing technology usually used by employers will only detect recent alcohol consumption, even though alcohol continues to impair cognitive performance long after consumption. Furthermore, because alcoholism is classified as a disability under the American Disabilities Act (ADA) testing for alcohol is limited and the employers options for inquiring into past rehabilitation for alcohol is restricted.

## Security And Drugs

Alcohol and drug abuse can create many security problems in the workplace, ranging from theft or destruction of company property to the compromising of individuals in sensitive positions.

Thefts are a plaguing problem associated with industrial drug abuse, and have tended to be primarily attributable to heroin-dependent persons. A heroin addict's habit costs from $50 to $150 a day, or more. Common company theft targets of addicts are tools, small office machinery, company products, uncashed pay checks, and petty-cash boxes. However, the increase of cocaine abuse may be contributing to on the-job-thefts.

Abuse of illicit drugs may result in additional problems for the employer. Some examples include: theft or misuse of company resources to purchase drugs; vulnerability of the employee to blackmail because of the fact of drug use; association of the employee with criminals during the procurement of drugs.

Theft of company property and embezzlement of company funds are common ways in which users support drug habits. Alarm systems, locks, and other security measures are therefore included in the estimated costs of substance abuse. The American Society for Industrial Security reported that in 1982, 25 percent of undercover assignments for police and private security agents were drug-related.

With so many well-documented aspects of the cost of drug use on the job, it's no small wonder that more and more companies are initiating drug-testing programs.

## Who Uses Drugs On The Job

Most employed users are white, young and have limited seniority. In the 1996 Household Study of Drug Abuse, 74 percent of all users (9.7 million) are white, 14 percent (1.8 million) are black and 8 percent (1.1 million) are Hispanics. When older workers experience drug problems, the drugs involved are usually alcohol, barbiturates, or amphetamine. Although the hiring of inner-city minorities is frequently cited in the literature as a cause of company drug-abuse problems, one study conducted by Halpern and reported to the American Management Association involving over 230 companies found no relationship between minority-group employment and an increased incidence of drug abuse. Men continue to have higher rates of illicit drug use than do women. Drug abuse cuts across ethnic, racial, educational, and class lines. On the other hand being unmarried—divorced, separated or never married—puts workers at greater risk of illicit drug and heavy alcohol use according to Substance Abuse and Mental Health Service Administration (SAMHSA) research.

Frequent job change seems to be correlated with drug use. Workers who report having three or more jobs in the previous five years are about twice as likely to currently use illicit drugs or have used them in the past year.

There is a sharp contrast between the profile of drug abusers in 1977 and that in the 1990s. In 1977, the average clients in treatment centers were addicted to heroin, were black adult males from the ghetto, and used mostly one drug. By 1990, abusers were predominantly lower-to middle-class whites, whose drug use stems from a recreational motive. By the mid-1980s, many people entering treatment—often at the behest of their employers—were polydrug abusers, using more than one drug. Their willingness to use whatever drug available was a symptom of the "let's party" syndrome.

Generations that grew up experimenting with illegal drugs now make up a large percentage of the workforce. The National Institute on Drug Abuse (NIDA) estimated that nearly two-thirds of those entering the workforce in the mid to late-1990s have used illegal drugs at least once.

Researchers at the Harvard School of Public Health studied physicians and medical students experiences with drugs, excluding alcohol. According to the responses, 59 percent of the doctors and 78 percent of the students said they had used psychoactive substances at least once in their lives. Recreational use was most prevalent among students and physicians under the age of 40, and most often involved marijuana and cocaine. There was a significant increase in cocaine use among medical students during early 1980s. Another problem that doctors have with drugs is self-treatment, usually with sedatives and opioids such as fentanyl, which are very hard to detect in urine analysis. How does drug use by doctors affect the welfare of patients?

In the survey 3.3 percent of physicians and 5.2 percent of students declared that they had become dependent on drugs, but only 1.8 percent of the doctors reported that drug use had caused them to give poor care. It should be noted, of course, that the doctors' response was based on their own judgment—not always a reliable indicator.

Illicit drugs use is highly correlated with educational status. People who have not completed high school have the highest use rate. Current employment status is also highly correlated with illicit drug use. 12.5 percent of unemployed adults were using illicit drugs in the mid-1990s, as compared to 6.2 percent of full-time employed adults. The rate of illicit drug use was 7.3 precedent in the West region, 6.9 percent in the North Central region, 5.5 percent in the South, and 4.8 percent in the Northeast.

## Jobs Associated With Drug Use

Some professions and types of jobs are especially prone to drug use. One is "shift work," or work between 5 p.m. and 8 a.m. Another is any particularly boring or tedious work. The professionals most likely to use drugs on the job are in the health professions. Health-care workers—pharmacists, nurses, physicians and dentists—are at risk for drug use on the job, because of such factors as access to drugs, shift work, and stress.

Unsupervised work and that with little supervision provides ample opportunity and research by National Institute on Alcohol Abuse and Alcoholism (NIAAA) revealed such jobs are associated with increased drinking problems, as are jobs with high mobility.

The highest rates of illicit drug use are reported by workers in construction, food preparation, and waiters and waitresses according to statistics from (SAMHSA). Use patterns were similar for heavy alcohol use, with the addition of auto mechanics, light truck drivers and laborers also having high rates of on-the-job drinking. Police and detectives, administrative support, teachers and child care workers were found to have the lowest rates of illicit drug use. State clerks, personnel specialists and secretaries were lowest in alcohol use.

# Reasons For Drug Use At Work

Motivation for most drug use in the workplace can be categorized as any of the following: performance facilitation, relief of boredom, physical and psychological pain, stress relief, drug addiction, or self-medication of side-effects such as hangover or nervousness from other drugs.

## Performance Facilitation

Some drug use is an attempt by the employee to work harder or to be more productive. Most commonly the drug is a stimulant of some form to combat fatigue. Piece workers may take amphetamine or opiates to enable them to work longer or faster without intolerable discomfort. Executives may use cocaine to allow them to work past their usual fatigue limits. Writers may use alcohol or cocaine to loosen up in an attempt to enhance their creative output.

Dr. Bobby Guinn, a professor of Health Studies at the Pan-American University, studied job satisfaction and amphetamine use among long-distance truck drivers. She found that more than 62 percent of the drivers reported at least occasional use of drugs while driving, but their reason for doing so was not for recreation, unlike the workers described in other studies. The truckers believed that using drugs was essential to meeting a delivery schedule. This does not indicate dissatisfaction with the job, but rather reflects a perceived necessity for the use of amphetamine in order to do one's job.

Stimulants, primarily amphetamines, are used extensively in the trucking industry, where individuals must stay awake and alert for extended periods of time. Guinn found that more than 62 percent of the drivers reported at least occasional use of drugs while driving, but their reason for doing so was not for recreation, unlike the workers described in other studies. The truckers believed that using drugs was essential to meeting a delivery schedule. This does not indicate dissatisfaction with the job, but rather reflects a perceived necessity for the use of amphetamine in order to do one's job.

There has been a tremendous concern that fatigue in the truck drivers might override the drug's effects and result in accidents. However, the Surgeon General's Report On Health Promotion And Disease Prevention and the President's Commission On Law Enforcement and Administration of Justice have reported no evidence of a causal relationship between amphetamine use and accidents.

## Relief Of Boredom And Stress

Many jobs are inherently routine and offer only rare opportunities for challenge. For example, watchdog jobs are structured to have a person available to take action if there is equipment malfunction or an atypical condition. With increasing automation of routine tasks by computers, the number of jobs having a watchdog function will increase. Watchdog jobs are extremely vulnerable to drug abuse. The employee's impairment may not be apparent until an emergency condition arises that may require high-judgment performance by the employee to divert disaster.

Drugs might also be used in order to bear stress or pain by individuals who have to perform difficult tasks such as shiftwork, or endure long periods of loneliness or withstand combat.

## Self-Medication Of Side Effects Of Other Drugs

With high-dose recreational drug use of alcohol or cocaine and other stimulants, users may have hangovers, depression, and nervousness that persists throughout the next day. They may attempt to offset these adverse effects by the use of sedatives or other medications.

## Other Reasons

Besides the reasons already listed, any number of factors could contribute to the use of drugs on the job. They may include performance anxiety, fatigue, or addiction due to non-job stresses, such as problems with families or relationships.

## Abuse Of Prescription Drugs

The National Institute for Drug Abuse (NIDA) estimates that abuse of prescription drugs causes 60 percent of hospital emergency-room admissions for drug overdoses, and 70 percent of all drug-related deaths. Usually drug abuse of prescribed medications occurs in one of two ways: prescribed medication comes to be used for recreation, or dependency develops from therapeutic treatment.

Patients may visit a physician claiming symptoms of nonexistent illnesses, or exaggerate symptoms of real illnesses, in order to convince the physician to prescribe the medication that the patient plans to use recreationally.

Therapeutic use of medication can result in addiction. Medication may have been initially prescribed for an indicated condition, but the patient discovers that the medication produces euphoria, and continues to use it for that purpose after the condition for which it was prescribed has been cleared up.

# Chapter 4

# Employer Liability

Employers have many solid reasons to be concerned about the behavior of employees. An employee with impaired functioning diminishes productivity and hurts the business. Furthermore, it is a matter of public safety when there is potential for accidents in which citizens could be injured. In cases where safety is involved, such as that of a surgeon performing an operation or a pilot flying hundreds of passengers, the company has a great deal at stake in avoiding accidents and being able to make certain that employees are fit for duty.

An employee acting on the job can be legally considered to be an extension of the employer so that employers can become liable for accidents caused by employees. An accident could be caused by diminished capacity due to drug abuse. Consequently, employers are compelled to detect and eliminate drug use in order to reduce their exposure to liability.

## Employers' Liability

Employers can be held directly responsible for negligence in screening and hiring applicants, and in supervising or retraining incompetent or dangerous employees. Because the behavior of drug and alcohol abusers can present serious problems to co-workers and to the public, an employer must pay particular attention to any sign that an applicant or current employee may present such a danger. An employer who does not act reasonably when such information is available *or could have been available* is exposed to substantial legal liability.

There have been some dramatic cases regarding employer liability. For example, in Texas, in *Otis Engineering Corp. v. Clark,* a wrongful death action against the employer was permitted when a supervisor sent an intoxicated employee home, and, on the way, the employee caused an automobile accident that killed two people. In another case, *Brockett* v. *Kitchen Boyd Motor Company,* cause of action for an automobile accident was permitted against the employer when an intoxicated employee left a prolonged company Christmas party and caused an accident. As these cases demonstrate, employers can be held liable even when the accident is caused by an employee after leaving the workplace.

# Employers Must Be Proactive

Lack of information is not a good defense, because employers are expected to be able to get information about the potential diminished capacity of employees. It is not surprising that employers have felt the need to perform drug testing in order to protect public safety and themselves. The greatest liability results from inaction by an employer who is aware of a drug abuse problem and the inaction results in the drug abuser harming another employee or a member of the public while in the service of the employer. As a consequence employers are under tremendous pressure to detect drug use on the job.

## Pitfalls Of Observation

Traditionally, drug and alcohol use was detected through observation of behavior and other work-related factors. However, employers have encountered problems with this approach, as illustrated by the experience of the Southern Pacific Transportation Company.

Bob Taggard, Director of Public Affairs, gave the example of a supervisor who observed that an employee seemed to have been absent often, was very irritable on the job, and had a constantly runny nose, all of which could suggest cocaine abuse. However, when the supervisor pulled the person off the job and wrote up a reprimand, the case came before the arbitration board. When asked the reason for the symptoms, the employee said, "I don't use cocaine. I had the flu. So of course I was absent and had a runny nose. And I was irritable because I had an argument with my wife!" As the example illustrates, the company may have a hard time proving that employees are actually using drugs; so they are sent back to the job. Drug testing attempts to give an objective answer to this problem.

Drug testing helps employers avoid many of the legal problems that could arise from observation of on-the-job performance problems by supervising personnel. The word "test" implies an objective measurement of fitness for duty and of the amount of drugs or drug metabolites in the body. Drug test results are much easier to use in court and arbitration than a supervisor's observations which can be dismissed as "speculations". For reasons such as these, many companies have implemented drug testing.

Carrying out drug testing is an action which demonstrates that the employer is taking responsibility in an objective way. Legal defense is served by evidence that the employer is making a reasonable effort to detect and prevent drug use on the job.

## Public Relations

Businesses respond to public values. Companies want to be perceived by their customers as responsible toward their community and reflective of the values of society. So as the larger society became more critical of drug use, business began to exhibit more conservative values as well.

Public relations is of particular concern in sports, since sports heroes are role models for young people. There have been several instances of widely publicized drug use by sports figures. The general public alarm about drug use by children who admired sports figures inspired the professional sports organizations to take up drug testing to restore the credibility of the players and teams. The sports employee assistance programs that developed reflect the intense concern of management about drugs.

For example, the manager of the Oakland A's baseball team said, "It's not just a question of occupational safety. We view drug testing as a way to make a statement that we are not on drugs, regardless of what the public thinks. We believe that testing acts as a deterrent."

# Everyone Is Suspect

Workers, however, usually have concerns quite different from those of their employers or the general public. Joel Youngblood, an outfielder who played for the San Francisco Giants, had not been implicated in the drug scandals that rocked baseball. Indeed, there was no evidence—not even a hint of rumor—that he was using drugs; yet because Youngblood balked at including a drug testing clause in his contract, he became baseball's black sheep.

What irked Youngblood was the proviso that the Giants could test for drugs at anytime, day or night, as often as they liked. "It puts you in a position of having to prove your innocence," his agent said. "It's like having the police coming to your house at 3 a.m. just to look around. No reason."

During the winter Youngblood's agent had worked out the details of the next year's contract. But when he objected to the drug testing clause, however, the Giants withdrew their offer to Youngblood. No one else in the league showed any interest in signing Youngblood, either. Suddenly, this nine-year veteran had become baseball's untouchable.

Professor of Law and Public Policy at the University of California at Berkeley, David L. Kirp said "Mandating drug testing turns the basic idea that people are innocent until proven guilty on its head. By testing everyone, including those about whom there isn't a whiff of suspicion, the presumption is that we are all guilty."

The American Civil Liberties Union opposes indiscriminate urine testing because they believe it is unfair and unreasonable to force millions of American workers who are not even suspected of using drugs, and whose job performance is satisfactory, to submit to degrading and intrusive urine tests on a regular basis. The ACLU questions the fairness of treating the innocent and the guilty alike.

*At issue in the dispute over drug testing is nothing less than whether workers may be subjected to "police state" tactics in the workplace, whereby their bodies may be seized and ransacked through the compelled extraction and analysis of bodily fluids without the fundamental protection of a warrant based on probable cause and in spite of common-law rights all supposedly enjoy. And because urine testing detects not on-the-job impairment or drug use, but **prior** exposure to drugs which could have occurred days or weeks before the test while the worker was off duty, drug testing effectuates a form of employer control of workers' personal lives **outside** the context of the workplace.*

*Random or mass urine testing reverses the presumption of innocence upon which much of our jurisprudence is built, and violates the strong prohibition of dragnet searches sweeping in the many who are innocent in order to find the few who are guilty which is the hallmark of a free and democratic society...*

*If the lessons of history are to teach us anything, it is that we must be vigilant against the public hysteria of the moment and adhere to basic constitutional principles and democratic values which are the hallmarks of a free society. The drug problem though real, must be distinguished from the drug **testing** problem.*

*Edward Chen & John True*
*Civil Liberties Attorneys*

# Reducing Liability

Drug testing has a Catch-22 element to it. You're damned-if-you-don't do drug testing—you can lose government contracts, for example. But you are also damned-if-you-do do drug testing! You might violate employee privacy and be sued. You certainly will face moral issues because most people, while they may agree in principle with the concept, they don't like having to pee in a bottle, especially if they're being watched by a co-worker. Potential liability is a fact of drug testing.

In a legal brief, David Evans, an attorney and advisor to the former head of the Drug Enforcement Agency (DEA) argues that utilizing a professional third party administrator (TPA) for random testing reduces employer liability, especially with respect to employee privacy. Use of TPA reduces concerns about management bias and discrimination because of the use of an objective third party to oversee the selection of employees for testing. The typical legal attack on random testing alleges violations of privacy because random testing is a search without first having evidence that there is a need for the search. The TPA has expertise in these issues and is skilled in responding to them.

Another area of legal vulnerability is negligence in conducting drug testing. The process is complex and getting even more convoluted with new laws like the American Disabilities Act and the Family Medical Leave Act. A professional TPA can oversee laboratory selection and selection of collection site. They can administer a program in compliance with the latest laws—Federal and State. On the other hand, hiring a team of consultants is always expensive. It is not an easy decision. There is no one right answer for all employers.

As this chapter demonstrates, even a brief examination of the legal issues surrounding drug testing yields complex and contradictory points of view. Behind the legal arguments are widely accepted ethical and moral values which, when it comes to the matter of drug testing, seem inevitably to come into conflict with one another—such as the apparent disparity between protecting the right to privacy and upholding public safety. Unlike some of the other problems surrounding drug testing, the advancement of technology, education, and level of experience of involved personnel will not necessarily make some of these more fundamental issues go away.

CHAPTER 5

# Drug-Free Workplace
# Becomes Law

President Reagan issued an Executive Order in 1986 calling for a "drug free workplace" and requiring each government agency head to establish a program to test for the use of illegal drugs by employees in sensitive positions. The word "sensitive" was vaguely defined and it was left to the agency heads to decide what it meant. Reagan insisted, in issuing the Executive Order, that it would not be used as a punitive measure to fire or otherwise hurt people. He promised that if people were discovered to be drug users, they would receive help. President Bush continued the Federal Drug Testing Program and, despite staff protest, mandated testing of White House personnel.

But when the Office of Personnel Management released its written regulations they departed dramatically from the assurances to Federal workers that drug users would not be fired. The administration began moving ahead with its program of drug testing of Federal employees, despite Court decisions that widespread random testing was unconstitutional, and despite reservations among some of the top advisors to the White House.

The regulations contained a dismissal provision. In fact, employees could be fired for a single incidence of illegal drug use, and were required to be dismissed for a second offense. The regulations did not require the agencies to prove in any way that the drug use affected the employee's work. Furthermore, the definition of "sensitive" position was so broad that more than half of the Federal workers were included. Under the regulations, disciplinary action was required to be taken against Federal workers other than those who voluntarily turn themselves in after a single confirmed positive drug test. Discipline could include a written reprimand, putting the employee on leave, suspending the employee, or firing, and those who refused to take the test could be fired for "failing to meet a condition of employment."

## Unions' Challenge

Several Federal employee's unions, including the National Federation of Federal Employees (NFFE), filed suit against the government in response to the new drug testing program. The constitutionality of the program was challenged on the basis that the regulations ignored the concept of the connection between the on-the-job performance and discipline. NFFE attorney Pierce said, "the law is very clear that there here must be a connection, 'a nexus' between a disciplinary act and an employee's performance. A nexus must show that there is an actual relationship between off-duty behavior and actual performance." For example, under the Civil Service Reform Act, if a Federal employee is caught shoplifting, that person cannot be fired simply because of that arrest, because there is no nexus, no demonstrable relationship between that arrest and actual performance on the job.

The regulations required that each agency offer counseling and rehabilitation to help employees overcome drug addiction and that employees who failed the test, refused to take it, or failed to complete treatment or counseling successfully could be reprimanded in writing, suspended for 15 days or more, or placed on leave. They also provided that employees must be notified 60 days before the actual testing could begin.

Shortly after the Executive Order, the Customs Service instituted a widespread program of testing custom workers that met with an instantaneous lawsuit, *National Treasury Employees Union* v. *United States Custom Service.* The suit was filed in New Orleans and Judge Collins ruled that the drug testing program run by the Customs Service was unconstitutional. He said that examining customs officials' urine constituted a "warrantless search" made in a "total absence of probable cause or even reasonable suspicion." Judge Collins issued a permanent injunction against the agency program.

The United States Supreme Court, in a narrow 5 to 4 vote, upheld testing of customs personnel carrying firearms or employed in drug interdiction, but questioned testing of clerks, lawyers and accountants.

# The Drug Free Workplace Act Of 1988

The Drug Free Workplace Act of 1988 requires Federal grantees and contractors having a contract for property or services of $25,000 or more to certify to the contracting agency that they will provide a drug free workplace. The Act is the first extension of Federal anti-drug legislation into the workplace of Federal contractors and grantees. The act neither requires nor prohibits drug testing. In practice, however, drug testing is a way of demonstrating compliance with the legislation.

# National Drug Control Strategy

In the Fall of 1989 President Bush announced The White House's drug control strategy on prime time television and followed it up with a text, *National Drug Control Strategy,* describing a comprehensive blueprint for controlling drug use and sales. Bush defended drug testing at work, despite of charges that it is an invasion of privacy and test results are often inaccurate.

Bush said:

> Despite broad public support for drug testing, the prac-
> tice remains controversial. The chief criticisms are that test-
> ing is an invasion of privacy, that the results may not be
> confidential, and that they are not sufficiently accurate.
> Federal guidelines published in 1988 respond to these con-
> cerns, providing significant protection for tested employees.
> By clearly specifying steps to be followed from specimen col-
> lection to reporting of results, confidentiality is maintained.
> If laboratories engaged in drug testing met standards equiva-
> lent to those prescribed from the Federal drug-testing pro-
> gram, the chances of an individual being wrongfully accused
> of using illegal drugs would be greatly reduced.
>
> 1989 National Drug Control Strategy

President Bush continued by setting forth a National Mission
Statement that has direct significance for employers and employees
alike.

> The Federal government has a responsibility to do all
> that it can to promote comprehensive drug-free workplace
> policies in the private sector and in State and local govern-
> ment. Employers will be encouraged to:
>
> • Develop and communicate to all employees a clear drug
>   policy setting out expectations of behavior, employee rights
>   and responsibilities, and actions to be taken in response
>   to an employee found to use illegal drugs;
>
> • Establish an Employee Assistance Program or other ap-
>   propriate mechanism;

- *Train supervisors on how to identify employees who use drugs*

- *Educate employees about the established plan; and*

- *Provide careful means to identify employees who use drugs, including drug testing where appropriate.*

*The Federal government will also move quickly to implement and strengthen regulations for the Drug-Free Workplace Act of 1988, which requires Federal contractors and grantees to have drug-free workplace plans in effect.*

*1989 National Drug Control Strategy*

# Information Management

In his National Drug Control Strategy, President Bush asserted that success in the war on drugs depends on "comprehensive information management." However, he cautioned that the necessity for greater information collection and control must be balanced with the protection of individual privacy and civil liberties. Nonetheless, some civil libertarians worried that Bush's information management is really people management in disguise.

*Success in the war on drugs depends in no small part on having comprehensive information wherever it is needed to make sound policy and operational decisions. The information management challenge is particularly acute given the number and diversity of Federal, State and local agencies involved in the drug war. It is not only a question of having enough information; it is also a question of making the information that is available, and that will become available, accessible to those who are involved in the fight against drugs.*

*Except for the small fraction of information in govern-*
*ment hands that is sensitive and must be closely held, wider*
*access to drug-related information is essential. Many agen-*
*cies are involved; each must be aware of the drug problem's*
*full range and complexity—coherent and coordinated*
*policymaking depends on it. Our national policy must be to*
*maximize the sharing and use of relevant information among*
*appropriate government organizations and to minimize im-*
*pediments to its operational use. All such information shar-*
*ing must of course be conducted with careful attention to*
*the protection of individual privacy and civil liberties.*
*1989 National Drug Control Strategy*

# Omnibus Transportation Testing Act

The Omnibus Transportation Employee Testing Act of 1991re-
quired the Department of Transportation (DOT)to adopt mandatory rules requiring private employers in the transportation industry
to adopt substance-abuse prevention programs, including drug and
alcohol testing. The law is very stringent and specifies each step in
the drug testing process, including how a person is asked to remove
clothing by the collection site person, how much urine constitutes a
sample, use of split samples, testing the sample for temperature within
4 minutes, which tests can be used for screening and which for confirmation, and so forth. These rules also include specific procedures
for testing for alcohol .

The DOT now oversees the Nation's largest workplace drug-testing program with approximately  8 million safety-sensitive Americans working in the aviation, motor, carrier, rail, transit, pipeline and
maritime industiries subject to drug testing. DOT requires workers
in safety-sensitive positions who test positive for drugs to be referred
to substance-abuse professional before returning to work. If substance abuse is diagnosed, the employee must receive treatment before resuming duties. This program—which also requires testing for
operators of commercial motor vehicles from Canada and Mexico—

has become a model for non-regulated employees throughout the United States and in other countries around the world.

If you have employees with commercial drivers' licenses the Federal government requires you to have a drug-and alcohol-free workplace policy. You must provide training about the consequences of drug and alcohol abuse and offer employees information about the policy and testing requirements and procedures. Employees testing positive must be referred to agencies that can help. Your supervisors must be trained to recognize the symptoms of drug and alcohol abuse. Your drug testing program must include random testing, use a SAMSHA-certified lab and use a specially trained Medical Review Officer.

Transportation employers, which includes aviation, railroad and transit companies, are responsible for conducting random unannounced drug tests on at least 50% of the safety-sensitive employees. You are required to keep detailed records of your alcohol misuse programs and submit annual reports to the appropriate DOT agency.

Transportation employers are expected to test at the following times: before applicants are hired, randomly, following accidents, when there is reasonable suspicion that an employee is abusing drugs or alcohol and when past violators return to performing safety-sensitive jobs, called "post-positive follow-up" testing. The Omnibus Transportation Bill has been so successful that in 1998 both the Federal Highway Administration (FHWA) and the Federal Aviation Administration (FAA) lowered the minimum annual random alcohol-testing rate from 25 percent to 10 percent for commercial drivers and aviation industry employees.

# Summary Of Laws And Orders

The ways in which the Federal government reponds to drug abuse and trafficking are outlined n the following laws and orders:

CHAPTER 6

# Search And Seizure

Even though indiscriminate testing may be the easiest way to identify drug users, there is a long tradition in the United States opposing general searches of innocent people. This tradition began in Colonial America, when King George's forces searched people indiscriminately in order to uncover those few who were committing offenses against the crown. These general searches were deeply resented by the early Americans. After the Revolution, the experience of the unfairness of the indiscriminate searches fresh in the new American psyche, the Fourth Amendment was passed. It states that authorities cannot search everyone, innocent and guilty alike, to find the few who are guilty. There must be reasonable suspicion of a particular person before subjecting him or her to intrusive or degrading searches.

Arguments surrounding the right to privacy hinge on the interpretation and application of several key terms and ideas. These include "search, seizure," "reasonableness" (as in "reasonable expectation of privacy" and "reasonable suspicion"), "probable cause," "compelling interest" (as in "a compelling interest to protect public safety" and "voluntary consent.")

*The fundamental legal question is whether drug testing in the workplace is compatible with the protection of personal privacy embodied in the Fourth Amendment's prohibition of unreasonable searches and seizures. Indiscriminate drug testing threatens traditional Fourth Amendment values. Perhaps more than any other provision of the Bill of Rights, the Fourth Amendment expresses an essential quality of democracy—the defense of personal dignity against violation by the State. We ought not experiment with these rights. They are fragile. Once damaged they are not easily repaired. Once lost they are not easily recovered.*

*Adherence to tested Fourth Amendment principles is particularly important when, as now, there is widespread clamor for a simple solution to a serious social problem. The saddest episodes in American Constitutional history have been those occasions, such as the internment of Americans of Japanese descent during World War II, when we have bent our principles to the zealotry of the moment. What is expedient is not necessarily fair, or Constitutional. A war on drugs is a good idea, but not if its first casualty is the Bill of Rights.*

Office of the Attorney General, Maryland

# Is Urine Testing A Search And Seizure?

A preliminary question is whether the collection and testing of a urine specimen is a "search" or "seizure" within the meaning of the Fourth Amendment. A *search* occurs when an expectation of privacy that society is prepared to consider reasonable is infringed. A *seizure* of property occurs when there is some meaningful interference with an individual's possessory interests in that property.

The Supreme Court ruled in *National Treasury Employees Union* v. *United States Customs Service* that taking a urine specimen for drug testing purposes *is*, in fact, a search under the Fourth Amendment. However, it is not necessarily a violation of that Amendment, because only unreasonable searches and seizures are prohibited; so an inquiry into reasonableness is essential. The greater or more demeaning the intrusion, the more substantial must be the reason for conducting the search. The right to "be free from unreasonable governmental intrusion" applies whenever an individual may harbor a *reasonable expectation of privacy*. An expectation of privacy is legitimate in Fourth Amendment terms if the person has an actual or subjective expectation of privacy, and the expectation is one that society is prepared to recognize as reasonable. The Maryland Attorney General concluded, "in our view, State employees as a group have an actual, subjective expectation that their bodily functions will not be subject to government intrusion. Nothing about State employment gives employees reason to suppose that their urination is subject to supervisory inspection and probing. It states the obvious to say that State employees, like everybody else, expect to dispose of their wastes in private."

## Reasonableness

It has been suggested that an employee's expectation of privacy at work can be rendered "unreasonable" by the simple expedient of the State's telling employees that they will be subject to searches. This argument has been challenged, however. A citizen who becomes a State employee cannot be compelled to give up his or her Constitutional rights as the price of gaining that employment. "The government could not avoid the restrictions of the Fourth Amendment by notifying the public that all telephone lines will be tapped, or that all homes will be searched" concluded *U.S.* v. *Davis* in the 9th Circuit.

Some people have suggested that drug testing will be less intrusive if the actual giving of the sample is not observed, since most people do not expect to be observed while they are urinating. However, the absence of supervision means that an employee who does use drugs may be able to substitute someone else's "clean" urine or otherwise tamper with the sample.

There are methods other than observation to ensure specimen integrity. However, to safeguard against this possibility, the Federal Testing Program calls for supervision of an employee's urination if "the agency has reason to believe that a particular employee may alter or substitute the specimen to be provided". For Fourth Amendment purposes, a less intrusive but also less effective program is as problematic as a more intrusive but more effective one.

> *If a blanket search program has little or no effectiveness, it is in substance merely a kind of harassment, a show of power, or a 'fishing expedition,' and therefore, per se, unreasonable under the Fourth Amendment.*
>
> U.S. v. Davis

## Determining Reasonableness

Reasonableness depends on two factors: the degree of intrusiveness of the search and seizure; and the public or private interests at stake. For a relatively innocuous search, or a very compelling public interest such as public safety in the case of an airplane pilot, the reasonableness of the search is greater.

Testing that does not involve observation of the sample is less intrusive, and therefore considered more reasonable. However, such testing is considerably less effective. The more effective type of testing, which involves actual close observation of the sample to prevent tampering, is more effective. It is also more intrusive and thus less reasonable, unless there is a very strong reason to actually suspect that person of using drugs.

## Probable Cause

It is impossible to fully define either "probable cause" or "reasonable suspicion" in the abstract. As a comparative matter, reasonable suspicion is less stringent than probable cause. Even reasonable suspicion must be founded upon objective facts and rational inferences derived from practical experience, rather than unspecified suspicions, and must be directed toward a particular employee to be tested.

Under a "for cause policy" a urine sample may be requested if a reasonable suspicion exists that an employee may be using drugs. *Reasonable suspicion* exists when there are specific objective facts and reasonable inferences from work experience that suggest the employee is under the influence of drugs. These may include slurred speech, an on-the-job accident, frequent absences, tardiness, or early departure from work. Since reasonable suspicion is established by combining fact and judgment, it is not possible to predict or describe every situation that may arouse reasonable suspicion.

There have been some significant Court cases around the issue of probable cause. For example, in *McDonnell* v. *Hunter,* the 8th Circuit Court declared unconstitutional on Fourth Amendment grounds the routine searches of prison guards and their vehicles by the Iowa Department of Corrections. In this incident, the Court directed the department to revise search procedures so that they would be based only on probable cause.

## Reduced Expectation Of Privacy

The context of the situation is very important in establishing the reasonableness or unreasonableness of a search. In part, context entails the particular requirements of performing a given job, and whether the employee could or could not threaten public safety.

Some categories of State employees can reasonably be expected to have somewhat diminished expectations of privacy, given the nature of their work. Someone who becomes a police officer or firefighter must know what the job entails and the special obligation of those who enforce the law to obey it themselves. Hence police officers may, in certain circumstances, enjoy less Constitutional protection than the ordinary citizen. But even where police officers and firefighters have diminished protection, they may be tested only if the reasonable suspicion standard is met. For example, in the

*McDonnell* v. *Hunter* case, in which prison guards' cars were being searched, testing was approved only on the basis of reasonable suspicions based on specific observable facts and reasonable inferences drawn from these facts in light of experience that a given employee was abusing drugs.

In the case of *Capua* v. *Plainfield,* an investigation began when officials in Plainfield, N.J., received an anonymous tip that some of the city's police and firefighters were using illicit drugs. The city cracked down, staging a surprise urine test for all 244 members of the police and fire departments. Twenty employees, including two cops, tested positive for marijuana or cocaine and were given the option of resigning or being suspended. Sixteen suspended firefighters filed suit in Federal court, and U.S. District Court Judge H. Lee Sarokin ruled that Plainfield's "mass round-up urinalysis" violated the Constitutional prohibition against unreasonable search and seizure. "The threat posed by widespread use is real. The need to combat it manifest," Judge Sarokin wrote in his decision, "But it is important not to permit fear and panic to overcome our fundamental principles and protections."

However, in the Plainfield case, the Court also held that testing of these employees under the "individualized reasonable suspicion" standard would meet Fourth Amendment standards. In other words, the mistake that the city of Plainfield made was conducting a wholesale mass testing unannounced, without any reasonable suspicion of particular individuals.

In *Amalgamated Transit Employee v. Suscy,* a Transit Authority employee came under suspicion by two supervisors who believed that he was under the influence and therefore had him tested. In the ensuing lawsuit, the Court held that the blood and urine testing of this municipal bus driver was permissible under the Fourth Amendment, citing the valid interest in protecting the public. This decision reinforced the notion that an employer should be able to test employees if public safety is an overriding concern.

In *National Treasury Employees Union* v. *United States Customs Service* and *Skinner* v. *Railway Labor Executives Associations,* both plaintiffs argued that "particularized suspicion" was essential to justify compulsory drug testing of employees. But the Supreme Court disagreed and found that drug testing can be Constitutional even without particularized suspicion that an individual employee is in fact a drug user.

Supreme Court Justice Anthony Kennedy, writing for the majority in the 1989 landmark *Skinner* v. *Railway Labor Executives Associations* decision, agreed that drug tests are "searches" according to the Fourth Amendment. But he concluded that the search was reasonable when the "diminished" privacy interests of railway workers were balanced against the "compelling" interest in deterring drug use on the rails. "The expectations of privacy of covered employees are diminished by reason of their participation in an industry that is regulated pervasively to insure safety," said Justice Kennedy. In the related decision of *National Treasury Employees Union* v. *United States Custom Service,* he concluded that Customs employees who carry firearms and those involved in drug interdiction have the same "diminished expectation of privacy."

## Compelling Interest

The reasonableness of a search, including a search by means of drug testing, is determined by balancing the employee's privacy expectations against the government's interest in conducting the search. In *National Treasury Employees Union* v. *United States Customs Service,* the Supreme Court identified three governmental interests:

1) Ensuring that front line drug interdiction personnel are physically fit, and have unimpeachable integrity and judgment;

2) Providing "effective measures to prevent the promotion of drug users to positions that require the incumbent to carry a firearm;" and

3) Protecting truly sensitive information from those who, under compulsion of circumstances or for other reasons, might compromise information.

The Court weighed the interference with privacy resulting from giving urine for testing against the government's compelling interests. The Court concluded that, while requiring urine samples could interfere with privacy, the governments need to conduct such searches of employees engaged directly in drug interdiction and of those who carried firearms took precedence.

In another case involving drug testing, *Skinner* v. *Railway Labor Executives Associations,* the Court characterized the government's interest in promoting railroad safety through drug testing as "compelling" and, therefore, "not an undue infringement on the justifiable expectations of privacy of covered employees."

While somewhat ambiguous, the Supreme Court's decision in the Customs case strongly suggests that protection of "sensitive information" related to drug enforcement investigation and national security are also compelling government interests. There is speculation that the decision may be applied to the broader context of commercially sensitive information. If future cases result in such rulings, then the range of employees subjected to testing could be greatly expanded.

## Voluntary Consent

In general, the Courts have supported the idea that voluntary consent to a search satisfies requirements of the Fourth Amendment. The Department of Justice has taken the position that when a public employee is told that drug testing is a condition of employment and does not quit, this is in fact consent to the testing. The Office of the Attorney General of the State of Maryland rejected this notion of consent, saying, "a valid consent to a search must in fact be voluntarily given, and not be the result of duress or coercion, expressed or implied. It flies in the face of economic reality to suppose that an employee voluntarily consents to a drug test when the alternative is losing his or her job, or, for that matter, that an applicant voluntarily consents when the alternative is being denied the job. Agreement to a search motivated by fear that refusal will lead to loss of one's livelihood is not voluntary consent."

Nor can voluntary consent fairly be inferred from a person's decision to accept a job with the knowledge that drug testing is a condition of that job. In both *McDonnell* v. *Hunter* and the *Security and Law Enforcement Employees* v. *Carey,* the prison employees were told at the onset of their employment that they would be subject to certain searches. In the McDonnell case, the employees actually signed a consent form expressing their agreement, among other things, to submit to a urinalysis or blood test when requested by the prison administrator. In the Carey case, they were given a rule book which stated that any employee on duty would be subject to a search. Nevertheless, the Court held that neither circumstance gave rise to voluntary consent. In both cases, the Courts ruled that it was coercion and not consent. If the choice to decline the search carries with it significant adverse consequences, then the alternative, submitting to the search, does not reflect voluntary consent.

"Consent" in any meaningful sense cannot be said to exist merely because a person (a) knows that an official intrusion into his privacy is contemplated if he does a certain thing, and then (b) proceeds to do that thing. Were it otherwise, the police could, for instance, use the implied-consent theory to subject everyone on the street after 11 p.m. to physical search, merely by making public announcements in the press, radio, and television that such searches would be undertaken.

## Two Views

*We're convinced that under the circumstances, this test will be proved to be Constitutional. We're in a situation . . . where the country has a real serious problem on its hands. And I think, under the circumstances, a drug testing program is appropriate.*

*Let me try to draw a parallel. A number of years ago, we used to be able to get on airplanes and fly from city to city without going through magnetometers and having our baggage searched at the gate. We developed a serious problem. We couldn't take an airplane flight without ending up in Cuba. We had to put in a fairly comprehensive program in our airports to stop this from happening, and the Courts, when weighing the problem against the intrusion in one's personal life, decided this was Constitutional.*

Stephen Trott
Justice Department

*If the government were to announce that all telephones would be hereafter tapped, perhaps to counter an outbreak of political kidnappings, it would not justify, even after public knowledge of the wiretapping plan, the proposition that anyone using a telephone consented to being tapped. It would not matter that other means of communication exist . . . it is often a necessity of modern living to use a telephone. So also it is often a necessity to fly on a commercial airliner, and to force one to choose between that necessity and the exercise of a Constitutional right is coercion in the Constitutional sense.*

U.S. v. Albarado

The question of whether or not testing is voluntary is very important, because a valid voluntary consent would excuse the need for a warrant or for probable cause prior to testing. In a private business setting, an employment policy posted publicly is generally taken to mean that all of the employees have consented to the policy. However, this may not be legally valid. An example is *Luck v. Southern Pacific* which was filed by a pregnant woman named Barbara Luck who worked for the company for six years as a computer programmer and refused to take an unannounced test administered to everyone in her department. Luck was fired because she did not consent to the test. She sued for wrongful termination. The jury was instructed that Southern Pacific had to show that it was "necessary" to test Luck "in order to achieve the public interest of safety in the operation and maintenance of the railroad." Southern Pacific failed to prove necessity and the jury awarded $485,000 to Luck in a unanimous verdict.

Southern Pacific appealed the ruling and in the Spring of 1990 the Court of Appeal decision upheld the jury award in favor of Barbara Luck. The California State Appeal Court ruled that employers must have a "compelling interest" when asking their workers to submit to random drug tests if the employees are not in safety-sensitive positions. The ruling applies to all California employers, public and private. However, it does not speak to the issue of testing job applicants. The "compelling interest" requirement for a person already employed is more stringent than the existing requirement used for job applicants. Applicants may be tested if the employer's right to know outweighs the applicant's right to privacy. Luck's attorney summaried by saying, "By this decision, employers (in California) must exercise extreme caution before they require any employee to submit to any test as a condition of employment."

The information in this chapter makes it clear that it is not always easy to determine whether drug testing is legal or Constitutional in a given situation. In many circumstances, an employer must weigh differing and sometimes conflicting interests against each other—for instance, an employee's "reasonable expectation of privacy" against the "compelling interest" of protecting public safety. When an employer's action is legally challenged, such issues are determined by courts. Important precedents are then set, which exert a significant—but by no means absolute—influence on future cases.

# CHAPTER 7

# Right To Privacy

Innocent people do have something to guard against: invasion of privacy. The "right to privacy" is, in the words of the eminent Supreme Court Justice Louis Brandeis, "the most comprehensive of rights and the most valued by civilized men." Obligatory urine testing may be considered an invasion of privacy because certain tests can disclose numerous details about one's private life in addition to illegal drug use, such as whether or not an employee or applicant is pregnant, legally consumes alcohol, is being treated for various medical conditions or is disabled.

## Who Has A Right To Privacy?

The Fourth Amendment was enacted in response to King George's indiscriminate searches of colonist's homes. It's goal was to prevent such excesses by government; it does not feature provisions directly relevant to the behavior of private individuals, organizations, or employers.

Federal and State Constitutions protect all citizens *against unreasonable government searches and seizures* of person and property. In general, the Federal protection applies only when the challenged action is taken by government officials. In fact, private employers often use the State action requirement as a defense against Constitutional challenges to their drug testing policy. On the other hand, if a private employer uses the police or other government officials in the search, and the counter-claim is that the employer is acting as an "agent" of the State, then the Constitutional standard is usually applied.

Privacy rights of private employees may be protected by special Federal or State laws or union contracts. In general, however, employees of private companies must look to their own State's laws to protect their right to privacy. For the most part, employees of private companies have little protection against the mandatory drug testing programs that have been adopted by many companies, including several in the Fortune 500. The ACLU believes that it is unfair that government workers are protected in their rights to privacy, but their counterparts in private industry are not.

## States Also Protect Privacy

Ten states—Alaska, California, Florida, Hawaii, Illinois, Louisiana, Montana, New York, South Carolina, and Washington—have express privacy provisions in their Constitutions. Some of these State Constitutions have a more developed right to privacy than the Federal Constitution. For example, the California Constitution under Article 1, Section 1, specifically guarantees a person's right to privacy, and this provision has been interpreted to apply to both private and governmental activities.

### California's Right To Privacy

*All people are by nature free and independent, and have certain inalienable rights. Among these are enjoying and defending life and liberty, acquiring, possessing, and protecting property, and pursuing and obtaining safety, happiness, and privacy.*

Constitution of the State of California
Article 1, Section 1

A leading California case addressing the general privacy rights is *White* v. *David*. The ourt ruled that the California right to privacy prevents government and business from secretly gathering personal information, from overly broad collection and retention of unnecessary personal information, and from improper use or disclosure of properly gathered personal information. The Court set forth a list of "mischiefs" that the right of privacy was intended to correct.

### White Mischiefs

• *Government snooping and the secret gathering of personal information.*

• *The overly broad collection and retention of unnecessary personal information by government and business interests*

• *The improper use of information properly obtained for a specific purpose, for example, use for another purpose, or the disclosure of it to a third party.*

• *The lack of a reasonable check on the accuracy of existing records.*

The White "mischiefs" may not apply to employee drug testing, however. The White Decision addressed secret or overly broad information gathering and improper disclosure.

In the first ruling of its kind in California, a State Appeals Court in 1989 upheld a private company's drug testing of its job applicants, regardless of the safety-sensitive nature of the position. The 3-to-0 decision upheld a pre-employment drug and alcohol screening program at Matthew Bender & Co., a subsidiary of the Times Mirror Co. The Court specified that its ruling applied only to testing of applicants and not to employees, whose privacy rights against testing may be greater.

# Compelling Interests

California privacy decisions after White have stated that the right to privacy is not absolute; it must be offset against other compelling interests. On the use of drugs, for example, at least one California Court has held that an individual has no Constitutional privacy right to use or possess cocaine at home (*People v. Davis*). In addition, California does not recognize a Constitutional right to use or possess marijuana in one's own home (*NORML v. Gain*). This ruling is now murky with the passage of a voter initiative allowing medical marijuana.

An infringement of a Constitutional privacy right must be justified by a "compelling interest" under traditional California Constitutional privacy analyses. Showing that the State's interest cannot be satisfied in a less intrusive manner is necessary in some instances. To meet the compelling interest test, the justification for the privacy intrusion must be very substantial.

Drug testing cases in California present competing Constitutional interests. The right to pursue and obtain safety, to preserve and protect property, and to pursue and obtain privacy are all protected by the Constitution. Drug testing cases in California often pit the Constitutional interests of employers, employees, co-workers and the public against one another.

How to resolve the clash of the Constitution rights of safety and privacy is an unresolved California Constitutional question. The use by police of drunk driver "checkpoints" that involve stopping and checking drivers at random, without any individual suspicion, was approved by the California Supreme Court (*Ingersoll v. Palmer*) and may help set the standard for the future of drug testing. The Court found that right to privacy was safeguarded by prior general public notice of location of the checkpoints and by stopping each motorist only very briefly if there is not suspicion of wrongdoing. However, as civil rights attorneys Edward Chen and John True point out, "no one has ever suggested that motorists be subject to random detentions and urine tests wherein they run the risk of losing their driver's license if such urine tests come up positive. . . . even sobriety check-points require probable cause based upon observation of behavior and appearance together with failed performance of a field sobriety test before the police can require the production of blood or urine."

## Privacy Off The Job

The concern that drug or alcohol testing may infringe on non-work activities merits consideration. The Courts must counterbalance the interests of the employer, co-employees, and society against those of the employee being tested for drugs. Tests can identify drug use during an employee's off-duty hours.  An employer's interest in an employee's personal matters is not compelling unless an employee's use of drugs affects the workplace.  But employees with traces of drugs in their system during working hours may violate the employer's anti-drug rules.  This is especially true if the rules require that employees be drug-free at all times.

Even though employees may not be impaired when tested, it is argued that they can be expected to be impaired at some future time when test results reveal past use.  Some employers feel that an employee's use of drugs while off-duty  is itself a hazard that they have a responsibility to curb.  On the face of it, use of drugs during off-duty hours is probably a weaker privacy interest than other personal matters not concerning the workplace.

*May employers exercise control over off-the-job conduct simply because there is some correlation with job performance? If so, employers would have the right to control many aspects of worker personal life which could influence performance and productivity, including domestic disputes, personal financial woes, sleeping and eating habits, cigarette smoking and indeed any personal condition which affects an employee's overall physical and mental health.  This argument has no logical limit, and it leads logically to fright-*

*ening consequences. If drug tests are permitted, why not*
*psychological tests and genetic screenings?*

Edward Chen & John True
Civil Liberties Attorneys

# Privacy Is Evolving

Differences can exist between Federal and State laws. For example, consider the Oregon election of November 1986, when at the peak of the national "War on Drugs," Oregonians could have legalized marijuana use in their state, even while in the rest of the Nation's employees in private and public business were being tested, put into treatment programs, and sometimes fired for the use of marijuana. The Oregon ballot contained an initiative signed by 90,000 Oregonians to legalize marijuana. While the initiative was defeated by a 2 to 1 vote, it was on the ballot nonetheless.

In the Oregon initiative, "private" means "not public." In common-sense terms, private means that marijuana could not be used in a location where it would intrude upon the sensibilities of other people who might be offended. This notion of private is comparable to the definition used in the statutes prohibiting public indecency or public drunkenness. Had the initiative passed, it still would have been illegal to possess marijuana in parks, school grounds, or any place visible to the public.

During the Oregon initiative process, Governor Vic Atiyeh rejected a proposal by the President's Commission on Organized Crime to test all State workers for drug use. Atiyeh was quoted as saying he would not require drug testing as a condition of employment in the State of Oregon, because in his opinion it was "not necessary," and that drug use by State workers in Oregon was not a "major problem." As far as Governor Atiyeh was concerned, what employees did in their off-duty time was none of his business as long as it did not negatively affect their job performance. The Governor further cautioned private employers against using drug testing on employees, because in his opinion, such drug testing "involves an unfair presumption of guilt."

Another dramatic instance of the different interpretation of privacy in a State versus Federal context is provided by the Alaska Supreme Court unanimous ruling on marijuana in *Ravin* v. *State*. The Court ruled that the Alaskan Constitution protects an individual's privacy, and agreed with the NORML and ACLU attorneys that marijuana did not represent a significant enough risk to society to allow the State to invade an individual's privacy. In the years following the Court's decision, several surveys indicate basic support for the reform. If anything, the surveys demonstrate support for legalizing the sales of small amounts of marijuana and perhaps total legalization.

The Supreme Court of Alaska discussed the Ravin decision, in *Harrison* v. *State*. A State trooper had been arrested in a dry county—a county where alcohol is illegal—with alcohol in his possession. The trooper claimed that the Ravin case provided a precedent for his possession of alcohol. He argued that if you are allowed to possess marijuana, you are surely allowed to possess alcohol. The Alaskan Supreme Court saw things differently, however. They examined the effects that alcohol was having in Alaskan society and compared that to marijuana. They found that there was no comparison, and that the State had more cause to regulate, even prohibit, alcohol than it did marijuana.

## Conflicting State Laws

Throughout most of this book we have been examining Federal drug testing mandates. Each state has its own laws for handling alcohol and drug abuse in the workplace. These laws can vary dramatically from state to state. For example, thirteen states and two cities ban, or significantly restrict random testing. The states include Alaska, California, Colorado, Connecticut, Iowa, Maine, Massachusetts, Minnesota, Montana, New Jersey, New York, Rhode Island, Vermont and West Virginia. Two cities, San Francisco and Boulder, prohibit random drug testing. Similarly, on-site testing is regulated by State laws. In some cases states limit companys' options in handling initial on-site positive tests. Other states outlaw on-site testing altogether. By

1998, states had begun to restrict hair-testing. In 1998 Iowa legislated a new drug testing law in which a new provision permits physician's assistants, nursed practitioners, and chiropractors to serve as MROs, as long as they have appropriate medical training. This provision is unique among State laws permitting non-physicians to act as MROs and is viewed as inappropriate by the Iowa Department of Public Health.

To complicate matters, each year there are new State laws and court cases. The Institute for a Drug-Free Workplace (www.drugfreeworkplace.org) in Washington DC periodically catalogs the State and Federal drug-testing laws, court cases and arbitration outcomes into a helpful publication entitled *Guide to State and Federal Drug-Testing Law.*

# CHAPTER 8

# Self-Incrimination
# And Due Process

Drug testing programs can be implemented in a way that can violate Fifth Amendment rights of employees. On the surface, for example, it seems that voluntary consent to drug testing forces employees into self-incrimination and denial of due process of law.

Blood and breath tests have been held not to violate a person's Fifth Amendment protections against self-incrimination. Therefore, urine testing is viewed as belonging in the same category as blood and breath tests. Self-incrimination defenses are not likely to stand. In fact, The Supreme Court, in *Skinner* v. *Railway Labor Executive* rejected the defense that urine drug testing is a form of self-incrimination.

## The Fifth Amendment

*No persons shall be held to answer for a capital, or otherwise infamous crime, unless on a presentment or indictment of a Grand Jury, except in cases rising in the land or naval forces, or in the Militia, when in actual service in time of war or public danger; nor shall any person be subject for the same offense to be twice put in jeopardy of life or limb; nor shall be compelled in any criminal case to be a witness against himself, nor be deprived of life, liberty, or property, without due process of law, nor shall private property be taken for use, without just compensation.*

## Polygraphs

The self-incrimination issue is central in the debates about polygraph testing. Lie detectors, known formally as polygraphs, are devices that purport to detect untruthful answers by measuring changes in blood pressure, pulse rate, and perspiration. Over the years, these devices have become more technologically sophisticated. Traditionally courts have not accepted the scientific claims for these machines, and they are barred as evidence. Some quarters of private industry, however, have embraced them.

In the 1980s, as many as 2 million polygraphs were administered in the private sector each year. Finally workers in the private sector brought suit, and the House of Representatives passed the Polygraph Protection Act, which prohibits private employers from giving lie detector tests to most current or prospective employees. Many utility workers, pharmaceutical workers handling controlled substances, day-care workers, and employees of private security companies could still be polygraphed, however.

In a California State Supreme Court ruling that outlaws the practice of forcing employees to take polygraph tests, Chief Justice Rose Bird wrote, "The device is designed so that an examinee cannot prevent a response to highly personal questions even by remaining silent. This method of interrogation thus strikes the very heart of the privacy guarantee." Even so, there are exceptions to California's Employee Polygraph Protection Act, including employees involved in national security activities for the Federal government, as well as security service firms and manufacturers, distributors and dispensers of pharmaceuticals, and employees of private firms who are reasonably suspected of involvement in a workplace incident such as theft or embezzlement that resulted in economic loss to the employer.

Whatever their scientific basis, lie detectors can serve as "scarecrows." Many people think the machines work, and when being threatened with the prospect of a test, blurt out confessions. Abuses have occurred. In Florida, for example, managers at a Zayre's Department Store discovered a $500 theft. They tested everyone who had access to the store safe, including an assistant manger named David. He failed twice and was fired even though he proclaimed his innocence. The investigation continued until another man who had cleared the polygraph was caught. However, Zayre's would not rehire David without an admission of guilt. He sued for defamation, and the store later settled for $250,000. Zayre's no longer uses polygraphs.

## The Honesty Test

In response to the expense of polygraphs and the controversy surrounding them, many employers turned to personality tests or written honesty tests. For obvious reasons, employers would like to be sure they are hiring honest persons, but it is virtually impossible to get to know people before they are hired. Honesty tests are specialized variations of personality tests. A large number of questions are usually included to increase reliability of the tests, but most questions simply represent different ways to probe for dishonest behavioral tendencies and attitudes. Interpretations are made by comparing an individual's profile with those of persons independently judged honest and dishonest by Courts of law or with polygraphs. Some tests measure an individual's test score against the response pattern of normal persons as well as those clinically diagnosed as suffering from such psychiatric disorders as depression, hysteria, paranoia, and schizophrenia.

## Typical Honesty Test Questions

Would you answer "yes" or "no" to the following:

- When you are wrong, do you usually admit it?

- Do you ever worry about what other people will think of you?

- Did you ever cheat in school?

- Have you ever thought about cheating anyone out of anything?

- Did you ever lie to a teacher or policeman?

- Have you ever stolen anything from an employer?

Stanton Corp.

Proponents claim that personality tests can predict which applicants are at risk of drug abuse, those who are unsuitable for employment in stressful positions, such as flight-control centers or nuclear plants, and even those who would function well in jobs that involve frequent rejections, such as sales, or physical threats, such as in psychiatric nursing. As Dr. Hommer B. C. Reed, a neuropsychologist at Tufts University New England Medical Center pointed out, the tests are often "disarmingly ingenuous." He singled out as an example from one of the tests, "The amount I stole from my employer was (a) 0, (b) $5, (c) $25, (d) $100, (e) $500." This was accompanied by a space for explanation. No single answer, or group of answers, is considered significant without taking into account the total pattern of responses. Sometimes the test determines that you are lying by the "no" answer to a question like, "Have you ever cheated?" or "Have you ever stolen anything?" The presumption is that everyone has cheated or stolen at least once.

Prompted by concerns that employers would use written tests to pry too deeply into an employee's background, as some lie detector tests have done, Massachusetts enacted a law that prohibits employers from giving honesty tests that amount to "paper and pencil" polygraphs. Considerable concern has been expressed about whom is actually being screened out by these devices. Not only could they screen out capable and honest employees, but they might also screen out people more likely to join unions or to challenge practices on the job as being morally or ethically improper.

> *The issue has serious repercussions. For example, a grand jury awarded $450,000 to an employee of a fast-food chain who was fired because a polygraph examiner said that the employee's denial of having used cocaine was untruthful. Aside from the polygraph results, the only "evidence" suggesting otherwise was "rumors" of drug use outside of work that the supervisor had heard.*
>
> *The next epidemic in America, which has already started, ... is test abuse. Let me put it to you this way. Would you want your doctor making a decision to operate on you on the basis of a single blood or urine test? Now, most people in America, I hope, would be horrified by that thought. Yet, everyday in America we are operating on our workers. We are severing them from their jobs and their livelihood, and sometimes from their freedom, on the basis of a single chemical test.*
>
> Dr. Ron Seigel

## Due Process

Denying an employee due process may be in violation of the Fifth Amendment. The question is whether or not the drug testing process and results are arbitrary. This question is usually answered by testimony regarding the accuracy of urine testing procedures and a factual demonstration that the procedure was followed.

The issue of abuse of drug testing has become very serious as a result of questionable practices by some employers. A very dramatic case of alleged drug testing abuse involved the Georgia Power Company. Leslie Price and Susan Register were two workers employed in a nuclear power plant. Register, a mechanical expeditor, and Price, a quality-control inspector, were concerned about plant safety and reported apparent violations to the Nuclear Regulatory Commission. Subsequently, the two were told they had been "hot lined," and were ordered in for drug tests. Susan Register testified to being forced by a nurse to drop her pants to her ankles, bend over at the waist with her knees slightly bent, hold her right arm in the air, and with her left hand angle a specimen bottle between her legs. She described sobbing, wetting herself, and vomiting. She was fired for insubordination for refusing to take the test. Price gave her urine sample and was told that her sample was positive for marijuana. She was fired for misconduct. Had she been fired for drug use, the Nuclear Regulatory Commission might have ordered the company to recheck, at great cost, all the work she had inspected as a quality-controller. This is a dramatic example of how drug testing might be used to punish whistle-blowers.

Employers are not the only sources of potential abuse. A spiteful employee, for example, could report having "heard" rumors that another employee was using drugs, causing that person to be tested. This could be considered harassment. Since these tests have a high rate of errors, that person could come up with a positive test, even though drugs were not used. Many are concerned that drug testing could be used in subtle ways to dissuade union organizing, or that particularly outspoken employees could be subjected to testing and have the future of their employment put in jeopardy.

Workers at Pacific Refining Company in Hercules, California, filed a class-action suit after the company ordered its employees to take urine tests. Hercules required all employees to come in, partly disrobe, and expose themselves so that a witness could verify the urine specimen. Three people refused to take the test and were fired, even though the company said that employees who tested positive would not be fired. The company said it had to fire those who refused because they needed 100 percent participation. The ACLU and Attorney John True of the Employment Law Center worked with the employees on the case and a restraining order was issued to halt the testing. It was one of the first tests of drug testing and right-to-privacy laws in California.

The plaintiffs asserted that there was no reason to believe that there was a drug problem at the refinery. The decision to do the testing was made at the home office in Houston, because of a belief that drug use is "pretty pervasive" in society. True pointed out that the test in no way showed anything about impairment on the job, but it could indicate pregnancy or ingestion of legal medications, which would be an invasion of privacy.

The right of employers to test employees for drugs has evolved since wide spread testing began. Testing of strongly suspected drug users, crews involved in accidents, and personnel in sensitive positions has been upheld by the Supreme Court. However, most employees do not use drugs, do not have sensitive positions, and are not involved in serious accident.s

Justice Scalia was with the 7 to 2 Supreme Court majority upholding post-accident testing in *Skinner* v. *Railway Labor Executives Association.* He dissented from the narrow 5 to 4 majority upholding testing of some, but not all, Customs employees. Justice Scalia noted that only five of 3,600 Customs employees tested positive for drugs. Of the 30,000 Federal employees tested in 1988 under the random spot checking program only 203 tested positive, a rate of 0.7 percent.

The Supreme Court seems to be shifting in its interpretation of the Fifth Amendment away from the negative requirement of "particularized" suspicion for reasonable searches. Civil libertarians warn about such erosion of privacy—especially that of the innocent. They say this shift prepares the way for dragnet office searches, blanket AIDS testing, or regular searches of travelers. Contrasting the documented record of alcohol and drug abuse among railroad workers with the data on Customs workers, Justice Scalia wrote that there is no "real evidence of a real problem that will be solved" by drug testing. He added, "Symbolism, even symbolism for so worthy a cause as the abolition of unlawful drugs, cannot validate an otherwise unreasonable search." Given the narrow 5 to 4 vote and limited scope of the Supreme Court decision in *National Treasury Employees Union* v. *Von Raab*, it is likely that there will be limits to drug testing. Responding to the Court's decision, Dr. Michael Walsh of NIDA, National Institute on Drug Abuse, said, "The issue in our program has always been who (to test). The most difficult decision is where to draw the line. Nuclear people are obviously in, and clerical people are obviously out, but there are a lot of people in the middle."

It will be years before the line is clearly drawn as to whom can be tested for drugs and under what circumstances. Good drug testing programs build in due process to protect employees from abuse and minimize employer liability. These include demonstrating a drug abuse problem exists in the company or within the industry, careful attention to how employees are selected for testing to prevent harassment or discrimination, strict adherence to forensic standards, preservation of the sample, permission for employees to use the lab of their choice for retesting, and advanced disclosure of the testing procedure to employees. California's testing program for applicants and employees (see Appendix) incorporates due process safeguards. Programs that are carefully crafted to include due process are less susceptible to legal challenge.

# CHAPTER 9

# Discrimination

The Courts have ruled that drug testing is a search—a search of one's urine or blood. In the process of such a search lawful prescription drug use can be revealed. The person tested is asked to disclose his or her drug use. And, as in the case of a positive test result, the person must do so in order to explain lawful drug use, which may be being taken to treat a disability. Once this information is known it can be used to discriminate against the disabled person by denying employment on the basis of the disability, when the person is otherwise qualified to do the job. This is a serious problem because it violates the civil rights of the disabled and deprives the workforce of needed skilled workers who desire to work. In 1990 the American Disabilities Act (ADA) was enacted to correct this situation.

## American Disabilities Act

The American Disabilities Act, which applies to government agencies and employers with 15 or more employees, expands equal employment law by creating a new "protected class" of Americans—individuals with disabilities—which is estimated to be 43 million people or about one-sixth of the population of the United States. The law is complicated and impacts on personnel policies, programs and hiring, including drug testing and medical review of testing results.

Among the people protected by the ADA are people with diagnosed psychological disorders such as depression and schizophrenia. Alcoholism and drug addiction are considered disabilities under this law. This is important to the issue of drug testing because people with psychological disabilities often use prescribed psychiatric drugs, the use of which is protected by the ADA, provided it is under the supervision of an appropriate health professional. Testing for prescription drugs and probing into a person's medical information to uncover the use of such drugs is prohibited because this information can be used to discriminate. This same protection extends to recovered or recovering alcoholics and drug addicts because they are disabled. The ADA does not protect individuals currently using illicit drugs or using prescription drugs illegally, however. These behaviors are specifically excluded from coverage.

## Past Versus Present Drug Use

The ADA makes a distinction between past and present drug use, and between legal and illegal prescription drug use. Illicit drug use in *the past* by a *drug addict* is considered a disability and is protected; whereas *current* illicit drug use is not considered a disability and is not protected by the ADA. Illicit drug use in the past by a casual user who was *not* addicted is not protected because causal drug use is not considered a disability. Use of a prescription drug under the supervision of an appropriate health care professional is legal drug use and protected, however, improper use of a prescription drug is illegal and not protected by the ADA.

These distinctions unfold in confusing and sometimes contradictory ways. The person most at risk of abusing alcohol and using illicit drugs is the person who has already done so in the past because the recidivism rate among recovered substance abusers is extremely high. However, employers are prohibited from considering *former* drug or alcohol abuse when hiring or in managing employees because alcoholism and drug addiction are defined as disabilities by the ADA. Asking job applicants about their *former* drug or alcohol use, including addiction or treatment, is a violation of the ADA and can lead to a discrimination suit—even if the person is subsequently hired. On the other hand, asking a job applicant about *current* use of illicit drugs is permitted because such use is illegal and not protected by the ADA.

#### QUESTIONS TO AVOID DURING A JOB INTERVIEW
- What  prescription drugs do you use?
- Have you ever abused drugs or alcohol?
- Have you ever been in drug or alcohol treatment?
- Are you an addict or alcoholic?
- Have you ever been arrested for driving under the influence (DUI)?

#### QUESTIONS PERMISSABLE DURING A JOB INTERVIEW
- Do you drink?
- Do you currently use illegal drugs?
- Have you used marijuana in the last 30 days?
- Have you ever been convicted of a DUI?
- Have you ever had your driver's license suspended or revoked?
- Have you ever been convicted of a felony related to drug or alcohol use?

## What is Current Use?

The ADA does not clearly define current versus past use.  Current use is not limited to the use of drugs on the day, or within a matter of days or weeks before the drug test or other employment action in question. Rather the Equal Employment Opportunity Commission (EEOC) has clarified it as "the illegal use of drugs that has occurred recently enough to indicate that the individual is actively engaged in such conduct." This includes current on-the-job use and job impairment due to illicit drug use.  It also includes a positive urine drug test which is equated with current usage. Past drug use is generally considered to be use prior to six months in the past.

While the time distinction between current and past is not fixed, "current" is broad enough that it precludes a person who has gotten a positive drug test from claiming that he or she has a disability—and is thereby protected from discipline—by enrolling in a rehabilitation program.

Employers are allowed to give drug tests to disabled people, provided they are testing for current illicit drug use and disabled people are not singled out for the testing. That is, abled and disabled alike are tested. Employers are not allowed to test for prescription drugs, except when the person is believed to be using prescription drugs improperly, such as taking someone else's prescription, in which case it is illegal drug use.

## Drug Addiction Is A Disability

It is a violation of the ADA to discriminate against recovering drug addicts and alcoholics. "Recovering" is defined as participating in or having successfully completed a supervised drug rehabilitation program and no longer using drugs illegally. This doesn't mean that employers must hire job applicants who have been drug addicts. That would be absurd. But rejecting a person solely on the basis of their disability—drug addiction or alcoholism—is illegal. The law does allow for exceptions, however. A person who is not currently using drugs but who has a history of drug abuse can be fired or refused employment in certain occupations such as law enforcement, for example, when it can be demonstrated that the prohibition is job-related and a business necessity.

The American Disabilities Act also protects people who are erroneously regarded as using drugs illegally. For example, suppose based upon a rumor, which turned out to be false, an employer believed that an employee was a drug addict using illegal drugs. The person is protected by the ADA and regarded as an individual with a disability. On the other hand, if the employer did not think the person was an addict but was using illegal drugs recreationally, the person would not be regarded as an individual with a disability and would not be protected by the ADA.

In other words, employers are prohibited from rejecting job applicants and taking adverse action against people on the basis of a disability, even when that disability is drug addiction. Employers are permitted, however, to not hire and to fire or otherwise discipline employees who are shown to be currently using illicit drugs or illegally using prescription drugs. Because the penalties for violating the ADA are so severe, employers must be very careful to take action based solely upon the person's current behavior, i.e., drug or alcohol use, and not upon a disability, including drug abuse in the past if the person has been rehabilitated.

## Medical Examinations

Under the ADA employees and job candidates with disabilities have enhanced privacy protection for medical information. Employers can not probe into employees' and applicants' medical histories or legal use of prescribed drugs—except when there is a genuine safety or health reason for doing so—because knowing this information could be used to discriminate. Since alcoholism and drug addiction are considered disabilities under the law, employers are restricted as to when and how they can probe into employee and applicant's past alcohol and drug use. This includes urine testings, reviews of positive drug tests by a company's Medical Review Officer, and questions asked during interviews.

American Disabilities Act enhances the medical privacy of people with disabilities in order to prevent job discrimination. The ADA places restrictions on when and how medical examinations, which includes urine testing, can be administered by employers. The distinctions are important because violations carry severe penalties. Urine testing for alcohol use is defined by the law as a medical examination and restricted, whereas drug testing to detect the use of illegal drugs is not a medical examination and permitted provided it is applied to abled and disabled alike. The distinction in the law was made because alcohol consumption is legal and the use of illicit drugs is not.

The ADA states that a medical examination of a disabled job applicant can only be performed *after* an offer of employment and *before* the employee begins employment duties—and only if required of *all* entering employees. During this brief window the employer can administer a drug test for alcohol use without violating the American Disabilities Act. Urine testing for illegal drugs, on the other hand, is not defined as a medical examination under the ADA which means that drug testing of job applicants is permitted as long as it is applied uniformly and not just to disabled applicants.

If a job applicant gets a positive drug test and that applicant is disabled, then things get even more complicated. Because some positive tests results have a legitimate explanation, such as having taken a prescribed medication, people testing positive are asked to meet with the company Medical Review Officer (MRO) to discuss the result and provide their explanation. Under the ADA such a meeting is considered a medical examination and prohibited, except after extending a job offer to the candidate. In order words, it is legal to perform a pre-offer drug test, but it is not legal to perform a pre-offer MRO inquiry—which is required by Federal drug-free workplace laws. Getting caught in this catch-22-like situation can be avoided by doing drug testing after extending the job offer, but before the person begins working. The EEOC recommends such post-offer, pre-employment testing.

## Testing for Alcohol

Testing for alcohol, unlike testing for use of illegal drugs, is defined as a medical examination under the ADA. This means that all of the requirements and restrictions applying to medical examinations apply to testing for alcohol. Alcohol testing can *only* be performed post-offer and pre-employment. Stated in another way, employers can test for alcohol only after they have offered the applicant a job and provided that the offer is conditioned upon the test results.

To further complicate matters, a positive alcohol test alone is not a sufficient basis for denying employment, except for safety-sensitive jobs. This is because use of alcohol is legal and the person may be a recovered or recovering alcohol which is a disability protected by the ADA. Whether or not an employer can take action against an employee because of a positive alcohol test must be handled on a case-by-case basis. To deny an employee work on the basis of alcohol use, the employer has to have a broader basis of evidence than simply a positive test result. The employer might demonstrate that the employee or job candidate cannot perform the essential functions of the job and is therefore not qualified. Another approach is to show that the use of alcohol is likely to pose a "direct threat to the health or safety of others in the workplace". Thirdly, the employer might demonstrated that the person is not actually a recovered or recovering alcoholic and therefore not disabled, and therefore is not protected by the ADA. Finally, employers can take adverse action against employees who violate posted company policy such as "no drinking on the job", so long as the rules are applied to all employees equally. In all of these cases, it is vitally important employers keep documented records of all matters pertaining to the actions taken.

## Prescription Drugs

The ADA explicitly protects the lawful use of prescription drugs. Employers must be extremely cautious in any regulation of prescription drugs because, in the case of any litigation, it will probably be presumed to be discriminatory and to have a disparate impact on the disabled—unless a compelling "business necessity" for such rules can be demonstrated. In the early days of drug testing employers often required job applicants and employees to report their use of prescription drugs. This type of blanket disclosure requirement is not likely to withstand a legal challenge and should be avoided. There is a loophole and that is health and safety—when the use of prescription drugs may cause impairment that could lead to dangerous situations. Employers need to be very conservative in this regard because Section

102(c)(4) of the ADA places the burden of proof on the employer. The employer must prove that such medical inquiries are job-related and consistent with business necessity.

## Exceptions

There are two exceptions to the rule that an employer cannot discriminate against a disabled employee or job applicant. An employer can refuse to hire a former drug abuser if the employer can show that its decision is job-related and consistent with business necessity. One Court has indicated that some employees of rehabilitation centers who previously used drugs may be discharged if they relapse into addiction. An employer need not place an employee in a position where he or she could pose a threat to the health or safety of that individual or others in the workplace if he or she suffered a relapse. Similarly employers are free to discharge, discipline or deny employment to an alcoholic whose use of alcohol adversely affects job performance to the extent that the person is not longer qualified to perform the job.

Employers may prohibit employees from using drugs and alcohol while at work, or from coming to work under the influence of drugs and alcohol. Employees who violate their employer's drug-free workplace rules may be disciplined or discharged without violating the ADA, and substance abusing alcoholic employees may be held to the same standard of conduct and performance that the employer demands of non-disabled employees.

# CHAPTER 10

# Drug Abuse Prevention

 A sound drug use prevention program for a plant or office has six basic elements, each of which is ideally linked to the other.

## Recognizing The Problem

It is essential not to ignore alcohol or other drug abuse in the workplace. Failure to address the problem is likely to cost an employer thousands of dollars. When left unaddressed, these problems usually do not solve themselves. Rather, they progressively worsen, until they cause absenteeism, tardiness, industrial or home accidents, poor job performance, friction between workers or with supervisors, loss of business, excessive claims for sickness and accident benefits, or a combination of these problems.

## Conduct A Survey

It is helpful to make a detailed survey of the workplace to discover the types of drug related problems that exist. Review of employee records is a good place to start. Absence of reported employee problems could be a danger signal. Failure to document work related problems on employee records increases the difficulties of discovering and correcting these problems. Attorney William Adams suggests a number of direct and indirect indicators of drug use in the workplace in Chapter 11, Deciding On A Drug Testing Program.

## Tour The Workplace And Talk With Employees

Look for employees who appear particularly unhealthy. Look for visible signs of loss of sleep, lack of alertness, bloodshot eyes, inattention to work, failure to meet reasonable schedules, flushed faces, or use of breath fresheners. Be sensitive to the smell of marijuana or alcoholic beverages. If a person is suspected, but there is no proof, do not jump to conclusions. Serious, adverse legal consequences could follow. When there is a record of impairment, safety violations, and broken work rules, the employer might first confront the employee and offer help such as time off, counseling or a drug rehabilitation program. Additionally, the employer can observe the employee's behavior and talk to co-workers. A word of caution, employers need to be especially careful not to equate being unhealthy with having a disability and thereby single out disabled employees for special scrutiny—which would be a violation of the American Disabilities Act (ADA).

## Prevention

Prevention of drug problems starts with pre-employment screening. Because of the restrictions imposed by ADA it is adviseable to delay drug testing and reviewing of the prospect's records (most especially medical records) until *after making an offer of employment but before the person actually starts working.* Alcohol, like any other drug, should be banned from company meetings, including sales meetings.

## Formulate A Company Policy

Have a sound company policy and work rules. The corporate policy should strictly prohibit the possession of intoxicants or illegal drugs on company premises. The company should have rules that impose stiffer penalties on employees who sell intoxicants or illegal drugs than on those who are using them. There should be a specific rule against coming to work under the influence of any drug, including alcohol, and the company should have separate rules regarding work safety and the operation of machines and vehicles.

Special precautions are advisable for isolated work stations and night shifts. For example, employees working on drilling platforms in the ocean should be systematically inspected for readiness to work prior to going onto the worksite, and there should be routine inspection of the worksite itself, sometimes even with use of drug sniffing dogs. Finally, actions should be taken to reduce the entry of drugs into the workplace. This may include policies for outside vendors, delivery trucks, shipping department, and even security guards.

## Contain The Problem

Companies can contain drug problems by cracking down on drug dealers, investigating the cause of employee accidents, monitoring sickness and accident benefit claims, and uniformly enforcing company policies and work rules. A good containment strategy will not wait for the later stages of drug problems to develop. Positive health promotion, including the opportunity for physical exercise appropriate to overall health, is beneficial. A drug awareness program and efforts to motivate employees toward positive, drug-free goals is useful.

Drug users seldom hide contraband in their lockers or at their work stations, because they do not want to risk being caught in possession of the drug. They hide the drugs somewhere in or on the premises, so that they will have access to them. A good containment strategy minimizes opportunities for unobserved employee drug use and eliminates hiding places, by restricting access and increasing the prospect of the discovery of hiding places.

# Offer Assistance

The key to the early identification of problems in the workplace is for supervisors to listen to employees and to understand their requests for help. People who are experiencing a problem, including addiction problems, will drop hints of their concerns and problems. A good listener will offer to assist the employee with personal problems to get appropriate help. Maintaining confidentiality is essential. Make it clear that the employer is not going to use personal information against the employee.

Supervisors should never try to diagnose the employee's problem, or discuss the use of inappropriate chemical substances. A problem of misguidance should be avoided. Covering up the problem with well-intentioned, sympathetic tactics is not helpful. Assistance may require constructive confrontation, because most drug users, including alcoholics, minimize their drug use, delude themselves about the seriousness of their problems, and deny much about their addictions. Employees with physical symptoms or behavioral patterns consistent with drug use should be routinely referred to a physician, psychologist, or an Employee Assistance Program (EAP).

Focus on documented instances, witnessed behavior, and impaired work performance. The supervisor, personnel director, and manager—sometimes with the help of the spouse and other peers—can confront the employee, and give him or her a choice between assistance or job action leading to termination. However, any counseling should be left to trained professionals, and it is a good idea if the company refers employees to either a program it has investigated or its own Employee Assistance Program.

Drug use rarely occurs in isolation. It is usually a response to home pressures and personal problems. Often, drug use on the job can be prevented by EAP programs that offer counseling for non-drug problems such as legal, marital and financial difficulties.

# Educate Employees

Drug education is both a form of prevention and a means for involving employees in early intervention. Set aside 15 to 20 minutes for a face-to-face presentation to employees. A presentation given by a recovered abuser or an individual with a drug treatment experience is very helpful. Such a person can share relevant personal experiences, and point out that everyone is prone to personal problems that adversely affect work performance. Confidential assistance should be offered in a nonthreatening manner. Encouraging employees to ask questions, and share their personal experiences is important.

Employee Assistance Programs are enhanced by the use of wall posters, materials, newsletters, employee benefit fairs, informational payroll stuffers, and direct mailings to the home. At least one direct mailing to the home is important, because it can insure that the family has access to information. It can provide information about confidential, low-cost or no-cost intervention, and outpatient care. Intensive training of key employees is also a good idea.

# Identify Drug Dealers

Cocaine and heroin users frequently become drug dealers to sustain their habit. Marijuana users often sell a joint to a friend. Drug dealers must come into contact with other persons to ply their trade. Hence they seek out exposure to co-workers. Employees who leave their work stations or who seek jobs that bring them into contact with many people are a higher-risk group for drug dealing than other employees. Cocaine, crack, and heroin users are more likely to be selling drugs than other types of drug users. The most common places for drug sales are high-traffic areas, such as cafeterias, restrooms, and toolrooms, which are used by numerous employees. Transactions may be made by mail-delivery personnel, forklift drivers, or others who routinely travel throughout the plant.

Dealers and users can be identified by a variety of techniques, such as  a confidential employee informant "hot line," undercover investigators, video surveillance (excluding bathroom stalls), and supervisor surveillance of bathrooms, offices, and private areas.

# CHAPTER 11

# Deciding To Test

Alcohol and drug use has caused problems at work for a long time. Many employers are unaware of the extent of their own company's problems. Some estimates say that 50 percent of the executives from leading insurance, banking, and financial, and transportation companies believed that alcohol and drug use was "not really a problem for their organization."

Supervisors are usually reluctant to accuse someone of abusing drugs. Many employers would like to look the other way, preferring to avoid the possibility of legal action. There is a common belief that problem employees, those who do abuse substances, will be screened out during pre-employment interviews. However, that does not always happen, even now that many companies implement pre-employment drug testing. With the passing of the American Disabilities Act (ADA) employers are prohibited from basing a hiring decision on past drug use if the person has been in a treatment program because drug addiction is now defined as a "disability".

The tendency is often to deny the whole issue. To initiate a drug testing program is perceived to imply that there may be drug users in the company, which is a serious social stigma that companies do not want to bear.

On the other hand, employers who ignore alcohol or drug use in their companies can face other problems, such as "vicarious liability," which means that the employer is liable for the employee's actions. For example, if a blue-collar worker has an accident on the job because of substance abuse, that employee can sue the employer! Additionally, if an employee has an accident on the way home after work, the employer can be sued for negligence for keeping a drug- or alcohol-dependent person on the job without rehabilitation.

On the other hand, an employer should be extremely careful never to terminate an employee for anything other than job performance. If an employer fires a worker for drug addiction or alcoholism, and communicates that reason to someone else, the employer can be sued under the ADA and possibly for defamation of character.

There are cases in which employers have been held directly responsible for failure to screen applicants carefully or for retaining incompetent or dangerous employees. The behavior of drug or alcohol abusers can present serious problems for co-workers and others. An employer must be alert to any sign that an applicant or current employee may cause such danger. Failure to act reasonably when information was or *could have been* available can expose an employer to substantial liability. Even when there is no evidence of negligent screening or supervision, an employer may be held vicariously liable for the negligent or violent acts of an employee.

# Drug Testing Pros And Cons

"Many companies jump into drug testing blindly, and realize after the fact—after they've collected samples and taken adverse action against employees—that they haven't really thought about the many parameters involved in developing a drug policy," comments Dr. J. Michael Walsh, Chief of the Clinical Behavior Pharmacology Branch of the National Institute on Drug Abuse (NIDA). "Drug testing is a deceptively simple solution. People think, 'All we have to do is start drug testing, and we'll get rid of this problem.' Probably the main point is that drug testing can be a useful tool within . . . an overall program of treatment, prevention, and education. It is not a necessary tool, but it could be a useful tool in identifying people with drug problems."

Positive identification of drug use is the main reason for implementing a urine testing program—because drug use is difficult to prove without the support of objective drug test results. A testing program can also identify drug use early, potentially reducing harm to the employee, the employer, and co-workers. A pre-employment screening program can reduce the number of drug users that enter the company's work force. Drug testing makes it difficult for an employee to deny drug use, and test results provide strong evidence if employee disciplinary action is necessary. Urine testing may allow employers to identify the causes of other sorts of problems, such as absenteeism and decreased output. Random testing may have a deterrent effect on drug use.

## Determining The Extent Of Drug Use By Employees

### Direct Evidence

- Substantial observed or known drug use by employees

- Security department or undercover investigation reports indicating substantial drug use or drug transactions

- Drug paraphernalia found on premises

- Complaints of drug use by co-workers

- Employees arrested off-duty for drug use

- Medical claims implicating drug use

- Results of fitness for duty examinations

- Drug use at other company sites

### Indirect Evidence

- Accidents on the job

- Accidents off the job

- High absenteeism

- Employee difficulties in concentration

- Decreased employee productivity

- Employees with poor interpersonal relationships

- Increased medical/benefits claims

- Increased wage garnishments/personal bankruptcies

William F. Adams, *Controlling Drugs and Alcohol in the Workplace: A Summary of Drug Testing Law and Legislation and Guide to Corporate Policy Development*, Orrick, Herrington & Sutcliffe, San Francisco, October,

## Direct Impact On Business

Drug testing takes time, costs money and can impact adversely on employee morale. Employers who institute drug testing programs with little planning can find themselves accused of violating employees' right to privacy.

Consequently, establishing a clear relationship between drug use and damage to the company is essential. When employers cannot demonstrate that its business is being or would be directly affected by drug abuse on the job, the testing program is unlikely to survive scrutiny.

In deciding whether or not to institute a drug testing program, employers must establish a connection between drug use and business concerns. The employer should gather direct and indirect evidence of drug use in the workplace from all reasonable sources. Next, the employer should identify the areas of the business that are at risk. Finally, the employer should be prepared to demonstrate the ineffectiveness of less objectionable methods.

# Employee Morale

When considering a drug testing program, employers must weigh the effect of a drug testing program on employee morale. For example, Tom Peters, author of *In Search Of Excellence*, says that if "future competitiveness depends on treating people as an important part of the institution, the least respectful thing I can imagine doing to a human being is telling him to piss in a bottle once a month."

Louis L. Maltby is vice president of Drexelbrooks Engineering Company, a small instrumentation company in Horsham, Pennsylvania, which decided not to have any drug testing. He argued, "We just don't think you need to test to keep the workplace drug-free. After all, drugs are just a symptom of something else. What you really want is a committed, dedicated workforce, people who like their jobs and care enough not to come to work stoned. What we do is select and nurture employees who are going to do a good job. We think that if we do that, the drug problem takes care of itself. We're incredibly careful about the people we hire. You're saying you can have a drug testing program and have the kind of employee relations I'm talking about. I say you can't. The two are inimical. Ours is based upon a relationship that doesn't come from a paycheck. When you say to an employee, 'You're doing a great job, but just the same I want you to pee in this jar and I'm sending someone to watch you,' you're undermining that trust."

# Cost

Cost justification is an important factor in any business decision. The bottom line is whether drug tests are worth the money they cost, and any employer considering a drug testing program must weigh the costs of the program against the benefits. For example, if there are serious potential liabilities because of public safety, as there is with transportation or manufacturing of chemicals and explosives, an accident caused by one "stoned" employee could cost the company and the surrounding community an extremely high price. In those cases, an effective drug program is probably worth its cost. On the other hand, if the goal of the program is to deter drug and alcohol use in a workplace where such safety concerns are not at issue, there may well be other, less expensive ways in which to accomplish that end without instituting an expensive company-wide testing program.

## What Tests Actually Show

The chief concern in drug testing is usually not the accuracy of the test, but the degree of the job-relatedness of the test results. Therefore, when a company is considering implementing a drug-testing program, it is important to have a good understanding of what a positive urinalysis result does and does not show. *A positive urinalysis indicates that a person has used a certain substance at some time in the past* (which might be hours, or it might be weeks), *but it does not show whether the person was intoxicated or under the influence of the drug at the time the urine was given.* This is a critical point, as some companies have learned after the fact.

For example, in one arbitration case in a mining company, a one-time mass test led to the firing of a few employees. However, the Court ordered that the employees be reinstated because they were fired under a company policy that prohibited employees from being under the influence of a drug or alcohol. The tests showed only that they had used a drug or alcohol, but not that they were under the influence. The arbitrator recognized that the positive urine tests only showed recent drug use. Had there been a written policy prohibiting the use of controlled substances altogether, the firing probably would have been upheld.

Drug tests cannot detect causes of worker impairment *other* than drugs, which may be costly to the company, such as fatigue, domestic problems, financial woes, grief, low worker morale, or organic disease.

There are a number of concerns to be weighed when a company is considering whether or not to implement a drug testing program. The employer must consider whether or not there is sufficient evidence that drugs are a problem in the workplace; whether such drug use does or would pose a direct threat to business or to safety; whether the potential benefits of a drug-testing program would outweigh its costs both in terms of dollars and morale; whether or not there may be more cost-effective ways of deterring drug use; and the relevance of test results to what is actually occurring in the workplace. The answers to these questions—and the resulting balance of the pros and cons of drug testing—will vary greatly from workplace to workplace.

# CHAPTER 12

# Reasons For Drug Testing

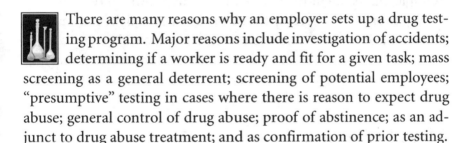 There are many reasons why an employer sets up a drug testing program. Major reasons include investigation of accidents; determining if a worker is ready and fit for a given task; mass screening as a general deterrent; screening of potential employees; "presumptive" testing in cases where there is reason to expect drug abuse; general control of drug abuse; proof of abstinence; as an adjunct to drug abuse treatment; and as confirmation of prior testing.

## Investigating Accidents

Testing for drugs is very common following an industrial accident. Drug testing after accidents has been successfully used by Southern Pacific Transportation Company who found that drug testing after accidents substantially reduced the number of accidents. In the 24 months preceding the initiation of their testing program, there were 15,082 accidents. In the 24 months following the introduction of drug testing, the number of accidents dropped dramatically, to 4,865, a reduction of 69 percent. Personal injuries dropped 24 percent after the implementing of drug testing.

There are two considerations to note with post-accident testing. If the person has been receiving psychotropic medication under prescription, that medication or its metabolites will appear in the urine, and impairment may be inferred when none existed. Second, drug metabolites can be detected in the urine long after the period of intoxication or impairment. This could occur with some medications or when the employee has smoked marijuana several days before, but not the day of the accident; yet the presence of cannabinoids in the urine can be construed as marijuana intoxication, and claimed as a contributor to the accident. Thus, post-accident testing does not necessarily yield data which is reliably relevant to the accident in question.

# Work Fitness

Testing for drug use may determine if a person is fit to work. For example, pilots might blow into a breathalyzer, which records alcohol vapor on the flight recorder, before assuming flight command. If measurable levels of alcohol are present, that fact will be displayed to both the intoxicated pilot and the crew members. Recording the breathalyzer results assures that crew members will not be tempted to cover for an intoxicated pilot.

# Mass Screening

The word "screen" can be used to refer to an inexpensive test administered prior to employment or at random. It can also refer to an inexpensive or easy-to-analyze test for an initial testing prior to selecting positive samples for more rigorous testing. The military and many corporations randomly screen employees to detect drug-using individuals and to assess the need for drug-abuse prevention. Personnel to be screened are selected at random, not because there is any reason to suspect drug use. People included in mass screenings are usually pulled from all positions and levels of the organization and not solely from high risk, safety or security jobs. Urine is generally first "screened" with an inexpensive and easy-to-analyze test.

Many experts argue that random testing is the most effective deterrent to drug use because each employee has some chance of being tested on any given day. Proponents argue that it is fair because there is no stigma or accusation attached to a particular employee who is selected for testing and because the decision to test is not influenced by supervisor biases.

Many civil rights attorneys reject this argument which asserts that random testing "reverses the presumption of innocence upon which much of our jurisprudence is built, and violates the strong prohibition of dragnet searches sweeping in the many who are innocent in order to find the few who are guilty which is the hallmark of a free and democratic society."

Mass screening programs have drawn the most criticism and have been the main source of legal attacks on drug testing programs. People who have no history of drug use resent being treated with suspicion. People using prescription and over-the-counter drugs often test positive and must defend themselves to prove their innocence. Furthermore, mass screening programs are responsible for most of the instances of false positives and inappropriate confirmations.

## Pre-Employment Screening

Screening urine of job applicants to detect drug use in order to avoid hiring drug users is a common function of drug testing. There is a danger that people will be denied jobs even though they are only occasionally use drugs off the job with no resultant work impairment. Also, capable applicants may be deterred from seeking a specific job if they know that the employer has a policy of pre-employment screening. This could be true of those who only occasionally use illicit drugs as well as those who oppose drug testing in principle.

## Presumptive Testing

A presumptive situation is one in which there is some strong reason to suspect—or presume—a person is using or abusing drugs. A test is administered to detect or confirm the presumptive. For example, a supervisor might notice that the person smells of alcohol and walks with a staggering gait; or a person might display signs of sedative use such as lethargy. In such cases the supervisor might request drug testing. Presumptive testing, sometimes called probable cause testing, is also used after accidents.

# To Confirm A Positive Result

Confirmatory tests are used to check the results of the initial or screening test. They yield fewer false positives and are more elaborate and expensive. Samples that test positive are retested or "confirmed" with a more powerful and accurate testing method.

Whether the confirmatory step is necessary depends on the intended use of the results. For monitoring in a drug treatment program, where the goal is detection of early relapse, and a positive result has no disciplinary consequences, screening methods alone are adequate and confirmation of a particular sample is not needed. On the other hand, in situations in which a single positive urine test could result in discipline, termination of employment, or loss of professional license, "forensic" or legal standards of testing positives using a different confirmatory method are essential.

Generally, a second urine sample is not necessary for confirmatory testing. Usually a portion of the sample is preserved and used for the confirmatory test. The important point to remember is that a different, more powerful test is used to confirm the initial positive result.

# Controlling Abuse

Rear Admiral Paul J. Mulloy told the Senate Subcommittees on Defense Manpower and Personnel and Defense Preparedness in 1983 that urinalysis is the most effective element in the Navy's "war on drugs." He said that implementation of urinalysis resulted in a decrease of detectable drug use among enlisted Navy personnel. Positive tests dropped from 48 percent in 1980 to 21 percent in 1982. Marijuana was the most common drug detected. However, he downplayed the finding that, following implementation of urinalysis for drug use, there was a notable shift to increased alcohol use.

Southern Pacific Transportation Company reported a decline in positive tests after implementing their drug testing program. In the first testing, they found 23 percent of those tested were reported positive: 60 percent of these were positive for marijuana; 20 percent for cocaine; 14 percent for alcohol; and 6 percent for other drugs. In comparison testings two years later, only 6.5 percent came up with positive results. Proponents of testing argue that using drug testing as a way to control drug use is legitimate, because after frequent urinalysis is implemented and expected among the population being tested, continued positive tests occur only in drug abusers who have lost control of their drug use.

# Proof Of Abstinence

Drug tests can be a positive indicator for a person who wants to prove that he or she has been drug-free. Such documentation can provide substantial legal protection for both a recovering drug abuser as well as the employer. For example, an anesthesiologist recovering from chemical dependency would give a urine specimen following any operation with anesthetic complications. If a lawsuit were filed and the plaintiff's attorney discovered the anesthesiologist's history of drug abuse, the attorney would probably claim that the mishap occurred because the anesthesiologist was intoxicated. A negative result on the drug test helps document that the complication did not result from drug use by the anesthesiologist.

# As An Adjunct To Treatment

Often a drug abuser will make a contract to be tested for drug use regularly as a condition of rehabilitation. Such testing is a valuable adjunct to treatment. Users fail in their program most commonly when they attempt to return to controlled use of the drug, which typically occurs in the first 3 to 6 months. Drug testing can catch use before the person returns to an abusive level. In short, regular testing helps the individual to break the habit and avoid the drug. Most treatment professionals believe drug testing is a positive tool for monitoring recovery of the chemically dependent.

# CHAPTER 13

# Establishing
# A Drug Testing Policy

In order to decide what levels of drug testing are appropriate for a given environment, a company should first define the severity of the problem. A 10 percent problem should be addressed differently than a 50 to 70 percent abuse problem. One approach is to conduct a sample screening of the work force population from the top down or a representative sample of the employee base by a "blind" screening (with no way to identify individuals who test positive). Once the extent of the problem is defined, one or all of the procedures can be implemented by a company if properly managed.

## Approaches To Drug Testing

There are five basic approaches to drug testing: the military approach, the medical approach, the security approach, the business approach, and the legal approach.

### The Military Approach

Unlike companies in the private sector, the military does not conduct pre-enlistment drug testing. The military believes that it can take its recruits and shape them up into good troops The centerpiece of the military testing program is that it is stringent. Entire units can be screened for drugs without notice, and individuals can be randomly selected for tests as well. Any commander who thinks there is a probable cause can have subordinates tested. For an officer who fails a drug test, dismissal is all but automatic. However, it is questionable whether or not the military model can be applied to the private sector. The military is an authoritarian organization, subject to its own legal structure, known as "military justice." The kind of stringent measures that it employs would undoubtedly cause an uproar in a private corporation or a university.

## The Security Approach

The security approach is based on the notion that drug users pose a risk to company security and to co-workers' safety, and on the belief that drug users must be quickly and permanently removed from the company's work environment. The approach calls for immediate dismissal or punitive actions. Here, firms actively look for drug use by urine-screening the employees, and by random searches of work areas by private security officers, often using trained dog patrols and undercover agents. This approach is expensive, usually lacks support from labor unions, and contributes to strained relationships between employers and employees.

## The Medical Approach

The medical approach involves treating troubled workers primarily through Employee Assistance Programs (EAPs), which provide treatment services or refer individuals to professional rehabilitation sources. Here a company demonstrates concern for its employees' health and well-being, and can save money by rehabilitating workers rather than firing or replacing them.

EAP programs usually work by employee self-referral. Some people believe that this is why they are less effective than they might be, because even a successful EAP might be missing half the employees who need help because of substance-abuse. In the security approach, substance-abuse is viewed as a crime; in some other approach it might be considered an immoral activity. In the medical approach it is viewed as a disease that is treatable, with high recovery rates, although long-term relapse rates are also substantial.

## The Business Approach

The business approach takes a broader view of substance-abuse in the workplace, and combines considerations of company policy, security, and treatment in setting up a substance-abuse program. Here the concern is with the performance of the individual and the cost of drug abuse. If employees are under the influence of drugs or alcohol, they are costing the company money because they are not working efficiently, because of absenteeism, and because of safety and security problems. The view in the business approach is one of the bottom line and the health of the entire organization.

## The Legal Approach

Here, the underlying concern has to do with protecting the organization from potential liability for accidents caused by employees who have been abusing substances on the job. Employee rights must be honored; yet, at the same time, the company must be sheltered from liability. The legal approach, like the business approach, involves planning and developing a comprehensive company program.

# Establishing A Company Policy

The first step, if the organization does decide that it is going to have a drug testing program, is to formulate a company policy.

### Points In A Company Drug Testing Policy

- An argument for a substance-abuse policy

- The company's position on use and possession of substances on company premises

- Responsibilities of both the company and the employees to insure public trust, public safety, and fitness for duty

- What sanctions will be taken if the policy is violated

- Which job categories will be subject to testing

- Circumstances under which employees will be tested

- Consequences of refusal to undergo testing

- Consequences of a positive result [see RED note on hard copy; I don't quite follow what it's asking]

- The company's position on rehabilitation opportunities

- Responsibility of employees to seek treatment

- Provisions for confidentiality

A company policy is a clearly articulated statement that spells out the company's attitude toward drug use on and off the job as it affects employee productivity. The policy is publicized throughout the company, and is included in the employee handbook, the supervisors' handbook, and the supervisory training program. How drug users will be dealt with is clearly spelled out, and usually rehabilitation through an EAP is offered.

A company drug testing policy statement is a vehicle for communicating the company's expectations regarding drug use to its employees. It describes what urine tests will be performed, under what circumstances samples will be requested, and how test results will be used. Such notice is vitally important. An employee's expectation of privacy can be reduced if they know that all employees are subject to urine testing in certain circumstances. If employees can show that they were not fully informed about such a policy, disciplinary action may be overturned.

The policy and procedures should clearly advise employees of the circumstances under which they will be tested, the consequences of refusing to submit a urine sample, and the consequences of a positive test result. Again, if the employees can show that they did not know about the policy and procedures, or if the employer cannot demonstrate that employees have been advised, disciplinary action may be overturned.

The question of who can be searched, and when, is important for a new substance-abuse policy. A union contract may affect the policy and must be considered. The contract may prevent the company from implementing a new drug abuse policy unilaterally. It may be necessary to negotiate the policy with the union. Any changes, even in the enforcement of the existing policy, should be reviewed alongside an existing labor agreement, and agreed upon by union representatives. Dramatic changes abruptly and unilaterally carried out can generate problems that will delay implementation of any effective drug control policy.

*Employment Law Update*, a newsletter published by Rutkowski and Associates, contains an alcohol and drug abuse policy that can serve as a model for developing a company policy (see Appendix B). Of course, it is important that each provision be carefully tailored to the unique needs of the company in consultation with its attorneys and not just "boiler-plated."

## Searches

A company should develop and publish explicit guidelines on searches of employees' lockers, vehicles, packages, and personal property, as well as when investigatory interviews with security personnel and other employees will be permitted. There should be a policy decision on whether undercover investigators furnished by law enforcement agencies will be utilized and what the arrest procedures will be.

Generally, searches are less likely to draw legal attack when they are conducted only in situations where there is reasonable suspicion that drugs are present, rather than on a random basis. Abusive searches may be considered a form of harassment and should be avoided.

# CHAPTER 14

# What Is Tested

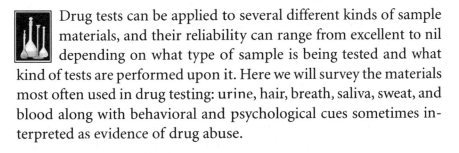 Drug tests can be applied to several different kinds of sample materials, and their reliability can range from excellent to nil depending on what type of sample is being tested and what kind of tests are performed upon it. Here we will survey the materials most often used in drug testing: urine, hair, breath, saliva, sweat, and blood along with behavioral and psychological cues sometimes interpreted as evidence of drug abuse.

## Urine

Urine is most commonly tested because of the ease of getting a sample, the speed of conducting the analysis, and the low cost. Urine tests can show the presence of drug metabolites or physiological by-products that usually indicate recent use. *The major drawback of testing urine is that presence of drug metabolites in urine does not indicate whether the person was actually under the influence of the drug at the time the sample was given.* The drug may have been used in the past, but not be actively affecting functioning. This is particularly common with marijuana, which can lead to positive test results two or three weeks or longer after use. The most commonly used method for screening urine is the EMIT® test, manufactured by the Syva Corporation.

# Breath

Breath testing is common for alcohol-testing on motorists by police. It has the advantage of being nonintrusive, inexpensive, and almost instantaneous. A positive breath test indicates the percentage of alcohol in the blood, which is a positive indication of intoxication.

Disposable breath analyzers for motorists, used by drivers to determine before driving if they're candidates for DWIs, have become a competitive business. BreathScan® from Prescott Technologies is a 3-inch tube filled with yellow crystals. The driver exhales into the tube, and the crystals turn blue-green if he is too drunk to drive according to legal standards. BreathScan® is available to the general public. Many other products can be found on the internet.

New rules for alcohol testing went into effect in 1995-96 which greatly increased the use of breath analysis which is required at collection sites with the use of "evidential breath testing" (EBT). The device costs between $2000-$8000 and a specially trained technician.

# Saliva

Testing saliva for marijuana can presumably determine recent use, whereas use of marijuana weeks in the past can sometimes cause a positive urine test in regular users.

Intravenously administered THC or tetrahydrocannabinol, the primary psychoactive ingredient in marijuana, does not appear in significant amounts in human saliva. Thus cannabinoids that are detected in saliva probably result from recent smoking or oral ingestion. Because THC metabolites can be detected in urine several days and sometimes weeks after marijuana has been smoked, a saliva test is a useful alternative to document recent marijuana use. In a study using a RIA (Radio Immunoassay) test, cannabinoids were detected in saliva four to 10 hours after subjects smoked a single marijuana cigarette.

# Blood

Blood testing measures the actual presence of the drug or its metabolite in the blood at the time of testing. Blood-test results are therefore the most accurate indicator of intoxication. However, blood testing, which requires trained medical skill and/or expensive equipment and is an expensive and intrusive method. The results of these tests tend to take more time than other tests.

A blood sample can be collected at the time of the initial test and later used to confirm an initial positive result of a screening test, such as from a urine or other test. This is especially important in accident investigations. A positive test can be confirmed by a Gas Chromatography (GC) blood test to detect whether or not the drug was present in the blood at the time the sample was taken. This test gives a greater indication of impaired function and intoxication than does urine testing, which indicates past drug use, but not necessarily present intoxication. For the confirmation of a screening test as well as a replication of the confirmatory test, it is important that the sample be frozen, since drug metabolites deteriorate. Depending on the dose, marijuana can be easily detected up to six hours after consumption by testing blood. After that, concentration falls rapidly, and marijuana is not generally detectable in blood after 22 hours.

# Hair

Until recently employers had to rely predominantly upon urine for testing. Since the late 1980s the National Institute of Justice (NIJ) has sought alternative techniques. Hair testing promises to fill the bill in providing a wider window of detection while being less invasive.

As hair grows drugs and their metabolites are absorbed into its structure. Once a metabolite is embedded in the sheath of the hair, a longitudinal record of drug use is created. Metabolites appear in detectable levels in hair about a week after drug use. Because hair grows about 1/4 to 1/2 inch a month, the shaft can be cut into lengths creating a sort of time line of drug use. Research reported by Dr. Tom Mieczkowski of the National Institute of Justice Research showed that at low levels of cocaine use the radioimmunoassay of hair (RAIH) detects about 10 times as many drug users at current accepted cut-off levels than does urine analysis; while at moderate levels of cocaine use the RIAH detects 3 to 4 times as many users as does urinalysis. Hair analysis does not pick up single or very infrequent drug use, however.

## Advantages of Testing Hair

Hair analysis offers unique advantages compared to other drug testing methods. It retains drug components for longer periods, and drug use can be detected in hair for weeks or even months compared to the 2 to 3 days that cocaine or heroin can be detected in blood or urine. Furthermore, hair specimens can be readily obtained without the privacy problems encountered with urine or the invasiveness of drawing blood.

Another practical limitation with urine analysis as a test medium is the frequency of collection. Opiates and cocaine are water-soluble and rapidly excreted from the body, generally within 48 to 72 hours. Fortunately for employers marijuana which is fat-soluble, has a slow, relatively long-term urine excretion rate so that regular users can test positive for several weeks. Urine-based data on cocaine and opiate use derived from a single urine test can greatly underestimate the true extent of drug use.

Hair testing solves these problems. It uses the same technologies as urine-based immunoassays; the difference is in what is being tested, urine or hair. Hair expands the window for detection of all illicit drugs. Whereas urine testing can detect drug use for several days to a week or two, hair testing detects presence of drugs for several months—or more with long hair. Importantly, brief periods of abstinence does not alter the test. Another advantage is that hair is easy to handle and because it is inert it does not require special storage conditions. Additional, there is less risk of transmitting disease with hair as compared to urine or blood. Hair lends itself to repeat testing because collecting comparable samples is quite easy. Finally, while urine samples can be manipulated in a variety of ways; it is practically impossible for people hoping to beat the test to foil hair analysis. In fact, hair analysis can be conducted on deceased people years after they've died which is impossible with urine and blood testing. Dr. Ron Siegel of UCLA, for example, analyzed strands of hair of John Keats, the nineteenth-century romantic English poet, and proved that Keats was, indeed, an opium smoker.

## Problems With Hair Testing

The major problem with hair testing is drugs bind into hair at different rates depending upon the hair. African-American's hair has been demonstrated to absorb drug metabolites 10 to 50 times greater than does the hair of Caucasians which can influence the likelihood of a positive drug test. Another problem is that hair absorbs contaminants from the air. A person exposed to drug smoke can have metabolites in his or her hair that can yield a positive drug test. This problem is particularly acute with marijuana because the lipophilic or fat soluble components of THC readily binds into the structure of human hair.

## Sweat

National Institute of Drug Abuse (NIDA) researchers argue that testing human sweat for drugs can be an effective method of monitoring drug use over extended periods. Sweat is a sensitive indicator of heroin and cocaine use. Usually urine is used in testing but it has the drawback that most drugs of abuse are cleared form urine in 2 to 3 days after use. In order to effectively monitor drug use on a continuing basis urine screening would have to be performed 2 to 3 times a week.

Analyzing sweat may prove to be cost-effective because testing could be less frequent and with less invasion of privacy than urine tests. Drug metabolites are excreted into sweat and then bind to hair, where they can remain detectable for months. Sweat is collected over several days or weeks by a small patch worn on the skin. Sweat testing is now being performed for cocaine, amphetamines, and opiates.

### The PharmChek® Drugs of Abuse Patch

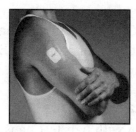

The patented "sweat patch" from PharmChem can be applied to the upper, outer arm or the lower midriff. After it has been worn, the absorption pad is removed from the sweat patch and sent to the laboratory for analysis. (Photos courtesy of PharmChem, Menlo Park, Ca.)

The Pharmchek® Drugs of Abuse Patch looks like a 2" x 3" bandage, and consists of an adhesive plastic film that hold an absorption pad in place against the skin. Larger molecules, such as drugs, are trapped in the absorption pad portion of the patch. Contaminants from the environment cannot penetrate the adhesive barrier from the outside, so the patch can be worn during most normal activities, including bathing and swimming.

The patch must be worn for a minimum of 24 hours to insure that an adequate amount of sweat is collected. The patch is tamper evident when applied correctly. A unique number is imprinted on each one to aid with chain of custody and identification.

The patch can be used to test for cocaine, opiates, including heroin, amphetamines, including methamphetamine, PCP, and marijuana. For most urine testing, the window of detection for drug use is 12 to 72 hours after the last use of the drug. The patch retains drug used at any time during its wear period until the patch is removed, up to 7 days later. In pilot studies the sweat patch was able to detect four times more cocaine users than intensive urine testing covering the same period. The parent drug as well as drug metabolites can usually be detected and identified in sweat. This is particularly important in the determination of heroin use. The heroin metabolite (morphine) typically found in urine may come from a number of sources. Heroin itself is rarely found in urine. Heroin *is* found readily in sweat and is only present when heroin is used.

The sweat patch can serve as a useful monitoring device for people in drug abuse treatment or under court supervision or probation. The patch is designed so that once removed, it cannot be reattached to the skin which prevents tampering. Patches can be frozen until subjected to testing.

Dr. Edward Cone and his NIDA research team demonstrated the usefulness of the sweat patch for testing. Their statistics revealed a comparison of urine, sweat and hair testing for testing cocaine and heroin.

| ISSUES | URINE | SWEAT | HAIR |
|---|---|---|---|
| Measure | Incremental | Cumulative | Cumulative |
| Invasiveness | High | Low | Low |
| Detection Period | 2-3 days | Weeks | Months/Years |
| False Positives* | Low | High | High |
| False Negatives** | High | Undetermined | Undetermined |
| Rick of Adulteration | High | Undetermined | Low |
| **Research** | | | |
| Screening Assays | Plentiful | Needed | Needed |
| Confirmation Assays | Plentiful | Needed | Needed |
| Cutoffs | Established | Needed | Needed |
| Control Materials | Plentiful | Needed | Needed |
| Cost | Low | Undetermined | High |

*False positives resulting from environmental contamination of the biological specimen during collection and handling, and from passive drug exposure as a result of, for example, contact with skin or exposure to cocaine vapors. **False negatives resulting form the drug detection "window" of the biological specimen. NIDA notes: Sept/Oct 1995

Sweat testing, especially in cases where on-going monitoring of drug use is needed, holds great promise. But it is still in the developmental stages. Assays and cut-offs levels still need to be determined and the cost of testing has not been established.

# Behavior

Observation of behavior is not commonly thought of as a drug test; yet most people do observe behavior to determine if people may be under the influence of a drug.

Behavior is often a better indication of intoxication than chemical analysis. Observation of performance, such as the ability to walk a straight line or maintain balance on one leg, is valuable. Slurred speech, unsteady gait, mood changes, and irritability are good indicators of drug intoxication. Quick-reflex tests used by police include walking the straight line, eye-hand coordination, balance, and standing on one leg. Observation of behavior from spouse, friends, work supervisors, or other individuals are another type of behavior assessment.

# Physiological Signs

The diameter of the pupils is a quick indicator of recent opiate use. Normal pupils are between 3 and 6 mm in diameter. However, following opiate use, pupils are constricted to 1 to 2 mm. In such instances, the pupils are called "pinned." Pupil constriction is a useful sign even in daily users, because tolerance to pupil constriction does not decrease even as drug tolerance increases with continued opiate use. Observations should be made under low-light conditions. Although opiate use is the most common reason for pinned pupils, medications used in the treatment of glaucoma, a disease that causes increased pressure inside the eye, also produces marked pupil constriction under low-light conditions.

In an opiate overdose producing unconsciousness, pupils may be dilated, because lack of oxygen in the brain, hypoxia, produces pupillary dilation which overrides pupillary constriction induced by the opiate.

*Nystagmus,* known informally as "eye-wiggle" is a persistent 1 to 2 mm back-and-forth eye movement when looking to the extreme left or right, is another sign of intoxication. To test for nystagmus, the person is asked to hold his or her head in a fixed position while tracking the examiner's finger, pen, or small flashlight with the eyes. The object to be tracked is moved across the visual field 12 to 20 cm from the face. It is easier to observe nystagmus if there is a light source diagonal to the subject's eye that reflects a small point of light from the sclera, or white portion, of the subject's eyes.

The back-and-forth movement can be seen by watching a circle of light reflected from a point on the sclera. Eye movement is characterized by a quick movement to the side of the gaze and a slow return movement toward the nose after the eye has moved to the extreme lateral position. When sober, most people's eyes will have one to three cycles of nystagmus and them stop. When people are intoxicated with alcohol or sedative hypnotics, the back-and-forth eye movements persist. This is called *sustained horizontal nystagmus,* and is strong evidence for alcohol or sedative hypnotic intoxication.

*Vertical nystagmus* is a similar disturbance in eye movement occurring in extreme vertical gaze. There may be a slight rotation of the eyes, called *rotary nystagmus.* PCP (phencyclidine) intoxication produces *central nystagmus,* severe back-and-forth eye movement when the person is looking straight ahead. Because sustained nystagmus is not under voluntary control, it is an objective, reproducible, and reliable test for intoxication.

## Pupil Size Indicates Drug Use

| Drug | Pupil Size | Nystagmus |
|------|-----------|-----------|
| Stimulants | Large | No |
| Marijuana | Variable | No |
| Opiates | | |
|    Intoxication | Pinned | No |
|    Withdrawal | Large | No |
| Alcohol & Sedatives | | |
|    Intoxication | Variable | Yes, horizontal |
|    Withdrawal | Large | No |
| Phencyclidines (PCP) | Large | Yes, central & horizontal |

*Source: David Smith & Donald Wesson,* Substance Abuse In The Workplace, *1984*

From the material in this chapter, it should be clear that several different kinds of biological samples—as well as behavioral and physiological indicators—can be used in determining drug use. These different approaches each have their advantages and disadvantages in terms of complexity, accuracy, length of time required for results, various substances and distinguishing between past usage and recent intoxication.

# Chapter 15

# Testing Technology

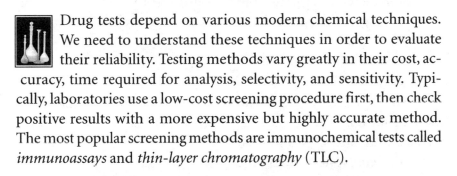 Drug tests depend on various modern chemical techniques. We need to understand these techniques in order to evaluate their reliability. Testing methods vary greatly in their cost, accuracy, time required for analysis, selectivity, and sensitivity. Typically, laboratories use a low-cost screening procedure first, then check positive results with a more expensive but highly accurate method. The most popular screening methods are immunochemical tests called *immunoassays* and *thin-layer chromatography* (TLC).

## Immunoassays

The screening method of choice when the objective of the drug test is to target a limited number of abused substances with a high degree of sensitivity and specificity is a test called an immunoassay. The most commonly used immunoassays are enzyme immunoassay (EIA), radioimmunoassay (RIA), and fluorescence polarization immunoassay (FPIA). All three tests work on the same basic principle in which utilizes binding antibodies capable of recognizing drugs or drug groups. When urine or hair extract containing drug is mixed in solution with the drug's antibody antibody, it binds to the antibody.

The immunoassay operates on the principle of antigen-antibody interaction. The basic principle is similar to that of the "rabbit test" for pregnancy. Drugs to be detected are coupled to large molecules and injected into rabbits or sheep. The animal's immune system produces antibodies against the specific drug. These antibodies are then purified for use in immunoassay tests. Competition occurs for available antibody binding sites between the tagged drug in the test and the drug in the unknown sample.

Immunoassay tests have many limitations. They can discriminate only between the presence and absence of the suspected drug so that they can yield only an estimate of the quantity of drug in an individual's system. Cross-reactivity, in which nondrug substances and over-the-counter drugs bind with the antibodies, is a serious shortcoming of this method and can cause lower specificity and inaccurate results.

## Cross Reactivity and Specificity

The  specificity of an immunoassay refers to the antibody to recognizing only the drug or drug group. Cross reactivity, on the other hand, is the tendency of antibodies to recognize substances other than the drug being tested for. In other words,  an antibody that has high specificity will be low in cross reactivity. The degree of cross reactivity varies widely among immunoassays. Although all three techniques are considered highly specific relative to other screening methods, they are not infallible. Immunoassays for amphetamines for example, will react with drugs structurally related to the amphetamines, such as the over-the-counter sympathomimetic amines phenylpropanolamine and ephedrine. Confirmation of positive immunochemical results by a fundamentally different technique such as GC/MS remains a necessity.

## Enzyme Immunoassay

The EIA assay uses an enzyme  to labeled the drug. When bound to the antibody, this enzyme is inactive and becomes activated as it is displaced from antibody binding sites by drug present in the specimen. The degree to which this reaction occurs is proportional to the amount of drug present in the specimen.

The Enzyme Multiplied Immunoassay Test (EMIT®) manufactured by Syva Corporation in Palo Alto relies on modifying an enzyme's ability to act on its substrate, lysozyme. An animal is injected with the drug or a drug metabolite, usually in combination with other chemicals. The injection provokes the animal to produce specific immune chemicals, called antigens, that will bind to the drug. These antigens are then harvested by extracting and purifying certain proteins (gamma globulins) from the animal's blood. The lysozymes or other enzymes are bound to the drug or metabolite of interest, such as morphine, amphetamine, or methadone. This drug-enzyme complex is inactivated as a functional enzyme when the drug antibody is placed in the same solution. If, however, an urine sample contains the drug in question, the antibody will bind less of the drug-enzyme complex, because the antibody will also bind to the free drug. Any unbound drug enzyme is active and loses the substrate bacterial suspension, clearing the solution. This clearing is measured as a change in absorption of light by using special testing instrument called a spectrophotometer.

EMIT® assays are available in a variety of kits for screening for amphetamine, barbiturates, benzodiazephines, cocaine metabolites, methadone, PCP, morphine, propoxyphene, ethanol, and cannabinoids. The EMIT® method can utilize several different enzyme systems available in different assay products.

## The Radioimmunoassay

Abuscreen is a popular radioimmunoassay is manufactured by Hoffman-LaRoche. It uses technology similar to the EMIT® test. The RIA also uses specially produced antibodies, but differs from the EMIT® by using radioactive isotopes, called tracers, to label and measure the results. How much of the tracer displaces drug bound to the antibody indicates the concentration of the drug present. Radiation emitted by the antibody bound tracer is measured using a gamma counter.

RIA is considered more accurate than EMIT®, but is somewhat more costly and requires more sophisticated laboratories due to the use of radioactive isotopes. Since EMIT® and RIA are both immunoassay techniques, one should not be used as a back-up or confirming test for the other. Instead, a positive test result should be confirmed by a nonimmunological procedure such as gas chromatography.

The most important weakness of immunoassays in general is their lack of specificity, because there are few antisera that are specific for a single compound. A more sensitive and more specific technique, fluorescent polarization immunoassy (FPIA) was developed by Abbott Labs and extended to testing drugs of abuse in 1986.

# Confirmatory Tests

Positive results on screening tests should always be confirmed because of the high risk of a false positive, which is a test that reads positive for drugs when no drugs are present in the sample. The confirmatory test should always be a more sensitive test based upon a different chemical principle.

## Gas Chromatography

Gas Chromatography (GC) and Gas Liquid Chromatography (GLC) are testing methods that separate molecules by use of a glass or metal tube that is packed with material of a particular polarity. The sample to be tested is

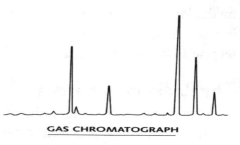

**GAS CHROMATOGRAPH**

Courtesy Hewlett-Packard, Palo Alto, Ca

vaporized at the injection port, and carried through the column by a steady flow of gas. Identical compounds travel through the column at the same speed, since their interaction with the column packing is

identical. The column terminates at a detector that permits recording and quantification. The time from injection until a response is
observed at the recorder is referred to as the "retention time." Identical retention time of substances run on the same column is strong
evidence that the substances are identical. The GC, as well as other
testing methods, require the use of standards of reference materials
to calibrate the tests.

## Gas Chromatography/Mass Spectrometry

Confirmatory tests are usually done with gas chromatography/
mass spectrometry which is the current state-of-the-art technique in
analytical toxicology. It combines two analytical techniques: gas chromatography and mass spectrometry. The reason to do a confirmatory test is double check for the human error. Gas chromatography
with a mass spectrometry detector (GC/MS) is the most sensitive and
specific procedure commonly used for drug identification. It is used
primarily for confirmatory tests and for tests that must meet forensic
courtroom standards.

GC/MS technique can be used both quantitatively and qualita-
tively. Depending on the drug measured, sensitivity can be measured
between nanograms and picograms. GC/MS is more specific and 100
to 1,000 times more sensitive than the TLC system. Most organic
molecules, including commonly used drugs such as marijuana, cocaine, and heroin, are readily identified.

GC/MS, GLC, and some RIA methodologies can be applied effectively to all biological fluids, including serum or blood. Blood levels of drugs are important because only these levels indicate *actual
levels of intoxication,* a fact that could have great legal significance.

GC/MS mixes a urine or hair specimen with an organic solvent.
The organic solvent is then evaporated to concentrate the drug prior
to introduction into the GC/MS. The technique consists of two steps.
First is the separation of drugs in a gas chromatograph followed by
mass spectrometry of the separated drug(s).

Gas chromatography forces a gas, usually helium, through a thin fused silica column with a crosslinked silicone polymer layer. Vaporized drugs are separated by interaction with the polymer and arrive at the end of the column separated in time, known as "retention time (RT)".

The sample is first separated into components by gas chromatography, and then mass spectrometry is used to identify the substances emerging from the gas chromatograph. The mass spectrometer subjects the components to an electron beam that breaks them into fragments and accelerates them through a magnetic field. A molecule of a drug always breaks into the same fragments, known as its mass spectrum. A mass spectrum for each drug is unique, like a finger print. Information on the fragmentation pattern is compared to a computer library, which lists that mass of the parent compound and its most likely fragments. A 98 percent match is considered confirmation of the presence of the compound.

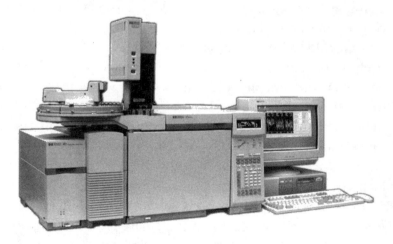

The Hewlett-Packard 5973 Mass Selective Detector. The latest generation of benchtop GC/MS system is accurate and reliable. (Courtesy of Hewlett-Packard, Palo Alto, CA)

Detection by GC/MS is highly specific, but the equipment for GC/MS is costly, and great technical expertise is required to interpret the analysis of the results. GC/MS devices provide state-of-the-art accuracy and are widely used in forensic, pharmaceutical, clinical, and industrial service laboratories.

The capillary fused silica column is then inserted into the mass spectrometer device which consists of a high vacuum chamber with quadropoles surrounding the end of the gas chromatograph column. Drugs are ionized by electrons as they exit the column and are forced into the quadropoles separating the fragments on the basis of their electrical charge and molecular weights. An ion detector converts the charged fragments into electrical pulses and feeds the information into a dedicated computer. Resultant mass spectra are extremely characteristic of the original molecule.

The use of GC/MS had been out of the reach of most laboratories because of the cost and the technical expertise needed for operation. However, advances in computerization, automated samples, and analytic technology have now placed GC/MS capability within the reach of most labs because the costs have come down and it is more automated. Many labs use the Hewlett Packard Mass Selective Detector connected to a Hewlett Packard gas chromatograph. The GC/MS is highly reliable.

## Cut-off Concentrations

Cut-off level is the value above which a specimen is considered positive and below which it is considered negative. Screening assays and confirmatory assays differ in their specificity and sensitivity so that screening (EIA) cut-off concentrations that are different than the confirmatory cutoff concentrations.

## Thin-Layer Chromatography

Thin-Layer Chromatography or TLC is a form of chromatography that is used less frequently in the 1990s than formerly. It is included here because readers may still come across references to TLC.

As in other chromatography, the urine is extracted with a reagent, and the extract is then subjected to a procedure that causes the components to separate. With thin-layer chromatography (TLC), results are created by the reproducible migration pattern of a drug on a thin layer of absorbent, usually a silica-coated glass plate. The plate is sprayed with a solution that reacts differently with different drugs, producing colored spots, that represent different drugs.

The sample is "spotted" by putting a drop of urine extract on the TLC plate, which is put in a solvent which runs up the plate by capillary action, carrying with it the drugs present in the extract. A specific drug will always migrate to the same spot or spots. After drying, the plate is analyzed for the position of drugs of interest. If cocaine is present in the sample, for example, the visualization solution is sprayed and reveals a specific spot on the plate that indicates where the cocaine has traveled. The spot location is identified by an "Rf" number which is a ratio of the distance traveled by the drug in question to the distance traveled by the solvent from the origin, where the sample was originally spotted. The plate can be illuminated by ultraviolet lights. Identical molecules are expected to migrate to the same Rf zone and to give identical color reactions. TLC often produces false positives in which certain over-the-counter and prescription drugs will travel to approximately the same spot in the testing device as illegal substances. Therefore, results of TLC must be interpreted by a skilled technician and positive results must be confirmed by a more reliable testing method.

TLC has been used most often in drug detoxification clinics, methadone maintenance programs, testing of parolees and prison inmates, and industrial screening.

## Problems With TLC Tests

Results from thin-layer chromography tests are qualitative, giving either a positive or negative result. Positive results cannot be quantified. While this is also true of the Immunoassay tests, using several tests with different cut off valves can yield a somewhat quantitative result. TLC is far less sensitive than other tests. Low levels of substance abuse are not readily detected by TLC so the meaning of screenings by TLC is confusing. Whether a sample is called positive or negative often depends on the concentration of the drug in the sample or the sensitivity cutoff of the test. The sensitivity cutoff of most TLC tests is between 1,000 and 2,000 nanograms per milliliter (ng/ml). Some drugs are detectable only when they reach a concentration of more than 2,000 ng/ml, which makes them difficult to detect. Cutoff points for immunoassay tests, in contrast, are often 100 ng/ml. and can be lower. A negative TLC result may simply mean that the method is not sensitive enough to detect the drug in the sample. TLC also suffers from low specificity, as do immunoassay tests. TLC is used as a broad screen for drugs because it is fast, inexpensive, and does not require sophisticated instrumentation.

TLC is often used in medical settings to detect recent high-dose drug abuse and toxic levels of drugs. It is an ideal test for an emergency room, where the drugs taken are unknown and quick measurement of toxic levels is necessary.

### Sensitivity Of Commonly Used Urine Analysis Methods

| Drug Group | Chromatography | | | Immunoassay | |
|---|---|---|---|---|---|
| | TLC | GLC | GC/MS | EMIT® | RIA* |
| Amphetamine | 0.5 mcg | 0.7 mcg | 10.0 ng | 0.7 mcg | 1.0 mcg |
| Barbiturates | 0.5 mcg | 0.5 mcg | 0.5 ng | 0.5 mcg | 0.1 mcg |
| Benzodiazepines | | | 0.5 mcg | 0.5 mcg | |
| Cannabinoids | | | 1.0 ng | 100.0 ng | 100.0 ng |
| Cocaine | 2.0 mcg | .75 mcg | 5.0 ng | .75 mcg | 5.0 mcg |
| Methadone | 1.0 mcg | 0.5 mcg | 5.0 ng | 0.5 ng | |
| Heroin/Morpine | 0.5 mcg | | 0.5 mcg | 0.5 mcg | 25.0 ng |
| PCP | 0.5 mcg | 150.0 ng | 5.0 ng | 150.0 ng | 100.0 ng |

Source: David Smith & David Wesson, *Substance Abuse in the Workplace. The values listed are not precise because many variables alter sensitivity.* *RIA levels are the lower limit of dectection.

# On-site Testing

The PharmScreen™ Drug Screen Card is a one-step on-site testing device that provides results in about 3 minutes, eliminating the need to send specimens to a laboratory for analysis—except for confirmation purposes. The absorbent tips are dipped into the urine sample. There is no mixing or adding of solutions. The results show in the viewing windows. One colored line indicates a positive screen; two colored lines indicate a negative screen. The results can be photocopied, providing a permanent record of the screen.

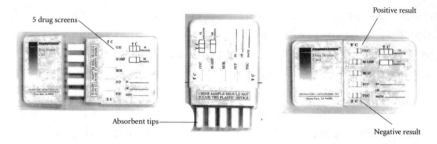

The PharmScreen™ Drug Screen Card tests for the presence of five drugs at one time—cocaine, methamphetamine, morphine, PCP and marijuana. (Courtesy PharmChem, Menlo Park, Ca.)

# Do-It-Yourself Drug Testing

As early as 1987, home-based drug tests began to appear on the market. One kit called AWARE® was developed by American Drug Screens of Dallas. The kit, complete with specimen bottles and mailing tubes, was marketed toward parents who are concerned that their children may be using drugs. Samples were mailed to a processing lab, with results returned within two weeks.

Rapid Eye Check® was a video course that instructs parents in how to examine their children's eyes for drugs with a special pen light. The eye test is essentially the same as the basic eye examination doctors use to gauge pupil size, nystagmus, response to light, and the eyes' ability to follow a moving object, all of which can be affected by drugs. Highway patrol use a similar roadside eye test for determining the sobriety of drivers.

Many labs offer testing on the internet. People fearing they will test positive get themselves tested to see if their drug use is detected. Drug abusers who plan to switch or adulterate samples use independent testing to try out their ploys in advance.

Drug testing technology and its accuracy is progressing rapidly. As this chapter has demonstrated, the various drug testing methods have differing advantages and disadvantages in terms of cost, convenience, specificity, accuracy and other concerns. Some of these disadvantages will decrease as technology advances.

# CHAPTER 16

# Drug Testing Basics

The goal of drug testing may be to detect drug use in the past or to detect current dysfunction. Pre-employment mass screenings, for example, are oriented toward detecting a pattern of drug use in the past rather than current impairment. Post-accident testing is intended to detect current impairment. Drug testing in a criminal context emphasizes accuracy, and forensic or legal standards are required.

## Terminology

Drug testing is a highly technical field, involving complex issues in both law and chemistry. Hence it is important to understand how common phrases are used. For example, "pre-employment screening" is used to refer to a testing program while "screening test" is used to refer to a preliminary and usually less expensive testing method which should be confirmed by a more sensitive and accurate method using a different technology.

## Observation

Observation of the urine as it is being collected is required to meet chain of custody requirements. Without observation one cannot be sure the urine has not been tampered with to create a false

negative, or that it is really the urine of the person in question. Whenever direct observation has been used in the workplace, there has been
a loud outcry. People feel humiliated and degraded by the process.
Indirect observation procedures can be used, together with other precautions, such as searching clothing, washing hands of the subject,
and measuring temperature of the sample.

## Drug Urinalysis

Urine drug screening is an analytical tool for detecting the presence of drugs and their metabolites in urine. The technology for performing urinalysis varies, and can be designed to meet the specific
needs of individual clients.

A major limitation of urinary drug tests is their lack of specificity, unless a GC/MS is used. Urine tests are less able to detect when
the drug was taken than blood tests. There is considerable individual
variability in detection times. Diet, urine flow, and dose dependency
can alter the test results. Some people test positive at lower doses than
others, for example.

## Direct Observed Collection

The Mandatory Federal Guidelines allow an immediate second
collection under direct observation when the temperature of the specimen is outside the acceptable temperature range and the donor either refuses to allow the collector to measure his or her body temperature or the donor's body temperature does not explain the specimen temperature. The collector can also demand a second sample
under direct observation when the collector believes that the donor
adulterated or substituted the specimen provided. This can occur
when there is bluing color in the specimen, when the collector hears
or smells something unusual while the donor is providing the specimen or when the collector sees an adulterating substance on the floor.

Direct observation with prior notice is also allowed when the
specimen provided by the donor on a previous drug test was reported
by the lab to have been diluted, adulterated, or the test was not per-

formed because the specimen was unsuitable for testing and the Medical Review Officer (MRO) determined that no medical explanation exists for the specimen's unsuitability.

## Dedicated Bathroom

A dedicated bathroom is one solution to the observation problem. This is a bathroom with all water supply cut off, so that urine cannot be diluted. Before entering, the person giving the sample leaves behind coats, purses, and any other obvious hiding places for "clean" samples or diluting agents. Such precautions increase the probability that the sample cannot be altered. However, the person can still wear a colostomy bag containing drug-free urine or hide contaminating substances under the fingernails. A substituted sample may be detected by measuring the temperature, unless it is given at body temperature. Most contaminants can be detected if they are suspected. But carefully planned attempts to foil the dedicated bathroom may succeed.

## Shy Bladder

Occasionally, a donor is unable to provide a specimen because he or she either urinated recently or has a "shy "bladder. Generally, the term refers to an individual who is unable to provide a sufficient specimen either upon demand or when someone is nearby during the attempted urination. The collector is required to keep records of each attempted urination. The donor is given large quantities of fluids, such as 8 ounces every 30 minutes up to 24 ounces and 2 hours. Donors who cannot provide a sample can be reported as refusing to provide a sample.

## Chain Of Custody

Chain of custody is a monitoring process to prevent tampering with the sample or the results. Chain of custody begins with collection of the urine, and continues through the final reporting of test results to clients. Sealing of sample containers, transport and control of samples, receipt of samples by the laboratory, and supervision of lab tests remain under strict discipline throughout the chain of custody. Authorized signatures are required at each step. Laboratory results can be effectively challenged in Court if there are weak links in the chain.

Standards regulate the handling, analysis, and collection of samples if they are intended to be admissible in a Court of law. Transfer of urine, blood, or saliva from the subject to the container must be witnessed. For example, if a person is taken to a physician for a blood sample, the physician becomes the first link in the chain of custody. Few physicians understand the legal chain of custody procedures. Unless otherwise instructed, they will usually follow clinical laboratory standards, which will not stand up to challenge by a knowledgeable attorney.

The person collecting the blood sample must be able to testify regarding the collection procedure. Likewise, the person collecting the sample must be able to testify to the accuracy of the container label, including the subject's name and other identifying information, such as date, time of the collection, and type of collection receptacle. The chain of custody must be maintained until the specimen reaches the laboratory—and through the confirmation of initial results.

## Custody and Control Form

Chain of custody forms became a nightmare because employers used different forms. This problem was corrected with rules which mandate the use of an approved Custody and Control Form (CCF) to be used to document the collection of a specimen at the collection site. The OMB-approved (Office of Management and Budget) CCF is usually supplied by the testing lab. The OMB-approved CCF may not be modified. The Urine Specimen Collection Handbook for Federal Workplace Drug Testing Programs can be ordered from the National Clearinghouse for Alcohol and Drug Information (NCADI) and is available at the NCADI web site (www.health.org/workpl.htm).

# Detection Period

The length of time a drug or metabolite can be found in bodily fluids is known as the detection period. Detection periods vary widely according to the inherent physical and chemical properties of the drug itself, the person's history of use, and characteristics such as age, sex, body weight, and health. For example, the cocaine detection period is very short (12 to 48 hours) whereas marijuana has a longer detection period, depending on drug-use history. Casual marijuana use can be detected from 2 to 7 days later; with chronic use, detection may be possible up to two months after the last use. However, a single puff of low potency marijuana is probably undetectable after 12 hours.

Detection times is of intense concern to employers because it indicates how long after illicit drug use that use can be detected and therefore how confident the employer can be that employees tested negative are actually drug free at the time of testing. For employees who have used illicit drugs, knowledge of detection times can mean the difference between being detected and slipping by. Drug using employees usually consult detections times tables to determine how long they must abstain from use when facing a drug test with the hopes of testing negatives. This cat-and-mouse game is found most often in pre-employment testing where an applicant will clean-up for a few weeks before applying for employment.

# Metabolite And Metabolism

After a drug is swallowed, smoked, injected, or snorted, it is distributed throughout the bloodstream. As the blood repeatedly passes through the liver and other parts of the body, the drug encounters numerous enzyme systems, which convert most of the drug into one or more end products called metabolites. Metabolites travel into various parts of the body, including urine, blood, and hair. How long it takes for this to occur depends on metabolism. The length of time the metabolites stay detectable in the system is called detection time.

# Sensitivity And Specificity

Test sensitivity is a measure of the smallest amount of the drug that can be detected in the urine sample. Specificity of a test is its ability to distinguish one drug from another. Sensitivity of the screening test should be set appropriately for the goals of the test.

# Cut-Off Level And Detection Limit

Cut-off level and detection limit are two factors influencing a test's sensitivity. Cut-off level refers to the concentration of a drug necessary to indicate a positive reading on the test. Detection limit of the test is the concentration below which a particular drug is undetectable by the method.

Typically the first test given is for broad screening and is inexpensive. These include the EMIT®, TLC, or RIA, which are relatively sensitive, and can detect most drugs or metabolites in the system. They give an on-off, positive or negative result. If there is a positive, it should be confirmed by a different test. The most credible confirmation is GC/MS, which is considerably more expensive. The confirmation test used should be more specific in its results. .

# False Positives And False Negatives

Clerical and laboratory errors can be made anywhere in the process from collection, identification of the sample, to reporting of the results. "False positive" means that a drug-free sample was reported positive for drugs. "False negative" means that a sample containing drugs was reported as drug-free. A "false positive" is not the same as an inaccurate or misleading result. For example, a positive screening result for amphetamines or opiates due to over the counter or prescription drugs is not a false positive if these over-the-counter medications were in fact consumed.

# Confirmation Of Positive Results

All urine samples reported positive should be analyzed a second time by a different testing method. Both tests must give a positive result before a positive report is made. This process is called confirmation.

# The Collector

The Mandatory Guidelines define a collection site person as a person who instructs and assists individuals at a collection site and who receives and makes an initial examination of the urine specimen provided by those individuals. The collector, who does not have to be a medical professional, must receive specialized training in collecting urine specimens. When a collection is required to be performed under direct observation, the collector must be of the same gender as the donor.

# Collection Site

The term collection site refers to the entire facility used to collect the urine specimen, which includes the rest room or toilet stall and the work area used by the collector. The site must restrict access to only authorized personnel and collection materials and supplies. The collector must ensure that the donor does not have access to items, such as soap, disinfectants, personal hygiene products and water, that could be used to adulterate or dilute the specimen. Unobserved entrance and exit from the site must be prohibited. The site must allow for secure handling and storage of specimens from collection until shipment to the testing lab.

In preparation of the site, any water supply available must be controlled to prevent the donor from diluting the specimen. Whenever possible bluing or other color agents must be added to any water supply available to the donor.

# Donor Identification

The donor must be positively identified as the individual selected for testing. Acceptable methods of identification are photo
identification including driver's license, and employee badge, positive identification by employer representative, or other identification
allowed under the employer's workplace testing program. Identification by a co-worker or another donor is not acceptable. Non-photo
identification cards such as social security card, credit card, pay vouch-
ers, or voter registration cards are not acceptable.

# Fatal Flaws

The following errors or omissions in the documentation for a
sample are considered fatal flaws that result in a specimen being rejected for testing by the lab. 1) The preprinted specimen I.D. number
on the CCF does not match the specimen I.D. number on the specimen bottle. 2) There is no specimen I.D. number on the bottle. 3)
There is an insufficient quantity of urine for the lab to complete the
test. 4) The specimen bottle label and or seal is massing, broken, or
shows evidence of tampering. 5) The specimen bottle is obviously
adulterated—color, foreign objects, unusual odor. Other errors or
omissions may be fatal flaws unless the information can be recovered
and/or provided by the collector to the lab in writing.

# Medical Review Officer

An essential part of the drug testing program is the final review
of results. A positive laboratory test result does not automatically
identify an employee of job applicant as an illegal drug user. An individual with a detailed knowledge of possible alternative medical ex-
planations is essential to the review of results. The Medical Review
Officer (MRO) fulfills this function by reviewing the results with the
donor and protecting the confidential nature of the donor's medical
information. The MRO is considered a critical safeguard in the Federal Drug Testing Program. The function of the MRO is described in

the Medical Review Officer Manual for Federal Workplace Drug Testing Program prepared by the Substance Abuse and Mental Health Service Administration (SAMHSA).

In 1998 Iowa legislated a new drug testing law. One of the new provisions permits physician's assistants, nursed practitioners, and chiropractors to serve as MROs, as long as they have appropriate medical training. This provision is unique among State laws permitting non-physicians to act as MROs and is viewed as inappropriate by the Iowa Department of Public Health.

# CHAPTER 17

# Problems With Drug Testing

 The appeal of drug testing at work is that it appears to be objective and scientific. But there may be problems with the tests, and results do not necessarily establish "proof" of drug use.

## Validity

Drug testing is far from perfect. For example, in the mid-1980s the Center for Disease Control (CDC) evaluated the performance of 13 laboratories conducting tests for methadone treatment facilities. The CDC prepared samples containing known quantities of barbiturates, amphetamines, methadone, cocaine, codeine, and morphine. The prepared samples were sent through as though they were patient samples, so that the labs did not know they were being evaluated. The results varied widely. The CDC reported error rates of up to 94 percent in false negatives (labs unable to detect drugs present in the samples) and up to 66 percent in false positive errors (drugs not present in the samples). Those early testing labs operated at a much lower standard than today's labs because methodology and reliability have improved considerably. But problems remain.

# Errors

The high level of false negatives showed that labs were often unable to detect drugs at the low concentrations called for by their contracts. However, the most dramatic result of this study was the astonishingly high level of false positives. The labs reported 152 false positives in 106 of the 160 samples, constituting an incredible 66.5 percent false-positive error rate! Commenting on the CDC study, David Smith, Director of the Haight Ashbury Free Clinic said, "in many cases the labs would have done a better job if they had poured the urine down the drain and flipped a coin." On the other hand, Bob Fogerson, Quality Assurance Manager at PharmChem, argues that "it is not valid to conclude drug testing can not be done accurately just because it has not been done accurately."

Problems of laboratory performance, faulty confirmation, legal action, and carelessness began appearing almost immediately in mass-screenings of enlisted military personnel for drugs. In 1984, the Army and Air Force began reviewing the results of 100,000 urinary drug tests. At that time, the American Civil Liberties Union estimated that as many as 30,000 military personnel might be eligible to have disciplinary charges against them dismissed. The Navy suffered similar problems which brought questions from Naval Commanders, who insisted on closer study. 6,000 positive urines were reexamined. The Navy found that 2,000 of these could not be "scientifically substantiated as positive." An additional 2,000 test results were of questionable validity because documentation was missing. One of the investigators, Lt. Commander Deborah Durnette, said that the use of the same test for both the initial screening and the confirmation made many of the Navy's tests invalid. The Navy labs used the EMIT® as a backup test to the RIA. This strategy is of questionable validity since the two tests are generally of the same type, both being immunoassays. Confirmation should be made by a different method, such as GC/MS. The Navy subsequently announced that it would discontinue the use of EMIT® as a confirmation.

The Army stopped using the Navy labs in 1982 because over 1,000 Army personnel had been affected by these lab problems. However, the Army also had problems at its own Fort Mead lab. A civilian lawyer aggressively defended soldiers disciplined for marijuana use as a result of drug tests, and the problems came to light. Many court-martials were dropped because lab records could not stand scrutiny. High percentages of errors were reported from the labs at Forts Mead (97%), Brooks (60%), Wiesbaden (75%), and at Trippler (20%). These error rates demonstrated a "basis for argumentation as to the legal and technical credibility or sufficiency of the testing process." The Army and Air Force were conducting 800,000 tests per year at these facilities. During the 20 months in question, approximately 1,320,000 tests were performed. Most errors were related to poor management, inadequate personnel, broken chain of custody, faulty maintenance of equipment, and faulty transmissions of reports and records, rather than to the tests themselves. Sometimes the problem is the contamination of glassware with positive urine caused a false positive rate of 3 to 5 percent.

False positives for opiates were a particular problem. Prescription drugs and poppy seed consumption as well as use of over-the-counter medications can give positive results for opiate use. Not only were many innocent people's work lives threatened, but the cost of large numbers of positive tests among non-illicit drug users was excessive. In response the government amended the Mandatory Guidelines for Federal Workplace Drug Testing Programs by increasing the cutoff (from 300 to 2000 ng/ml) and confirmatory levels for opiates taking effect May 1998.

## Human Error

Manufacturers of drug tests say that their instruments are 95 to 99 percent accurate at detecting traces of drugs in urine, when their own lab employees operate the machines while closely watched for proficiency. Manufacturers claim that the gas chromatography/mass spectrometry is nearly 100 percent accurate. But these high accuracy rates hold only when the lab operators are extremely proficient and diligent. Such ideal conditions hardly ever exist in practice. The reality is that the machines are only as reliable as the people operating them. Careless, overworked, or incompetent operators can misuse the machines in innumerable ways, yielding false positive results on clean urine specimens, or other errors.

# Regulation

At a California State Senate Hearing to evaluate the need for lab regulations, Dr. David Smith of the Haight-Ashbury Free Clinic was adamant in pointing out that "in a random or mass testing, without probable cause, error is inevitable." Because the methods used in mass testing are less sophisticated, unqualified clerks are often delegated the responsibility of obtaining samples. Typically, the cheapest tests are used. These give only a positive or a negative result, with no quantification, and are subject to some error. Consequently, erroneous results in mass testing are quite possible. Smith points out that many employers are not adequately informed by the manufacturers or companies selling the testing programs. Often the lab technicians themselves do not understand the testing process or how data is to be interpreted.

### Causes Of Errors in Testing

Improper laboratory procedures
Inadvertent switching of samples
Paperwork being lost or damaged
Passive inhalation
Cross-reactivity with other, legal drugs
Tampering with samples
Unknown reasons

# False Positives

"False positives" refers to a positive result on a drug-free sample. False positives may occur due to testing methodology or because equipment was contaminated. Of course, operator error is present to some degree in all technologies, but in drug testing it is common to have nonspecialist personnel carrying out on-site specimen collection at private companies.

A high false-positive rate is of lesser importance in research, drug abuse treatment programs, and nonpunitive situations. On the other hand, in a screening program directed at probationers, pre-employment or prepromotion examinations, or job-fitness evaluations, reporting a positive urine test takes on great social significance. The potential repercussions of a positive drug test result in an employment context can be catastrophic to the person tested positive.

As with most politically important terms, the use of the phrase "false positive" is sometimes confused and subject to tedious argument. In fact, some call them "unconfirmed positives," which implies that, although the positive result has not been confirmed, it still may be correct. Positives in "initial" or "screening" tests should be confirmed by using a test that is more sensitive than the initial screen and is based on a different methodology. That is, a chromatography test should be used to confirm immunoassay test results, because they utilize a different method, whereas *EMIT* *and RIA should never be used to confirm other immunoassays.* Using TLC to confirm an RIA result is valid because it is of the chromatography group. However, there are other considerations in using TLC. The TLC is ordinarily a first step or screening test, and subject to more error than the GC or GC/MS. If confirmation of a positive can have a significant impact on the person tested, then the most accurate test available should be used. This would call for the GC/MS, and sometimes a drug test on a blood sample would be indicated, especially in post-accident testing to determine impairment by drug use.

# Cross-Reactivity

Cross-reactivity was studied by Allen and Stiles, who tested 161 prescription and over-the-counter drugs with the EMIT®-d.a.u. screens for opiates, amphetamines, barbiturates, benzodiazepines, methadone, propoxyphene, and cocaine metabolite. They found that 65 of the prescription drugs and over-the-counter products showed some cross-reactivity, including values above cut-off. Fortunately, most of the positives required concentrations that are not achievable in human urine and do not present practical problems.

Appedrine® diet pills tested positive for amphetamines. Ibuprofen, the anti-inflammatory agent in Advil® and Nuprin®, is reported to produce false positives when testing for marijuana. About 150 legal over-the-counter medications, especially those containing synthetic compounds like phenylpropanolamine, have been reported as causing positives in amphetamine tests, and can also cause a false positive in a methedrine test. Some sources claim that the cocaine EMIT® test can yield a positive if the person being tested drank large quantities of tea. Antihistamines may cause a false positive for PCP.

Syva and Roche, which manufacture the EMIT® and Abuscreen® tests, say they inform labs purchasing machines from them that the tests are "class assays," designed to detect broad categories for drug-like substances in the urine. This is particularly true for amphetamines and opiates. For example, the heroin screen looks for substances *similar* in basic structure to morphine, the basic opiate molecule. Opioid substances include dextromethorphan, a nonintoxicating cough suppressant found in common, uncontrolled, drugstore nostrums like Nyquil®, Doco Children's Cough Syrup®, Comtrex®, Peda-care®, and Benylin®. EMIT® and Abuscreen® both yield amphetamine positives on phenylpropanolamine or PPA, a mild decongestant which is an active ingredient in dozens of drugstore medications, including Alka-Selzer Plus®, as well as popular weight-reduction preparations like Dexatrim® and Dietac®. Syva reported that ephedrine cross-reacts with amphetamines on both the EMIT® and the Abuscreen®. Ephedrine is a decongestant in common over-the-counter medicines.

## Cross-Reactivity With EMIT® At ≥100 MCG/ML

| Generic name | Brand name* | Cross-reactivity |
|---|---|---|
| Amitriptyline HCl | Elavil® | Methadone |
| Carisoprodol | Soma® | Methadone |
| Clindinium bromide | Quarzan® | Benzodiazepine |
| Cloxacillin Na | Tegopen® | Benzodiazepine |
| Diphenhydramine HCl | Benadry® | Methadone |
| Imipramine HCl | Tofranil® | Methadone |
| Isoxuprine HCl | Vasodilan® | Amphetamine |
| Orphenadrine citrate | Norflex® | Methadone |
| Perphenazine | Trilafon® | Benzodiazepine |
| Promethazine HCl | Phenergan® | Methadone & Opiate |
| Thiethylperzine maleate | Torecan® | Methadone |
| Tripelennamine HCl | Pyribenzamine® | Benzodiazepine & Methadone |

Values are equal to or greater than 100 micrograms per milliliter. Source: Allen & Stiles.

The Table shows the over-the-counter medicines that often cause cross-reactivity on EMIT® tests. This is serious because the medicines are widely used for common ailments. People who do not abuse drugs may be subject to positive results on a drug test which can result in suspicion and inconvenience. Cross-reactivity is a problem that has not been solved and is misunderstood by many companies that have drug testing programs.

The molecular diagram (on the next page) showing the sensitivity between phenylpropanolamine and ephedrine which are found in many over-the-counter medicines and amphetamine and methamphetamine. These similarities are the reason that many over-the-

**Phenylpropanolamine**     **Ephedrine**

**Amphetamine**     **Methamphetamine**

counter medicines cause cross-reactivity and false positives. (From John P. Morgan, M.D., "Problems of Mass Urine Screening of Misused Drugs," pg. 26 *Substance Abuse in the Workplace.*)

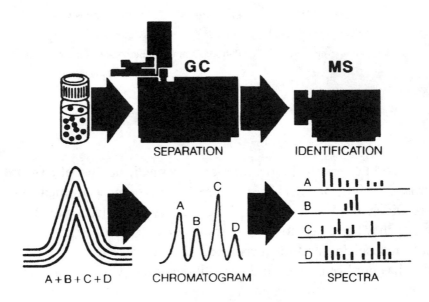

How GC/MS works. Left-to-right, the sample is separated into its components by gas chromatograph and then the components are ionized and identified by the characteristic spectra produced by the mass spectrometer. (From product literature for Hewlett Packard's GC/MS systems for drug confirmation.)

# CHAPTER 18

# Picking Tests
# And Selecting Labs

 The testing should be tailored to the employer's purpose in testing. The methodology and the detection limits as well as the selection of a laboratory are key factors.

## Drug Screening Tests

A drug-screening test is intended to determine whether or not a drug-like component is present in the sample. If the purpose of the drug testing is for screening a large number of samples where there is no known relationship between their performance or activities and the test taking, then the test needs to be inexpensive (because there will be many samples), easy to administer (possibly by people who have had minimal training), and relatively quick in yielding results, possibly on the spot. For example, some types of tests might even use colored dipsticks, although it would not necessarily be recommended for the employers themselves to actually do the testing. A drug screen test may also be used as an initial test, with positive results given a subsequent "confirmatory test."

# Confirmatory Tests

A confirmatory test is used to ensure that what is revealed by an initial screening test is actually an abused drug instead of, for example, an over-the-counter medication, an unusual food, or an error of some sort. Confirmatory tests may also be used when there is some behavioral indication, such as slurred speech, staggering, nystagmus, or even an accident. The cost of the confirmatory test is usually much higher than the screening test. The time it takes to yield the results is not as important as the specificity and sensitivity of the test. In "for cause" and post-accident drug tests with severe consequences, both urine and blood samples may be taken. The blood sample is used for a confirmatory test to the screening test on the urine sample.

# Sensitivity and Cut-Off Points

Another issue that must be determined before implementing a program is the sensitivity of the test. Sensitivity refers to how readily the test can detect the presence of a drug. Sensitivity may not be the same as the "cut-off" point, which can be calibrated, while sensitivity is inherent in the test methodology. The most common type of screening test is a test for the presence of the drugs in urine, although screening methods can be applied to blood and saliva as well. Police officers who stop motorists who appear to be under the influence may use saliva or breath tests, but employers typically use urine tests.

A "positive" or "negative" result is relative, not absolute. That is, if it is above or below the cut-off value, it is labeled "positive" or "negative." It is therefore extremely important to find out in advance what the laboratory's cut-off point for positive samples will be. The cut-off points should be reviewed to ensure that the laboratory can detect the drugs of interest within an appropriate length of time after use by an employee or job applicant.

The cut-off point can be rather high, making the test less sensitive, or low, making it more sensitive. The sensitivity of the test should depend on the company's purpose for testing. For a broad screening, employers have to have a somewhat less sensitive test or higher cut-off points. This would tend to detect only people who have used a drug very recently, or who have used a large amount of a drug. In a safety situation, employers might have a much more sensitive test and lower "cut-off" point, which would flag a wider range of people.

A confirmatory method should not only be as sensitive for the drug's presence as the screening method, but also permit specification of the drug that was detected. The confirmatory test should always be one that uses a different process than the screening test.

Sophisticated labs never use the same type of test twice for both screening and confirmation. The confirmatory test is usually based on a different chemical principle than the nonspecific screening method. These tests include the gas chromatography (GC) and the gas chromatograph/mass-spectrometer (GC-MS). These methods require extensive instrumentation and experienced operators. They provide the best means available to identify a specific drug present, but are expensive.

## Choosing Test Sensitivity Level

If the company decides to launch into a drug testing program, one of the questions is, "What kind of errors can you tolerate?" Another way of saying this is "what bias do we want in the test?" We have already seen in our exploration of the issues and the data that errors in drug testing programs are inevitable. There is no such thing as a perfect drug testing program. There may be innocent people who are accused of being drug users. And there may be guilty people, drug users, who will be undetected. So, does the company want a program that will catch only the extreme drug users and let many casual drug users by? Or does it want a program that will indicate all drug users, of even the slightest amount, but will also give a positive result on many people who are merely eating poppy-seed bagels, taking diet pills, or taking Nyquil® cough medicine?

Louisiana University, for example, set its initial screening cutoff level for marijuana at 100 ng/ml instead of at the 50 ng/ml to prevent false positives due to passive inhalation. This is probably reasonable considering how many university personnel might be exposed to such passive inhalation, as compared to employees in others industries.

In cases where public-safety is at issue, as with airline pilots and train engineers, it would perhaps be better to get a positive result on a person who is not abusing substances. On the other hand, if the program is being used to deter drug use, and public safety is not at issue, it might be better, in light of the serious consequences to the individual, to let some people escape who are occasional or recreational users, or even regular abusers, on the grounds that sooner or later they will be detected.

## Choosing Detection Limits

The *cut-off value* refers to the concentration of the drug that will be reported by a laboratory as a positive indication that a drug or its metabolites are present in the sample. Most tests for drug abuse have high cut-off values. A laboratory will usually be unable to detect, or will not report the presence of, a small amount of drugs or drugs taken more than a few days prior to the tests. To avoid detection, an employee generally needs to abstain from most drugs, including marijuana, for a week. Chronic marijuana users, however, may need to abstain for up to three or four weeks to avoid detection, depending on the potency of the marijuana and the individual's previous level of use and the sensitivity of the tests.

Some cannabinoid tests may be unreliably positive for employee testing, since they can react positively to a sample from a person who has been passively exposed to marijuana smoke, particularly when the results are reported at cut-off levels as low as 50 nanograms per milliliter. A higher cut-off value, for example, such as the use of a 200 ng/ml cut-off value in an EMIT® cannabinoid test, is less likely to result in the reporting of a false positive. The use of a high cut-off value increases the job-relatedness of a test. However, the test can not measure the degree of employee impairment. The smoking of a single joint by a nonuser is not analogous in effect to that of a single joint for a chronic user, much as one stiff drink to a nondrinker is more impairing than it would be to a moderate drinker. Yet the same drink may set an alcoholic off on a binge. Still, the use of a higher detection limit is a way of creating an error bias toward the negative.

The common tests for alcohol use have very short detection limits, and the correlation between the results of laboratory urine tests and actual blood-alcohol concentration is well understood. Thus, blood tests detect recent use of alcohol, as well as actual impairment.

Drug testing laboratories are very much aware of the consequences of reporting false positive test results. In practice, they may use higher cut-off points for positive results rather than use the full sensitivity that their methodology is capable of providing. This technique leads to a higher cut-off value in screening for drugs, so that fewer samples, those with high drug concentrations, will need to be confirmed.

Another way to reduce the chance of a false positive test result is to use a less sensitive method to confirm the initial screening results. Since the initial positive screening result cannot be confirmed, the overall result is reported back to the client as a negative result. In either case, the net effect would be an underestimation of the actual drug use, and many false negative test results.

## Choosing Your Errors

Errors in drug testing are likely. There are two main types of errors: a drug user can test negative, or a non-drug-user can test positive. If the consequences of the test are used as a basis for disciplinary action, employment, promotion decisions, or criminal investigations, then a false negative is the safest error. It is better to let a few of the "guilty" go undetected than to wrongly accuse the innocent. Chronic drug abusers who escape detection in one testing are likely to be detected in a subsequent testing.

On the other hand, a false positive might be preferred in a research or treatment setting or where issues of safety are paramount. If testing is intended to evaluate work fitness, such as that of a pilot commanding a passenger plane, then it would be safer to stop a functioning pilot from making a flight than to fail to detect an intoxicated one.

# Selection Of A Drug Testing Laboratory

Doing the initial drug screening within the company can reduce the cost of testing. By confirming only those laboratory samples that test positive at the company's initial screening, a company can significantly reduce the cost of its drug testing program. In this situation the training and skill of the person performing the analysis are crucial to the success of the program. People who have minimal training are likely to make mistakes, such as contaminating a sample and causing positive results for people who have not been abusing drugs. What effect might these positive results have on those persons' reputations? The in-house program can also suffer from problems of who has access to the tests, the test results, and samples. For these reasons, most companies conducting testing programs prefer to have a laboratory perform the drug screening even though it costs more. Confirmatory testing is almost always done in an off-site lab.

## Considerations In Choosing A Testing Laboratory

- The laboratory should be licensed, inspected, audited, and in good standing with state authorities. The laboratory should use the National Institute on Drug Abuse (NIDA) or College of American Pathologists (CAP). Guidelines as the standard for "good laboratory practices."

- The laboratory should confirm all positive results by a fundamentally different method of testing. Under no circumstances should a positive sample be screened once and then reported without a confirmation test being performed.

- The laboratory should adhere to forensic procedural standards, including strict chain of custody to guard samples from the possibility of tampering. Samples should be locked away when not going through the testing process. Visitors should not be permitted in the testing area, unless continuously escorted by authorized staff.

- The laboratory should have a substantive quality control program that dictates standard operating procedures to ensure the integrity and repeatability of results.

- The laboratory should be willing to defend its procedures with expert testimony, at a reasonable fee, if questions arise.

- The laboratory should save all positive samples in frozen storage for a reasonable time, at least one year, which would permit retesting if a question arises.

- The laboratory should participate in an outside proficiency test program to monitor the quality of its performance. Ideally, the program should consist of blind analysis of samples having known levels of various drugs, as well as totally negative (drug-free) samples.

## Test Procedures

No testing method is guaranteed to be error-free, but there are methods of selection and guidelines a company can follow to ensure the highest degree of accuracy in drug testing. A company should demand certain procedures, and monitor the lab to make sure these conditions are being met, so that both the company and its employees are protected from errors in test results.

Because of the tremendous revenue it can generate many laboratories have expanded their services to include drug testing. But not all labs are the same. Many labs that have been doing clinical testing can not meet the rigorous standards needed for drug testing. Results from clinical tests are used for treatment decisions and patient management whereas positive drug tests can result in loss of employment.

If a company is promised high quality results with returned reports in two to four hours, it should be aware that it is risking a high number of errors. Quality work takes at least 24 if not 48 hours from receipt of specimen.

Incidences of poor testing generally come from casual selection of laboratory vendors. Make sure that the laboratory managers are well versed in substance-abuse testing. Ask for references and call them.

## Questions To Ask Prospective Testing Labs

- Who has accredited the laboratory?

- How does it maintain quality control?

- Does the laboratory insist upon a release form from employees?

- Does it provide help with policy statements?

- Has it done work for treatment facilities?

- Does the lab insist on confirmation testing of all positives, or is it willing to provide reports from a single-method general screening?

- Does it follow forensic standards and how is the chain of custody maintained?

- Is the lab willing to defend its data in court?

- Does the lab participate in an external quality assurance program?

Be aware that drug testing labs may not have to be approved or certified by any State or Federal agency to conduct business. Even if a lab has been approved or certified, such credentials could mean only that the overall lab operation meets minimal requirements for personnel space and safety. However, NIDA or CAP Certification implies that the lab employs sound analytic methods and can perform tests reliably.

A good lab will attempt to minimize errors by having a quality assurance program. This should include internal measures to prevent breakdowns in procedures and participation in an external quality-assurance program, such as those conducted by the College of American Pathologists, the American Association of Bioanalysts, and the California Association of Toxicologists. These programs submit urine samples to laboratories at fixed times during the year and evaluate the accuracy of the results. Ask if the lab subscribes to any of these programs, and ask to review any evaluation made of the lab.

Another approach is to ask the lab to test a set of drug-free and drug-containing urine specimens before awarding a contract for services. Labs will often provide free analyses under these conditions to obtain the contract.

## Cost Of The Lab

Price in selection of a lab should not be the primary consideration. Labs who are completing for contracts are under pressure to give low bids. As a consequence labs are under considerable pressure to limit costs. You usually get what you pay for. Striving to be competitive, many labs have increased the numbers and speed of testing while decreasing the costs of testing. The results is a high number of false positives. The cost to a company of one badly botched lab test can be far greater than any savings in the lab testing fees. On the other hand, price alone is no assurance of quality testing. Companies establishing testing programs should look for technical excellence at a reasonable price.

## Evaluating The Lab

Any lab can provide drug testing services. There are no established standards or certifications, per se, for drug testing of private employees which leaves employers vulnerable. Because of the complexity of drug testing and the difficult of getting reliable performance data for labs, it's advisable to utilize a lab certified by NIDA (National Institute on Drug Abuse) and follow the guideline from the U.S. Department of Health and Human Services as is required of Federal agencies and certain private employers such as those involved with public transportation.

Once a lab has been selected, its performance should be continually re-evaluated. This can be done by requesting data from external quality-assessment programs, and by conducting a blind assessment of the lab periodically. One way this is done is to occasionally split a specimen and submit it under two different names or sample identifiers. Lab results should presumably be identical for the two specimens. However, the split sample technique has a flaw. If the sample screens as a marginal positive for the first split sample, it may well result in a marginal negative for the second split sample. This frequently happens for specimens that are at or close to the cutoff value concentrations. If the blind method is used, it is probably better to attempt to get a specimen that has known drug concentrations in it. These can be obtained from external quality-assessment programs, through consultants, or by recycling positive drug specimens identified by the lab itself.

# CHAPTER 19

# Responding To Positive Results

When positive results come back from initial, or screening tests, it is a mistake to assume that there are actually positives for drug use. Instead, view initial positives as a need to confirm results with a more sophisticated, more reliable test based upon a different testing methodology.

## Confirmatory Tests

The second test is called a *confirmatory test.* A confirmatory method ideally should be more sensitive than the screening test and permit identification of specific drugs. Many screening tests are not specific, but in confirmation a test which indicates which kind of substance was used is required. This is particularly important because the use of over-the-counter drugs may have caused the positive result on the first screening test. A valid confirmatory test requires the use of a testing method based upon a chemical principle different from that used in the less specific screening method.

Two confirmatory methods are gas chromatography (GC) and gas chromatography/mass spectrometry (GC/MS). These methods require special instrumentation and a highly skilled operator; therefore, they are more expensive, and require specialized labs. However, they provide the best means available to identify the specific drugs present.

The HP Mass Selective Detector ChemStation is the most sophisticated and accurate benchtop GC/MS available and is now in use at many durg testing labs. (Courtesy of Hewlett-Packard, Palo Alto, Ca.)

The terms "positive" and "negative" are used in a relative rather than an absolute sense in drug testing. Since different drug testing methods have different sensitivities for drugs, it is not surprising that one laboratory, using one method, might find a sample positive for a drug, but another laboratory testing the same sample, but using another method, might find the same sample negative.

An employee who feels that the urinalysis test results have not been properly confirmed or that the tests were improperly performed could bring a negligence action against the employer. The basis of such an action would be that the person conducting the test and the employer who ordered the test have a legal duty to see that the manufacturer's directions are properly followed, and that the screening test is confirmed in a proper manner. Failure to fulfill this duty and subsequent harm caused to the employee by loss of work or by other disciplinary action could be the basis for a lawsuit. Despite the additional cost of confirming a screening test, it is advisable for the employer to confirm all positives on screening tests by means of reliable and appropriate confirmatory tests.

To ensure that a specimen is available if a retest is requested either by an MRO or by an official administrative or judicial proceeding, HHS requires labs to place all specimens confirmed positive in properly secured frozen storage for a minimum of one year. This is generally a sufficient amount of time to allow for a retest to occur. The time, however, can be extended beyond one year by either the employer or an administrative/judiciary official to allow completion of any litigation or arbitration that may be ongoing with the donor.

If split specimens were collect, the lab is required to keep both specimen bottles frozen for one year. For a split specimen collection, the MRO must inform the donor of his or her right to request an analysis of the split specimen (Bottle B). the donor's request to have the split specimen tested must be made through the MRO. The donor is normally given a maximum of 72 hours to initiate the request.

## Medical Review Officer Review

The Mandatory Guidelines specify that the MRO reviews all positive results before they are forwarded to the employer. This review included a review of the Custody and Control Form (CCF) for completion and accuracy. Next the MRO is required to interview the donor to determine if the donor can provide a valid alternative medical explanation, such as the use of a prescription or over-the-counter drug. If all of the information on the CCF appears correct and complete, no problems are noted by either the collector or the lab on the CCF, and the donor is unable to provide a valid alternative medical explanation, a positive lab test result is determined as "POSITIVE" which is reported to the employer.

If the information submitted by the donor is sufficient to support the legitimate medical use of a prescription medication that would cause the positive test result for the drug reported by the lab, the MRO may immediately inform the donor that the result will be reported to the employer as a verified "NEGATIVE".

Ideally, the MRO is always able to contact the donor for an interview. However, this is not always the case. Occasionally, the MRO is unable to contact the donor. The MRO may verify a positive test as "POSITIVE" without having communicated directly with the donor when the donor expressly declines the interview, when the MRO has been unable to contact the donor within 14 days of receiving the positive result, and when the employer has instructed the donor to contact the MRO but the donor has not done so within 5 days. The MRO should establish guidelines as to what constitutes a reasonable effort to contact the donor and should document all attempts that were made to contact the donor.

The American Disabilities Act has made handling positive results more confusing. Employers are permitted to give disabled people drug tests. However, under the ADA testing for alcohol is considered to be a medical examination. It also defines an interview with the MRO to be a medical examination. Medical examinations of disabled people are prohibited prior to offering the person a job. Many employers resolve the confusion by giving drug tests *after* offering a job but *before* the person has begun work. Medical examinations and testing for both drugs and alcohol is permitted during this period.

## Positives for Prescribed Drugs

Executive Order 12564 used the term "illegal drugs" to refer to any controlled substance that was included in Schedule I or II of the Controlled Substances Act. The Executive Order also stated that the term illegal drugs does not mean the use of a controlled substance pursuant to a valid prescription. The purpose of the policy is to ensure that in a Drug-Free Workplace Program, drug testing does not identify an individual who is receiving legitimate medical care and, thereby, provide confidential medical information to an employer or anyone else.

There is, however, a public safety issue associated with information that a donor may provide an MRO during the review of a drug test result. That is, the donor may be taking a legal prescription medication as treatment for a medical condition. This medication may have possible side effects that may impair the mental and/or physical abilities required for the performance of potentially hazardous tasks such as driving a vehicle or operating machinery.

If the side effects of a legitimately prescribed medication have a possible impact on the safety aspects of the work performed by a donor, the MRO must decide what should be done with the information. Although the Guidelines require an MRO to verify a drug test result as a negative result if the donor has a legitimate alternative medical explanation, it is recommended that the MRO contact the prescribing physician to discuss the possible impact that the medication have on the safety aspects of the work performed by the donor. Additionally, some occupations have restrictions that prohibit an individual from taking specific medications which may, otherwise, be allowable for other occupations. In these instances, the MRO may inform the individual responsible for certifying that the donor is qualified to perform that job that the donor is taking a medication that is restricted for an individual in that occupation or that the medication may affect the individual's ability to perform a safety sensitive occupation.

# Discipline And Termination

The appropriate response to positive test results depends on a variety of factors, including the nature of the job, the employee's past employment record, whether drug use can be shown to have taken place on the job, and the severity of the employee's drug abuse problem.

If the drug test confirms other evidence that the employee was under the influence while on the job, there is a stronger case for termination or other serious discipline than if the employee's drug usage was not clearly job-related.

What the employee does off the job is usually of no consequence or concern to the company. There are exceptions to this rule, however. If the employer can show a relationship between off-duty behavior and the job, then disciplinary action may be taken. Even with illegal off-duty behavior, such as the use of illicit drugs, it is the employer's burden to establish a link between that misconduct and job performance, and this can be difficult to prove. There are several standards generally used to evaluate off-duty misconduct and whether it constitutes grounds for discipline.

# The Particular Problem Of Marijuana

Marijuana presents several unique problems in the workplace, reflecting its unique place in our society. It is illegal, but in many jurisdictions its use or possession is no more serious than a traffic ticket. It is the most used illegal drug in our country, particularly among younger people. In general, its use is not considered as serious as the use of cocaine, LSD, or so-called "hard drugs" such as heroin and methedrine. In the late 1990s several counties passes voter initiatives legalizing medical marijuana, further confusing the issue.

This ambivalence toward marijuana is manifested in arbitration decisions. Some arbitrators will sustain discharges for simple marijuana use on company premises, and others will not. The case for discharge improves where several incidents of usage occur, however, or when a large quantity is found in the employee's possession, since the issue of sale of the drug on company premises then becomes the major issue.

Another complication is that marijuana traces may appear in urine for days after use. This problem is substantially aggravated in jurisdictions that have decriminalized marijuana, and in which the community has relaxed attitudes towards its use. In such communities, an employee who uses marijuana at home without criminal implication can be penalized on the job for having done so.

Cannabis metabolites tend to be stored in the fat cells for long periods of time. The positive result could be indicating usage several days or even weeks in the past, and may not be correlated with impairment of job performance.

## Passive Inhalation

Another major problem with drug testing for the presence of cannabinoids is that people can test positive even if they don't inhale. Ferslew, Manno, and Manno demonstrated that people who were present while marijuana was smoked by others tested positive, even though they did not smoke any themselves. Researchers were exposed to 13 male subjects individually smoking marijuana cigarettes calibrated to deliver 0, 37.5, or 75 micrograms of delta-9 THC per kilogram of body weight. Urine was collected 2.5 hours after each smoking period, and just after waking the following morning (the first void) and measurable concentrations of cannabinoids were detected in the urine.

In a The National Institute on Drug Abuse study conducted by Cone it was demonstrated that THC, the psychoactive component in marijuana, accumulates faster in the fatty tissues of people passively inhaling the smoke than in the person actually smoking! Further, the greater the body fat of the passive inhaler, the longer the detection time. Cone documented detection times up to 9 days following exposure to passive, second hand marijuana smoke. Clearly, an employer has no right to discipline employees for the behavior of their friends, or to dictate where they may go for recreation and entertainment, if it is otherwise lawful. To discipline or discharge an employee for "dirty" urine under these circumstances could be to invite a lawsuit based on the torts of intrusion or defamation. Therefore, when drug screens for marijuana are used, it is imperative to look for more than a trace, which could be a result of passive inhalation. However, complicating any attempt to determine whether a positive result reflects actual use or passive inhalation is the fact that a concentration of metabolites sufficiently small enough to be attributed to passive inhalation could still be the result of actual marijuana use, depending on the amount of time that has passed since the drug was ingested.

## Evaluation Standards

- Does it cause injury to the employer's company? Has the company's reputation been harmed, or has a jail term or time off from the job led to a loss of production or deprived the company of the employee's unique skills?

- Does it lead to inability or unsuitability to perform work?

- Does it threaten the safety of the public or co-workers?

- Does it lead to negative employee attitude, such as other co-workers refusing to work with the person?

- Does it lead to adverse effects on the employee-employer relationship, such as confrontations and hostilities that make it difficult for them to work together?

## Follow Established Procedures

In order to avoid liability, an employer who discharges or disciplines an employee for suspected or proven drug use or abuse should act reasonably in accordance with the stated personnel policy and the employee's work record. The employer must follow the company's termination procedures when dealing with an employee suspected of illegal drug use in the workplace as it would for terminating an employee for any other reason. Restrictive laws affect employers the least when discipline relates to absenteeism, unacceptable performance, or safety violations. Employers are accorded particularly wide latitude if health or safety is at risk. Since drug and alcohol use is commonly linked to accidents, mishaps, and other incidents involving breach of safety, employers will have more freedom to discipline employees if the affected job involves safety risk to co-workers or the public, such as jobs related to public utilities, or transport, or involving machinery.

## Fairness

An employer should handle any termination for drug- or alcohol-related offenses in the same reasonable manner as other terminations. The Mandatory Guidelines require that the Medical Review Officer review the facts for objectivity and to ensure that proper procedures have been consistently followed. In particular, employers should beware of double standards in which executives or other key personnel are not subjected to anti-drug and alcohol policies, but other employees are subject to discipline.

An employer should be consistent in procedures and practices. A checklist of procedures can be reviewed with a legal counsel. Mistakes and inconsistencies can be minimized by using the checklist. If legal counsel is involved in the investigation, it is possible to protect the confidentiality of the process and documentation by use of the attorney-client privilege.

An employer should always provide an employee under investigation with a full opportunity to express his or her own viewpoint on the situation. It is advisable to interview the affected employee to determine the nature and substance of any potential claim. This will help avoid misunderstandings. This interview should be documented with a file memorandum made immediately afterward. Strong disciplinary actions, including termination, may be required and can be accomplished with minimal legal risk, so long as the action is based on fair and reasonable policies that have been communicated and followed in good faith.

## Progressive Discipline

A policy that emphasizes purely disciplinary sanctions in response to test positives may in doing so influence both the Courts and the arbitrators to favor the employee. The concept of "progressive discipline" offers a more constructive alternative. A purely disciplinary approach to drug use can damage employee morale, increase the company's training cost for new employees, and increase the adversarial relationship between management and labor.

Disciplinary decisions will be reviewed in a variety of forms, depending on the nature of employment (either public or private) and the presence or absence of a union agreement. "Employment-at-will" theoretically allows an employer to fire an employee whether or not there is a valid reason. In the private sector, an "employment-at-will" situation may exist if there is no union agreement or other specific contractual agreement between management and employees regarding termination procedures. However, many courts now give a discharged employee grounds for suit against an employer if the discharge is in bad faith, abusive, wrongful, or against public policy. In some cases of this kind, the employer's personnel manual or policy statement has been viewed as constituting an implicit employment contract, or as superseding a signed contract which provided for discipline-at-will. Therefore, even in an employment-at-will situation, an employer should ensure that the company policy and procedure accurately state the consequences of urine testing, and these policies and procedures should be followed carefully.

## Arbitrator Review

Labor agreements typically require that all discharges be reviewed by an arbitrator. The arbitrator will look at several issues. First, the arbitrator will decide whether the employer's description of the situation is accurate. One factor to consider is what kind of drug the result indicated. Was the test accurate enough to prove the use of the drug? Was the chain of custody of the sample clear? Was the test performed properly?

Second, the arbitrator will decide whether the employee violated a company rule or the terms of the labor agreement. In the absence of clear rules, the arbitrator may overturn the discharge on the basis that the employee lacked fair notice of the consequences of his actions.

Third, the arbitrator will decide whether the sanctions imposed are fair and equitable, or too harsh. An arbitrator who feels the sanctions are too harsh is empowered to reverse the sanction in favor of a lesser penalty. Here is where questions concerning off-the-job conduct, the employee's past records, severity of the conduct and other relevant information will be considered. The arbitrator may ask if progressive disciplinary actions were applied, and, if not, why not. Under labor agreements, compensation is generally limited to orders of reinstatement and back pay, whereas in the employment-at-will situation, damages may be awarded for categories such as mental anguish.

# Handling Refusal To Be Tested

An employer policy may call for termination of employees who refuse to undergo drug testing. In general, company policy should link the severity of the discipline for refusing to take the test to the nature of the job or the needs of the particular workplace. Employers should not require involuntary administration of a drug test. Employees who refuse to take the test may be permitted to resign instead, or be subjected to some predetermined discipline instead of taking the test. Employers might offer the option of undergoing rehabilitation instead of discipline, for example. Another approach might be to bar employees who refuse to take the test from particular job categories, for example, vehicle or equipment operations, until they have taken and passed the test.

# Termination

For instance, in workplaces where safety concerns are significant, an employee's refusal to be tested is more difficult to justify. Terminations of union members who refuse to submit to a test are carefully examined by arbitrators to ensure that the employee has completely understood why he or she had been fully informed. If there is any doubt about whether the employee was informed regarding policies requiring submission of urine samples, or about negative consequences for refusal arbitrations tend to be resolved in the employee's favor, especially when employee's job is at stake.

There are two key components to avoiding legal issues associated with refusal to submit to tests. First, the company needs to inform employees in advance of the details concerning when urine samples may be requested and the consequences of refusal.

Second, when a specimen is requested, it is advisable to remind employees of the requirements of the policy. If a union is involved, employees should be allowed to consult with union representatives in order to help prevent ignorance or confusion in regards to the policy.

When it is clear that the employee knew that refusal to submit a urine sample was grounds for discipline, the legal question becomes whether the company sanction was appropriate or too harsh.

## Rehabilitation

The National Institute on Drug Abuse (NIDA) report on drug testing states, "Employers should consider providing an opportunity for employees who test positive for drug abuse to enter a drug treatment program and be eligible for reinstatement in an appropriate position on successful completion of that program. It may also be appropriate, in certain situations of casual or infrequent abuse, to allow an employee to demonstrate by one or more future negative tests that the drug abuse has been stopped. An employer is justified in terminating the employment of employees whose tests yield results indicating substance abuse after appropriate opportunities for treatment for such abuse have been provided." These recommendations are particularly relevant in a situation where an employer is dealing with a recreational user who smokes marijuana on weekends and who tests positive. Such persons may not need rehabilitation, and the problem may be addressed in other ways than termination or drug treatment.

## Use Of Legally Prescribed Drugs On The Job?

Firing or disciplining the employee who uses legally prescribed drugs is not advisable, because the employee has done nothing wrong except, perhaps, failing to inform the company about the medical circumstance in question. In theory, discipline is possible in such cases but *only* if the company policy refers specifically to legally prescribed drugs and requires disclosure of such use; and, even given these conditions, the company should not impose any measures beyond progressive discipline. On the other hand, the underlying issue with legally prescribed drugs is the same as for illicit ones—their effect on job performance. If the prescribed drugs are found objectively to be interfering with job performance, then the issue is raised as to whether that person should remain in that job or be moved laterally or whether some other action should be taken.

## Abuse Of Prescription Drugs

Prescription-drug abusers are typically middle-class, or upper-middle-class, law-abiding citizens who obtain drugs from physicians rather than "dealers." These abusers are not thought of as criminals or individuals who are dangerous to their communities, and probably do not consider themselves drug abusers. But legal drugs can be dangerous. The National Institute on Drug Abuse has established that abuse of prescription drugs causes 60 percent of hospital emergency-room admissions for drug overdose, and 70 percent of all drug-related deaths.

An employee taking a legitimate prescription drug presents unique problems in the workplace. While the employee may have a legitimate medical need for the drugs, he or she has no right to report to work in an impaired state, especially if that impairment poses safety risks. In upholding the disciplinary suspension of an employee for being under the influence of prescription drugs and alcohol, arbitrator James C. Reynolds stated:

> *The union questions the fairness of a rule that results in an employee being disciplined for taking medication as prescribed by his physician.*
>
> *The rule clearly makes no exception for that situation. To provide such an exception would not be appropriate, in my opinion. The purpose of the rule is to safeguard the employee and fellow workers from injury which might occur as a consequence of the employee being under the influence.*
>
> *Whether that influence resulted from the employee taking medication as prescribed, or using drugs without benefit of prescription, is not relevant to the fact that the employee was under the influence and therefore a risk in the workplace.*

> *An employee who is taking prescribed medication which*
> *would diminish his capacity to work safely should take sick leave*
> *rather than report to work under the influence.*
>
> *James C. Reynolds, Arbitrator*

Some consultants advise employers to require every employee on prescription drugs to report the use and duration of such prescriptions to the medical or personnel departments, so that decisions can be made about what tasks the employee can perform safely. Employers following this guideline should make sure that they impose it across the board. They should be particularly careful that no group, such as the executives, is excepted and that the information is held in confidence and is in no way used to treat people with disabilities (discriminate) from abled employees. Moreover, supervisors should *never* confiscate prescription drugs from an employee who has a prescription. An employee with a prescription has rights under the American Disabilities Act, which has severe penalties for violations.

When the employee has no prescription, otherwise legal drugs become contraband and may be treated as illegal drugs. Company drug abuse policies should specifically define illegal drugs to include legal drugs obtained without a prescription.

# CHAPTER 20

# Employee Assistance Programs

Employee Assistance Programs (EAPs) have enjoyed spectacular growth and acceptance. The reason for this growth at a time when many other kinds of employee benefits are being scaled back is that EAPs are financially beneficial to the employer. If employees are successfully rehabilitated, the cost in dollars as well as hardship is usually far less than that of tolerating poor performance, absenteeism, industrial accidents, worker's compensation cases, turnover, retraining, increased medical costs, and other expenses attributed to the impaired employee. Employee Assistance Programs offer confidential assistance to workers troubled by either personal problems or substance abuse.

## History Of EAPs

The first EAPs were established by businesses in the 1940s to combat alcoholism affecting performance of white collar workers. These early EAPs were staffed primarily by recovering alcoholics or other lay people who could refer troubled employees to community treatment programs or Alcoholics Anonymous. Today, more than 5,000 U.S. companies now have EAPs. Most of these programs have been established since the early 1970s in response to the rise in employee substance abuse and increasing awareness of its impact on job performance and absenteeism. Many contemporary EAPs provide counseling services for family problems, marital and sexual difficulties, legal and financial troubles, and social or emotional dysfunction. These programs are referred to as "broad brush" in scope because they attempt to deal with a wide variety of problems that can affect worker performance and productivity.

Certain EAPs have demonstrated both strong success rates as well as cost-effectiveness for the companies that use them. For example, according to a three-year study, approximately 70 percent of the employees who enter General Motors Corporation's treatment and aftercare program recover sufficiently to resume work satisfactorily. In addition, lost work time for these GM employees has been reduced by 40 percent, sickness and accident benefit payouts by 60 percent, and job accidents and disciplinary actions by 50 percent. GM estimates that for every dollar spent on its EAP and outside treatment, two dollars are returned in regained work productivity, during the period of this study.

## A Model Employee Assistance Program

*GM tests all job applicants for drugs. If the result is positive, the individual is rejected for employment and must wait six months before he can re-apply. If an employee exhibits a decline in work performance, unexplained prolonged absences, or other erratic behavior, his supervisor may report such observation to the company's medical department. Following a consultation with a company physician, a medical evaluation may be required, including, at the physician's option, a drug test. Employees in "safety-sensitive" positions cannot continue to perform their jobs without a drug test, and refusal to take one could result in termination. When there is a positive result, and no medically-acceptable explanation can be found, the company assists the employee in seeking treatment. In order to return to work, the employee must become and remain drug-free, participate in an appropriate rehabilitation or treatment program, and consent to be monitored by the company physician, including periodic, unscheduled urine testing.*

*1989 National Drug Control Strategy*

# Advantages of EAPS

Creation of an EAP which allows the employee with a drug problem to participate in a treatment program helps the company retain qualified and productive employees. Furthermore, a drug/alcohol policy that tempers discipline for substance abuse with opportunities for rehabilitation tends to increase arbitrator's support for urine testing programs. In a case involving a bus driver, for example, an arbitrator upheld a company's screening policy, and noted with favor that a first positive urinalysis result would not lead to termination, but to identification of a problem and need for treatment. Once adopted, however, a rehabilitation first policy must be followed through lest employees fight disciplinary action by claiming they were denied an opportunity for treatment, or were discriminated against for refusing treatment. For example, in one case, the firing of an alcoholic employee who admitted to alcoholism but sought treatment only when asked to leave, was overturned as being a violation of the company's policy.

# Guidelines For Establishing An EAP

The goals of an Employee Assistance Program are the identification of troubled employees, the offering of incentives for such employees to identify troubled employees to seek and accept help, and the selection of the most appropriate treatment and cost-effective care.

# Assign An EAP Coordinator

The position of Employee Assistance Program Coordinator can be a full-time or part-time position, depending on the size of the company. Generally, a full-time coordinator is needed only for companies with more than 2,500 employees. Thus, the coordinator can often be selected from current staff. The coordinator must understand the problems associated with drug or alcohol abuse and emotional or mental problems, and act in an evaluation and referral capacity. The coordinator estimates the nature and the scope of an employee's problem, and may provide limited counseling. The coordinator, especially if selected from current staff, must be someone in whom all employees, whatever their position, can confide.

# Formulate A Policy

Management must define the program and the types of problems it will deal with and assure confidentiality for all employees. This policy should be readily available, posted on employee bulletin boards, and printed in the employee manual. Once an EAP and policy is set up and put into place, employers should follow it. Any deviation, particularly a significant one, may result in liability for breach of contractual obligation. If an EAP of some type is offered, participation by affected employees should be strongly encouraged but not be made mandatory.

# Decide On Implementation Procedures

Managers should never presume a drug problem based solely on their own observations. However, they should know their employees well enough to be able to identify changes in behavior that are related to job performance. When they suspect an employee has a problem that is interfering with work, the manager typically meets with the person and then refers him or her to the EAP coordinator, who then evaluates the problem and decides how to handle it.

# Decide On Appropriate Treatment Programs

The EAP coordinator should survey local resources to find out what type and quality of services are available. These may include outpatient clinics, counseling groups, private practice, medical professionals, and credit counseling. The coordinator should also examine the company's medical insurance plan to see what types of treatments are covered by insurance. The company may want to change its coverage to include these types of services.

# Train Managers And Supervisors

Training generally includes an overview of the kinds of problems employees suffer from and their causes, the kinds of behavioral signs to look for and techniques for approaching and referring problem employees. Employers should also train supervisors to intervene when work performance first becomes noticeably affected, even if the cause is not positively known to be drug- or alcohol-related. Absence from the workplace, decreasing work performance, wide mood swings from depression to short-fused anger, injuries at work, disappearance during work hours, or severe family problems are often symptoms of substance abuse. Employees with physical symptoms or behavioral patterns suggesting drug use should be referred to the EAP. Managers and supervisors should never attempt to conduct drug counseling themselves.

# Promote The EAP Program

Employees and their families must be made fully aware of the program. Its preventive aspects can be stressed, thus encouraging employees who need help to get it before it affects their work.

# Evaluate The EAP Program

Criteria for assessing whether goals are being met and whether the program is cost-effective. Work performance should be evaluated independently of EAP participation, although such participation can be considered a positive sign of an employee's willingness to improve.

## Use A Multidisciplinary Team Approach

Ideally an EAP involves the family of the troubled employee both in preventive education and in treatment. A model EAP recognizes that identification, intervention, and treatment require a multidisciplinary team approach because drug abuse is a physical, emotional, and cultural disease. A team approach is important in deciding on the type of treatment called for and in helping the troubled employee develop new coping skills to replace drug-dependence.

Alcoholism and other drug addictions are relapsing diseases. A model EAP should both anticipate and be prepared to deal with this phenomenon. Supervisors and others involved should understand that a relapse is not invariably treatment failure, but may be another step in the recovery journey. However, the program should not allow an attitude of relapse permissiveness. Relapse requires further structure and self-discipline, as the key to recovery continues to be personal accountability. A model EAP has carefully structured aftercare, based on the belief that alcohol and other drug addiction can be overcome with appropriate treatment.

Arbitrators have a history of favoring EAPs. In the absence of an EAP, arbitrators tend to order reinstatement in cases where the employee has sought post-discharge treatment, and has demonstrated an awareness of and progress with the drug problem. Arbitrators are less sympathetic toward employees who suffer relapses after treatment. It is to the advantage of the astute employer to define the EAP treatment as a "last chance" and to have the employee sign a "last chance agreement."

## The Family And Medical Leave Act

The Family and Medical Leave Act (FMLA) covers private employers with 50 or more employees who each work 20 or more calendar workweeks. It requires employers to give employees unpaid leave of absence for birth or adoption of a child, to provide care to a family member with a serious health condition or for the employee to recover from a serious health condition which prevents working. Eligible employees are entitled to 12 workweeks of unpaid family and medical leave per year and can be taken all at once or on an intermittent basis. In most cases the employers is required to restore the employee to the original position or an equivalent position.

FMLA includes leaves of absence to receive treatment for substance abuse. In certain cases, the employer can take adverse action against an employee who wishes to enter a treatment program and who has violated the company's established substance abuse policy. Absence due to use of illegal drugs is not covered by FMLA. Eligibility for a leave of absence under FMLA for rehabilitation depends upon whether or not the substance abuse is a *serious health condition*. Model certification forms are available through the Department of Labor. Employers would be wise to consult an attorney prior to using such forms in order to ensure that employee privacy and medical confidentiality are protected.

# CHAPTER 21

# Protecting Employee Rights

Consideration of employees' Constitutional rights is imperative when setting up a company drug testing program. The program must be designed in such a way that it does not violate, and in fact protects, employee rights. This strategy will minimize exposure to lawsuits, maximize the company's ability to have its program upheld in Court if a lawsuit does occur, and is less likely to have negative effects on employee morale.

The mechanisms used by employers for selecting which employees to test is an extremely important consideration. The legality of the testing program is often determined by the way in which individual employers are selected for testing. Random testing programs are most likely to encounter legal resistance. For example, testing of job applicants or employees in connection with periodic physicals has drawn little attention in the Courts. Similarly, testing under conditions of reasonable suspicion, when employers were clearly informed of the policy beforehand, has withstood legal challenge.

Employer attorney William Adams recommends that random testing be used only in high risk, safety-sensitive jobs, especially those in which it is difficult to supervise day-to-day work. Even in such cases, he cautions employers to be prepared to demonstrate the ineffectiveness of less objectionable methods.

## How To Limit Exposure To Legal Challenge

- Develop a specific drug abuse detection program. This program should be developed in consultation with all parties of the company that might be affected, such as union representatives, occupational safety and health personnel, security staff, and legal advisors.

- Modify private employment contracts and collective bargaining agreements as well as policy statements, employee manuals, and all other relevant corporate literature and documentation, to reflect the company's policy.

- Formulate and document a strong argument showing the relevance of possible drug use to job performance, safety, security, etc.

- Use random testing only in high risk, safety-sensitive jobs, particularly where it is difficult to supervise day-to-day work performance.

- Demonstrate the relative ineffectiveness of potentially less objectionable methods of drug detection.

- Inform all job applicants of the policy. Employees should be given advance notice of any disciplinary action that might be taken as a result of confirmed drug use on the job. If drug tests are to be administered, employees and job applicants should consent to these tests. If penalties are to be imposed for failure to take tests, these penalties should be described in advance.

- Establish a grace period announcement of the policy and its implementations.

- Notify employees of positive drug detection results, and give them an opportunity to contest disciplinary action based on the results. Consider referring employees to medical help or employee assistance programs before taking punitive action.

# Privacy

Privacy is one of the fundamental employee rights that must be protected when devising and implementing a drug-testing program. Employees have a "reasonable expectation" of privacy. For example, people using a toilet or urinal usually have an expectation of privacy. Observation of these activities can be considered in violation of that reasonable expectation. If an employee can demonstrate that this expectation of privacy has been violated, the company may face legal action. However, the employee's expectation of privacy can be reduced if the employer clearly informs all employees about the drug testing program, when and how it will occur, and so forth. This notification reduces but does not eliminate expectation of privacy. Such information should be included in both the employee manual and in documents given to job applicants.

For example, drug testing programs that gather samples without disclosing that they will be tested for drug contents probably constitute an invasion of privacy. Also, drug testing that unnecessarily focuses on off-duty conduct may be open to a privacy challenge, more so than testing that detects only drug use that would affect work performance.

## Off-Duty Behavior And Privacy Rights

Most people have a reasonable expectation that what they do in their off-duty time, away from the job, is their business and not the business of the employer. Generally, the Courts would support that opinion. There are exceptions, however. For example, when the employer can show a relationship between off-duty behavior and the job, disciplinary actions may be taken. Even for illegal behavior, such as the use of illicit drugs, it is the employer's burden to establish the link between that misconduct and the employee's job performance. For example, what link can be shown between occasional weekend use of marijuana and the job of a stock boy, clerk, or even a professional? It could be argued that casual use in this situation is no more damaging or job-related than casual use of alcohol. It is important for the employer to keep in mind that the burden is on the employer to prove this link. There are several standards generally used to evaluate off-duty misconduct and whether or not it constitutes grounds for discipline. These standards include injury to the company, inability or unsuitability to perform, safety of the public and co-workers, and interactions with other employers.

# Injury To The Company

A jail term leading to the loss of production or depriving the company of the employee's unique skills could harm the business. Claimed harm cannot, however, be merely be speculative. The employer must show that the employee's drug use would constitute real and actual harm. For example, the company's reputation might be damaged by an employee going to jail. However, unless the nature of such harm is virtually self-evident, demonstrating its existence in concrete terms, such as loss of sales, can be difficult. Showing the need for high public confidence in the employer is one approach. For example, a Court upheld the firing of an air traffic controller who was found in possession of cocaine at a concert, because drug use and possession would detract from the public's confidence in the agency. In assessing the damage to the company, the Courts will take into consideration the degree of notoriety of the incident and the relationship of type of conduct in question to the employee's position in the company.

# Inability Or Unsuitability To Perform

Absence without authorization, including a jail term, can provide the basis for discipline. Absence or physical inability to perform often go hand in hand with damage to the company. Additionally, dishonesty or breach of trust can render an employee unsuitable for a job. When such a standard is used, arbitrators usually review the employee's previous record, which can lead either to lessening the severity of a punitive action or justifying termination.

# Safety Of The Public And Co-Workers

For employees whose jobs are directly related to the safety of others, such as pilots, vehicle drivers, crane operators, and railway workers, the relationship between safety, job performance, and drug use seems clear. However, even where the safety is concerned, Courts generally look at the extent of the employee's drug use when considering the legality of a discharge. For example, in one case, firing of an employee was upheld because evidence showed extensive drug use; however, a second case was dismissed because the employee had a good record, and it could not be shown that he had endangered other employees.

## Relations With Co-Workers

Cooperation and team work are vitally important to productivity and morale in most companies. Drug abusers may exhibit attitudes toward the company and co-workers that can lead to conflict, dissent, and discharge. Employees also may be discharged if co-workers refuse to work with them as a result of off-duty conduct.

## Adverse Effect On The Employer-Employee Relationship

The most difficult case standard involves serious confrontation between employee and employer that creates a situation in which they are unable to work together. Such ill-feeling may be brought about, for instance, when an employee is identified as a drug user but refuses to participate in a drug treatment program.

# Reasonable Suspicion

It is sensible for an employer to respect the employee's notion of privacy where possible and appropriate, even if the law might permit the employer to engage in various observational methods. Testing only when there is reasonable suspicion greatly reduces the degree of legal risk. Labor attorney William Adams reports that an employer's testing policy is likely to be upheld when there is a strong indication that a particular employee has recently used or is under the influence of drugs or alcohol. Generally, employers should probably avoid intrusive monitoring of employees, such as the use of cameras, unless there is real justification for these methods.

## Factors Affecting Reasonableness Of Drug Tests

Here is a checklist of factors that may affect the reasonableness of a drug testing program:

• Accurate test methodology

• Reliable chain of custody

• Need for tests due to safety, security or integrity of company business goals

• Documentation of past drug use in company

• Inappropriateness of ineffectiveness of other, less intrusive means of achieving the company's goals

• Efforts to minimize intrusiveness of specimen collection

• Procedures for protection of confidential records and test data

• Availability of rehabilitation option or periodic monitoring before discipline results

• Existence of clear notice of the program and its requirements that may result in discipline or termination

• Existence of other safeguards against error, such as permitting employees to explain positive results that might be in error and retesting the same sample in questioned cases

• For random testing there should be additional justification on the basis of substantial safety or security factors; difficulty in monitoring employee performance for signs of drug use

From William Adams, The Dos, Don'ts and Whys of Drug Testing, Labor and Employment Law Update, Orrick, Herrington & Sutcliffe.

# Reasonable Suspicion Standards

In cases where reasonable standards of suspicions can be satisfied, mandatory testing of a public-safety employee do not violate the Fourth Amendment's protection of privacy. Reasonable suspicion may be based on indications that an employee is under the influence of drugs. Indications may include slurred speech, accidents, frequent absences, tardiness, and early departures from work. Since reasonable suspicion is established by combining facts with judgment, it is not possible to predict or describe every situation that may create a reasonable suspicion.

Even when reasonable suspicion or probable cause exist, it is not wise for the employer to attempt to forcibly extract a sample from the employee. For example, UPS was sued in 1986 because a company nurse demanded that an employee who had been a drug user, and had been through a drug treatment program, provide immediate samples of his blood and urine for testing when he returned from vacation. When the employee objected, the nurse disregarded his protest and "plunged a needle into his arm and extracted blood." Such a use of force constitutes blatant violation of principles of privacy and consent. Samples should always be obtained with the consent of the employee.

## Gathering Confidential Information

The gathering of information should be performed for a particular purpose with a particular employee. In California, for example, the State Constitution specifically protects privacy from what is called "overbroad and unnecessary" information gathering. For instance, in California law requires the employer establish a compelling need for the test and that there are no less intrusive ways of meeting that need.

Employers investigating drug or alcohol abuse by workers may wish to obtain an employee's medical records to see if there is a history of drug or alcohol abuse. However, doing so can be dangerous, since most states set a premium on the right to privacy of medical records. Access to and release of medical information is highly regulated. Information containing medical, psychiatric, or psychological material is classified as "confidential information." It simply cannot be obtained without the prior written voluntary consent of the individual to whom the records pertain. Furthermore, the American Disabilities Act regulates medical examinations, which includes medical records, of disabled people. Therefore, an employer should not depend on having access to these records; if they do become available, the employer must be scrupulous in maintaining their confidentiality.

Employers who do obtain positive drug test data on an employee must maintain the privacy of that data. They cannot give data to other employees or employers. Claims for defamation of character may arise if an employer investigates an employee and shares the findings or suspicions with third parties, including other employees who have no need to know, particularly if the findings turn out to be incorrect. There may also be grounds for defamation lawsuits if the employer explains to third parties the reason for any adverse actions, such as termination against an employee, especially if the third party is a prospective employer. The wisest policy is to issue no information without a signed release from the affected employee.

## Due Process

When implementing a company drug testing program, the company must be thorough in making sure that employees are given due process. Due process means that legal procedures are followed that guarantee a person's rights, and that decision making is not arbitrary. The most important way in which a company can ensure that employees are granted due process is to disseminate a written company policy on drug testing that specifies the rules about drug use on and off the job, what kinds of testing procedures will be use and when they will be used, how they will be used, and what sanctions will be taken if controlled substances are found. It is also important to be sure that the drug testing, the actual taking and analysis of the sample, and the use of the results are not in any way arbitrary.

# Nondiscrimination

Title VII of the Civil Rights Act prohibits discrimination based on race, creed or religion. This statute says an anti-drug policy may not single out minorities, women, or disabled persons or other protected groups. Therefore, an employer may be required to demonstrate that the drug policy is job-related and not discriminatory or violating the American Disabilities Act (ADA). One way to demonstrate that the program is not discriminatory is to give the test to all applicants or to all persons in a particular job category. Also, discipline based on positive test results should be meted out in a balanced fashion. Providing that context, job duties, and various other factors are all equal, a positive test result should have the same consequences for a employees regardless of race, gender, disability, creed or religion.

# For Cause

Another way that the employer may ensure due process is to make sure the drug testing is done "for cause." This means that testing may occur when reasonable suspicion exists that the employee is using drugs, that is, when there are specific objective facts and reasonable inferences in light of work experience that suggest the employee is using drugs. Staff members trained in recognizing signs of drug or alcohol abuse are able to make this kind of decision more reliably than untrained staff members, and their judgment will be more likely to withstand the scrutiny of a Court arbitrator.

# Forensic Standards

Use of forensic standards in the gathering of the samples and in conducting the analysis of the sample is an effective way to ensure due process. Unless proper forensic procedures and forensic standards are followed, an employee can argue in Court that the results are tainted by procedural errors and are therefore unreliable.

## Consent

Due process can be demonstrated when an employee actually consents to the test. Of course, consent must be voluntary, not forced. There is some debate over this issue, because people naturally wonder whether consent is genuinely free if the possibility of being fired is implicit in the situation.

### Inform Employees

Informing employees, either in their employee handbook or by placing notices on employee bulletin boards, about the drug testing program, how it will work, and what the sanctions will be taken for positive results is another way to guarantee they have been granted due process.

## Employee Rehabilitation

Employers should be aware that people who have abused alcohol or drugs, who have been involved in formal rehabilitation, and who have been certified as having been "cured," are protected by Title V of the Federal Rehabilitation Act of 1983, which protects handicapped people from discrimination by Federal employers. This protection was extended to employees in the private sector by the American Disabilities Act. The drug or alcohol abuser who has been in a program is usually considered to be handicapped. An employer cannot legally refuse to hire such individuals solely on the basis of their history of addiction. However, once hired, these people can be tested, and can be reprimanded or fired if the employer can establish a clear connection between unsatisfactory on-the-job performance and some kind of drug use as indicated by the testing.

## Search And Seizure

If the employer is going to conduct a search, the search procedure should be announced well in advance as company policy, and described in detail in writing to all employees. Whenever possible, the employer should seek written consent from employees to search before proceeding with an intrusive search. Searches should always be conducted so that employee dignity is preserved. Without a properly announced search policy, it may not be possible for an employer to search a purse or lunch box stored in a locker. In fact, searches are a very legally sensitive issue, and usually employers should avoid searching altogether.

Employers should exercise caution in taking possession of any incriminating evidence that belongs to the employee. It is usually wise to call in the police, and have the police take possession of the evidence; if the employer takes any evidence before police involvement, criminal prosecution might be affected by mishandling of the evidence.

The information in this chapter is intended to make clear the importance of protecting employee rights when formulating and implementing a drug testing program. Proper consideration of employee rights, especially privacy issues, is not only ethically desirable, but also serves to minimize the threat of future legal challenge to an employer based on drug testing activities. Additionally, incorporating such protections will help maintain employee dignity—and therefore loyalty and morale—in the face of potentially invasive drug testing. However, the boundaries of privacy required by a given work situation vary greatly, and must be determined by taking several factors into account, including the relevance of off-duty behavior to job performance, the potential injury to the company presented by employee drug use, and issues of safety. Rights to privacy are ensured by clearly stating solid reasons for instituting drug testing to begin with, the confidentiality with which information resulting from drug testing is handled, maintenance of due process, and other significant considerations.

# CHAPTER 22

# Getting Union Support

Getting support from all parties involved in the company's drug testing program is critical to its acceptance and success. Support of unions is particularly important. Unions can be of great benefit, or they can resist a drug testing program bitterly if they feel that the testing may be used to harm, fire, manipulate or dominate employees unfairly.

## Unions Are Concerned

A study of union opinion revealed that unionists felt at that time that drug use in the workplace was a serious problem and is likely to increase. Of the executives responding to an inquiry about union cooperation, 31.5 percent said that unions associated with their company were cooperative with management. Most of union literature shows concern with labor's involvement with drug programs, which labor leaders support because they want to seek alternatives to termination of unionists detected as users. In order to garner union support, management needs an alternative to automatic termination of detected users. Joint programs, with active participation of both labor and management, have been found to be more effective than programs run solely by management or the union. In such cooperative action, management program resources and union reassurances of protection to the user can be successfully combined.

Most unionists feel the most effective approach to the drug problem is preventative education in the workplace, school, and community. While there is a trend toward less primitive reactions to detected drug users, the respondents in the study mentioned above perceived that terminating users was the most typical management policy for dealing with drug users. Managers usually view drug use as a problem arising outside of and "imported" into the regular workforce. Similarly, unionists believe that drug use normally begins prior to joining the workforce through peer associations made in school and in the military.

However, even though they believe drug use begins in the social arena, unionists feel that the problem is best confronted within the workplace. Specifically they feel that management and union efforts would be most effective if directed toward preventative education rather than toward in-house counseling or referral to outside agencies.

## Get Union Support

Employers as well as unions should be concerned about the well-being of employees. When introducing drug-testing programs to unions, it is best to emphasize that the program is aimed at preventing drug abuse. Control of alcohol and other drug use in the workplace makes it safer for all employees by preventing abusers and substances from getting into the workplace or by removing abusers from the work station.

Any changes, even in the enforcement of existing policies, should be reviewed alongside an existing labor agreement and agreed upon by union representatives. A union contract will probably affect a company drug policy. It may prevent a company from implementing a new policy of drug testing unilaterally, for example, requiring that the policy be negotiated with the union.

There has been a marked change in attitudes regarding drugs among union members. According to Gunter Neurenburg of the Crowley Maritime Corporation, a large transportation and oil exploration company with 4,000 employees, "Something has changed. The employer is all of a sudden the good guy. Seafarer [the union] came to us and demanded we begin drug testing." Mr. Neurenberg recommended that employers obtain a copy of the master trade agreement of the Teamsters or other unions regarding drug testing to see how they deal with union policies and agreements about drug testing programs. An example of a bargained agreement is found in the Appendix.

According to George Cobbs, the Northern California Alcohol Representative for the International Longshoremen's and Warehousemen's Union, unions will generally support pre-employment screening for detection of drug use in job candidates, but typically do not support random testing of those on the job. It is very important that companies look at their union contract if random testing is under consideration because most union contracts will not allow random testing without bargaining for it. Unions typically feel that the random testing is an avoidance of the problem and violates the rights of employees. However, where a job involves public safety issues, an employer working with the union can often bargain for random testing because of the union's concern for the safety of lives and property.

On the other hand, unions will often support testing for probable cause, provided that it is across-the-board testing of all employees including management and executives. One source of discontent is that, in many companies, only blue-collar workers are subjected to testing, whereas the management is rarely subject to testing. Unions feel that this is a subtle form of discrimination and control.

Unions often fear that drug testing can be used to weaken unions or interfere with strikes. Typically, they will support drug testing when it's used for rehabilitation purposes—that is, if the employer does not use test results for punitive actions.

In a typical union labor agreement, the discharge of an employee is reviewed by an arbitrator. The arbitrator's job is essentially three-fold. First, the arbitrator must decide whether the employer has accurately described the facts of the situation. For example, was the urinalysis for the employee positive for the drug in question? Was the test accurate enough to prove the use of the drug? Was the chain of custody of the sample clear, and was the test performed properly? Second, the arbitrator must decide whether the employer has violated the labor agreement. Third, the arbitrator must decide whether the sanction imposed was fair and equitable, or too harsh. An arbitrator who feels that the sanction was too harsh is empowered to reverse the sanction in favor of a lesser penalty. Labor agreements generally limit compensation by employers for punitive actions judged unfair by arbitrators to reinstatement of the job and back pay. Here, the employer's liability is somewhat limited compared to the that of the employment-at-will situation, where damages may be awarded in categories such as "mental anguish."

# CHAPTER 23

# How Employees Beat The Test

Passing or failing is a matter of considerable concern. For many employees it means loosing their jobs. Even when not fired, a positive result can mean probation, having to admit to drug abuse and entering a drug rehabilitation program. People employ a myriad of strategies when faced with testing, including abstinence, flushing one's system, masking the drugs in the sample, substituting another sample for one's own, adulterating the sample and diluting the sample. Some of the strategies are more effective than others. All are a form of evading detection.

## Abstinence

The best way to avoid detection is abstinence. Employees using this ploy simply do not use any drugs—legal or illegal—for a long enough time for the drugs they habitually use to clear their systems. Abstinence includes refraining from using any over-the-counter medications because they can come up as positives.

False positives, however, are still possible even for people who use no drugs at all. In most cases, a false positive casts suspicion on the unfortunate employee and results in further testing. This fact is particularly alarming to employees facing testing given that their livelihood and reputation are on the line.

# Detection Periods

The required length of abstinence to test negative varies, because different drugs are metabolized and excreted by the body at different rates. Clever drug users school themselves in the time periods—known as *detection periods*—after which particular drugs become undetectable. With this knowledge in hand, the drug user knows how long before testing that he or she must stop using in order to come up clean on the test. The following table lists the average detection periods published by PharmChem Laboratories headquartered in Menlo Park, California.

## PharmChem's Drug Detection Periods For Urine

| Drug | Detection Period |
| --- | --- |
| Amphetamines—Stimulants | |
| Ethanol—Sedative Hypnotics | |
| Amphetamine | Up to 72 hours |
| Alcohol Very short** | |
| Methamphetamine | Up to 72 hours |
| Methadone—Narcotic Analgesics | |
| Barbiturates—Sedative Hypnotics | 1-4 days |
| Amobarbital | 2-4 days |
| Methaqualone—Sedative Hypnotics | |
| Butalbital | 2-4 days |
| Quaalude | 2-4 days |
| Pentobarbital | 2-4 days |
| Opiates—Narcotic Analgesic | |
| Phenobarbital | Up to 30 days |
| Codine | 2-4 days |
| Bensodiazepines—Sedative Hypnotics | |
| Hydromorphone | 2-4 days |

| | |
|---|---|
| Diazepam (Valium) | Up to 30 days |
| Morphine for Heroin | 2-4 days |
| Chlordiazepoxide | Up to 30 days |
| Phencyclidine—Hallucinogens | |
| (Librium) PCP | |
| Cannabinoids—Euphoriants | |
| Casual use | Up to 5 days |
| Marijuana | |
| Chronic use | Up to 14 days* |
| Casual use | 1-4 days |
| Chronic use | Up to 14 days* |
| Cocaine—Stimulants | |
| Benzoylecgorine | Up to 72 hours |

---

* In rare instances, an individual may be at a detectable level for up to 30 days.

**Alcohol is excreted at the rate of approximately one ounce per hour.

The length of time for which drug metabolites are retained by the body can vary dramatically from person to person. Relevant factors include the person's weight, fat level, and speed of metabolism, as well as the frequency and duration of drug use and the dosages involved. According to Dr. John Morgan, Medical Professor and Director of the Pharmacology Program at the City University of New York, a heavy marijuana smoker who was incarcerated continued to secrete the metabolite for more than two months. PharmChem says that cannabis delectability at 30 days happens, but is rare.

The length of the detection period is also influenced by the sensitivity of the test used. The EMIT® has two cut-off sensitivities, high and low. The low cut-off level detects a concentration one fifth of the high level.

# Flushing The System

With this strategy, the person facing a test puts as much liquid through his or her system as possible, in order to eliminate drug metabolites through urination prior to the test. Removal of 100 percent of the metabolites in the system is unlikely. However, prior flushing can dramatically reduce the concentration of metabolites in the sampled urine.

Employees who know they are going to be tested might drink large quantities of water and other nonalcoholic liquids the night before and during the morning before the test in order to flush out evidence of drug use. This dilutes their samples and thereby reduces the possibility of a positive result on a broad screening test.

The first urine in the morning after waking from sleep is called the "first void" and has the highest concentration of metabolites. Underground literature advises drug users to avoid giving a sample from their first urine of the day. Abby Hoffman, in his book *Steal This Urine Test,* tells readers to not sleep the night before testing or to get up earlier than usual in order to provide an opportunity for a greater number of urinations, each of which further empties the body of metabolites in the hours before the test.

There is a way of detecting this ploy. Employers can request a urine osmolarity which measures the kidney's concentrating and diluting ability. The normal range is 50 to 1200 osmol per liter, averaging 300 osmor liter. Few employers request this test.

# Using Diuretics

Another method of flushing is the use of a diuretic known as Lasix. Its generic name is furosemide. Diuretics cause the kidneys to step up the secretion of water. Simultaneously, employees using this evasion strategy increase their water intake. Furosemide is a prescription drug, but not a controlled one. Family physicians often give a prescription for it without much thought. Some drug users drink large amounts of coffee, because caffeine is a mild diuretic and is believed to cause similar effects.

Consuming large quantities of liquid makes urine nearly color-less. To avoid suspicion employees who have been flushing their system to conceal drug use often take  large doses of Vitamin B complex for several days before the test since it imparts a deep yellow color to urine.

# Masking

Masking is another favorite strategy for defeating the test.  In this technique the employee ingests a substance that masks or covers the presence of drug metabolites in the urine so that they are not detected by the drug test.

Street-lore cites many ingestants that people have tried, but these methods have questionable, if any, results.  Golden seal, cranberry juice, vinegar, and aspirin are sometimes mentioned. U-R-KLEAN is a commercially sold tea claimed to clean urine.  A study of 50 herbal teas failed to support claims that they mask drugs in urine.

Vitamin C has been demonstrated to effectively mask marijuana, amphetamines and barbiturates according to Holtorf author of UR-INE TROUBLE, one of the popular underground beat-the-test books. He says that  taking 8,000 to 10,000 mg of the vitamin 4 to 6 hours before the test, followed by a second dose 2 hours before testing masks marijuana use. Large doses of vitamin C acidifies urine which increases excretion of amphetamines, cocaine and phencyclidine. Utilizing this information, some people take vitamin C for several days before drug testing to eliminate these drugs from their system.  This strategy is tricky, however, because when vitamin C is taken j*ust before testing* by users of amphetamines, cocaine and phencyclidine, its propensity to increase excretion can actually increase metabolites of these drugs in urine, thereby increasing the likelihood of a positive test.

Another favorite is ingesting bicarbonate and antacids like Tums® and Rolaids® which decrease the excretion of amphetamines, cocaine and PCP and reduce getting a positive test. Other masking agents include Tolmetin®, a prescription NSAID similar to ibuprofen, which can hide cannabinoids and opioids in urine tests. Ciprofloxicin, a common antibiotic, may be able to hide opiates, cocaine, amphetamines and benzodiazepines on immunoassay tests.

# Substitution

Some particularly daring, and probably desperate employees sneak in a sample of clean urine which they substitute for their own. They may have obtained it from a friend whom they believe has been drug-free, or it may have come from a vendor of powdered urine.

## How Samples Have Been Substituted

When the sample is given in a situation that is not observed and is relatively lax, such as a family doctor's office, substitution is a simple procedure. The person just goes into the bathroom and puts the substitute sample into the container. However, most testing is conducted in a testing facilities at the place of employment, in testing labs, or in even more rigidly controlled Court-monitored situations. In these situations, people who are substituting become cunning in their elaborate attempts to sneak in and switch samples.

### Containers and Bags

Some people have used a catheter bag hidden under a shirt, with a tube running down a sleeve to deliver the bogus sample. A body pat-down, or undressing to put on a gown, will reveal the intent to deceive.

Pharmacy or hospital supply centers sell Bard Dispoz-a-Bag® which are inexpensive drainage bags used by ambulant patients. Usually the drug user has gotten advice as to how these products can be used for substituting urine from a sympathetic pharmacists and clerks in pharmacy supply stores.

Some bold employees have used a large bag hide around the middle of the body, with a long tube extending into the groin area. A short piece of rubber tubing and a valve are added for dispensing of the sample.

Sometimes the bag is held in place by wearing incontinence pants that are purchased at a pharmacy or hospital supply store. When the person gives the sample, the fluid flows down.

Employees hoping to substitute a sample usually use a bag taped to the body rather than attempting to carry the sample in a jar, since such a bag is likely to be discovered only in the event of frisking or strip-searching. When employees are closely observed, the risk is higher, but motivated people have learned to hide and use the bag even while being observed.

Another approach is the use of a reservoir-tipped, nonlubricating condom. One condom is filled and then a second one is pulled over it to prevent bursting. This bag is taped in the crotch area. When it is time to give the sample, the employee uses a sharpened fingernail to puncture the tip.

People carrying a concealed container with substitute urine in an observed situation have successfully avoided direct observation by claiming they just can't "go" when being watched. This is a common phenomenon which is referred to in the medical community as "blushing kidneys" or "shy bladder".

Some desperate employees have attempted to substitute cat, dog, or other nonhuman urine, or to manufacturing a facsimile of urine by using water and artificial coloring. These ploys are easily detected.

## Temperature

Some programs call for testing the temperature of the urine. When Federal Guidelines are being followed, the temperature must be tested within four minutes of giving the sample, and if it is not within 90.5 to 99.8 degrees Fahrenheit, a new sample is to be taken, with the collector directly watching the person giving the sample.

Employees avoid this by warming up samples before the test by holding a bag or condom containing the substitute sample close to the body which keeps it at body temperature.

# Adulterating The Sample

Another approach that is commonly attempted is adulterating the sample by adding a substance that can prevent the sample from testing positive. The most common adulterant used is salt. Very little salt is required. The EMIT® test is most easily nullified by this approach. Small quantities of lye, common table salt, or household ammonia will neutralize the enzyme activity, causing a negative result.

Many consultants advise that the pH factor of each urine sample be tested, because some contaminants can follow the pH factor of the sample outside the normal range for urine. Employees suspected of tampering with their samples should be questioned and asked to give a second test in which collection is rigidly observed.

Some people have smuggled salt and other substances into the testing bathroom on their hands or under their fingernails. However, if the test is being conducted under the Federal Guidelines, employees are required to wash their hands and scrub their nails in the presence of a monitor. If the Federal Guidelines are not being followed, then a person might be able to hide salt under the nails.

## Other Commonly Used Adulterants

Bleach and ammonia are two commonly used adulterants. When liquid bleach is added directly to urine it will oxidize and destroy THC and other cannabinoids. Alternatively, hydrogen peroxide, which is odorless, causes a chemical reaction and can alter the urine to the point where there will be a negative result. Research has shown that Liquid Drano® will cause false negative test results for cocaine, barbiturates, amphetamines, opiates, and marijuana. When first put into the urine sample it bubbles and fizzes which can give the adulteration away. Another give away is that Drano increases urine pH to outside the normal physiologic range. Vinegar, another commonly used adulterant, has been shown to cause false negative test results for marijuana.

One or two drops of a liquid soap dropped into a urine sample can make the EMIT® test record negative. A readily available adulterant is blood. If while giving a sample, the person pricks a finger and drop in three or four drops of blood, the sample may then test negative for cannabis, according to Dr. John P. Morgan, Medical Professor and Director of Pharmacology at City University of New York.

# Diluting The Sample

The basic strategy is diluting the sample by adding water to it, so the concentration of any drug metabolites present is reduced. This technique is actually more effective than trying to dilute the sample by drinking a lot of water, primarily because the amount of water put into the sample can be controlled. Usually the employee puts some urine in the sample because the test can determine when only water is present. Monitors should be trained to watch for water on the outside of the cup is an indication of tampering with the sample.

The diluting strategy can be foiled by filling the toilets where samples are given with a blue dye. When the toilet contains the blue dye, some people open the back of the toilet to gain access to the clean water in the reservoir. In the back of the reservoir there is usually a plastic spout or tube, which carries the fresh water in from the pipe. Pushing the float down causes the mechanism to turn on the water. Monitors should be trained to listen for the sounds of opening and closing the lid of the reservoir.

Diluted samples can be detected if the temperature is not high enough or not within the acceptable range. Some employees counteract this by rubbing the outside of the specimen cup with the hands to warm it up.

A second signal of dilution is the coloring of the sample. A lot of water in the sample makes it lose its yellow color. Clever employees get around this problem by taking Vitamin B before the tests so that the portion of the sample provided is very deep yellow in color and when it is diluted, the sample will show the typical pale yellow coloring.

# The Dry Room

Some testing programs battle the problem of diluting the sample with what is called the *dry room*. In a dry room, access is prevented to water that could be used for diluting samples. This includes sealing off water taps and leaving a minimum of water in the toilet bowl which contains a colored dye. Usually, the reservoir tank is also secured, so there's no access to clean water from that source.

# Using Saline Solution

Some employees have used an IV (intravenous) saline bag taped under the arm where it stays warm. A tube is taped down the front of the body to the pubic area. At the time of the test, a small amount of urine is put into the testing cup, then the cup is filled by squeezing the saline fluid out of the bag. Usually the observer is on the other side of a partition, or stands behind the person giving the sample, and so cannot observe the tube easily.

With careful planning, most testing programs can expose employees trying to substitute or adulterate their sample. Flushing is probably the most difficult ploy to catch. Drug testing labs maintain that beat-the-test products sold on the internet and elsewhere are tested regularly and do not work. Nebraska and Texas have enacted criminal laws that punish people who attempt to falsify drug-test results. In 1998 a Pennsylvania bill became law that criminalizes selling, sharing or using drug-free urine for the purpose of evading a positive drug test.

# Chapter 24

# How Employees
# Foil The Paperwork

The sample is only one target for the employee trying to defeat the test. Each person tested has to fill out a variety of papers and forms. Several underground books offer employees advise on how to complete forms in such a way as to lay a foundation for a defense against a positive result.

## Consent Form

On the Consent Form, the person being tested gives permission to have his or her urine tested for drugs. It must be signed either by the person giving the sample or a legal custodian. Of course, anyone can refuse to take the test, and make a formal objection, but few employees do so because it invites suspicion.

The Consent Form typically has the name of the company performing the test and the employer (in cases when these are different), the date, the name of the employee being tested, job title, and employee ID number. The employee signs a statement that the information given is complete and correct to the best of his or her knowledge. It says that the employee understands that the urine sample is going to be analyzed to determine the presence of illicit drugs and alcohol, and it usually states that the signer is aware that the results will be given to the employer.

# Disclosure

The employee being tested is usually asked to fill out a form in addition to the Consent Form, that discloses what medications or drugs that have been taken in the past week. The form requests that the employee write down the name of the medication, the reason for having taken it, how much was taken, when it was prescribed, and who prescribed it. Finally, the employee is asked to sign it.

## Disclosing Cross-Reactants

A sophisticated strategy used by drug users is to disclose over-the-counter or prescribed remedies that can cause positive test results. This creates a potential loophole for drug user. Employees using this approach write down over-the-counter or prescription drugs whose cross-reactivity would cause a false positive for the controlled substance that may have been ingested. If a positive is revealed, the employee then points to the disclosure form where the over-the-counter or prescription substance was indicated. In this situation the employer should schedule a confirmatory test which will be more specific about which metabolite was in the urine. Nonetheless, disclosure of the cross-reactant before the first test provides the employee's attorney with some leverage in the situation, should it escalate into the legal arena.

## Cross-Reactivity

| Positive for | Cross-Reactivity | Examples |
|---|---|---|
| Marijuana | Ibuprofen | Advil®, Nuprin® |
| Amphetamines | Phenypropanolamine | Diatec®, Dexatrim® |
| | | Cotylenol®, Triaminic® |
| | Ephedrine | Primatene®, Bronkotabs® |
| | | Nyquil® |
| Opiates | Dextromethorphan | Vicks Formula 44-M® |
| | Amitripyline | Elavil® |
| | Meperidine | Demarol® |
| | Imprimine | Tofranil® |
| | Perylamine | Mydol®, Permensin®, |
| | | Primatene-M® |
| Barbiturate | Phenobarbital | Primatene® |
| Methadone | Diphenhydramine | Benadryl® |

Source: Abbie Hoffman, *Steal This Urine Test*

# Having A Legal Prescription

An common alternative strategy is obtaining a legal prescription from a sympathetic doctor for the substance the person may have taken or a substance that has a positive cross-reactivity for the one taken.   That prescription is then  disclosed on the form.  For example, a doctor may prescribe a codeine-based cough syrup to an employee who has been using opiates. If an opiate has been used, the cough syrup is ingested before the test and disclosed on the form, stating that it was used recently.   The doctor is then available to substantiate that the employee has a legal prescription for a drug that could be responsible for the positive result. Some employees with legal prescriptions may not want to disclose certain medications such as an anti-depressant or other psychiatric for fear that they will be suspected of suffering from a mental illness that could interfere with his or her capacity to perform the job competently.

Disclosure of prescription medication is regulated under the American Disabilities Act (ADA). Disclosure of prescription medication reveals a medical condition. It is presumed that employers will use information about medical conditions to discriminate against disabled people. Employers are prohibited from asking for medical information from job applicants, for example. Employers need to be careful not to violate any of the stringent provisions of the ADA which could lead to a law suit.

# Filling Out The Form Improperly

All steps of the drug testing process must be able to withstand a Court challenge. An improperly completed form, one with missing information or crossed out writing can negate forensic standards and, thereby, weaken charges against the drug abusing employee. Of course, this is a very risky strategy, since employers will demand that the employee provide another sample along with properly completed paperwork. But for a desperate employee with a positive result, it does provide one more chance.

# National Drug Control Strategy

Following is a reprint of sections of the *1989 National Drug Control Strategy,* which is still enforce, as it pertains to the workplace.

## Federal Implementation

Translates the general policy statement into specific steps that the Federal Government will undertake.

### Implementation Steps in the Workplace

OBJECTIVE: Ensure a drug-free Federal workforce through implementation of Executive Order 12564.

Each Federal agency will expedite the implementation of a drug-free workplan. Those agencies with certified plans will fully implement them, consistent with recent court decisions, by January 5, 1990. This implementation is to include Employee Assistance Programs or other appropriate mechanism, training for supervisors, rehabilitation for drug users, and drug testing. Agencies without currently certified plans will complete certification by January 5, 1990, and fully implement the plans by April 5, 1990.

In carrying out their responsibilities under Section 3 of Executive Order 12564, agency heads should review their testing designated positions periodically as significant new decisions on drug testing are issued by the courts.

OBJECTIVE: Promote drug-free workplace policies in the private sector and the State and local government that include clear penalties for use and drug testing where appropriate.

The Administration will issue final regulations for the Drug-Free Workplace Act that will require Federal contractors and grantees to:

a) adopt policies banning illegal drug activities in their workplaces;

b) individually notify employees working on covered Federal contracts of grants that they must abide by this policy;

c) establish an ongoing drug-free awareness program emphasizing education about drug use and providing information about counseling and rehabilitation; and

d) report convictions of employees resulting from drug offenses occurring in the workplace and appropriately penalize such employees.

ONDCP (Office of National Drug Control Policy) will convene an interagency working group to draft model legislation for drug-free workplaces in State and local governments and for their contractors and grantees. This model will reflect the key components of the Drug-Free Workplace Act of 1988 and the President's Executive Order for a Drug-Free Federal Workplace.

Further, Federal agencies which conduct workplace inspections including those in the Department of Labor and Transportation, will investigate whether the use of illegal drugs was involved in accidents in the workplace.

## Recommended State Legislation

States and localities are already doing many good thing in the fight against drugs. They provide the lion's share of resources and many of the best ideas.

The Anti-Drug Abuse Act of 1988 contained numerous Federal provisions that might profitably be adapted to State and local purposes. Several such provisions—and other recommended State legislation pertaining to the workplace—are briefly discussed below.

## Drug-Free Workplace Statutes

All State and municipal employers, including agencies, contractors, and grantees, should be required to take personnel action against employees found to be using drugs, or to be under the influence of drugs at work. Such action could include suspension, termination, or enrollment in a drug treatment program.

States are encouraged to examine the model Uniform Controlled Substance Act (UCSA) closely and to determine what changes to their existing laws might be appropriate.

States should review their labor laws to ensure that private employers are not legally precluded from implementing drug-testing programs (including pre-employment screening).

State board and agencies responsible for professional licensing should adopt policies whereby individuals would immediately lose their licenses if convicted for sale or distribution of illegal drugs. These policies should also call for the loss of licenses by individuals who use drugs, with reinstatement only after treatment and monitoring.

States should enact a range of penalties for persons caught using or possessing even small amounts of drugs, among them suspension of drivers' licenses for 1 - 5 years.

# Sample Alcohol And Drug Abuse Policy

## I. Statement Of Purpose

XYZ Company is committed to maintaining the safety and health of its workers, and will not tolerate any drug or alcohol use which endangers the health and well-being of its employees or threatens its business. To this end, company employees and supervisors will be educated on:

1. The Company's Drug and Alcohol Abuse Policy;
2. The danger of abusing drugs and alcohol in the workplace.
3. The medical treatment available for persons who seek treatment and counseling; and
4. The action that the company will take when employees violate the Alcohol and Drug Abuse Policy.

It is this company's belief that the use of illegal drugs and the abuse of other controlled substances, on or off the job, is not consistent with the law of the land. When employees use illegal drugs or abuse other controlled substances or alcohol, on or off duty, they threaten the company's business by tending to be less reliable, less productive, more accident prone, and less likely to report to work regularly in a mental and physical condition fit for work. This results in increased costs to the company, and jeopardizes the reputation of the company and the quality of its products, as well as the well-being of involved employees, their families and their co-workers.

Employees have the basic right to work in an environment that is free of drugs and alcohol, and to be able to rely on the fact that co-workers are not impaired by substance abuse. In the interest of maintaining a safe and healthy workplace that is free of alcohol and drug abuse, this company is committed to strictly enforce its drug and alcohol policy and to comply with the requirements of the Drug-Free Workplace Act of 1988 and the special Drug-Free Work Force Rules of the United States Department of Defense.

## II. Procedures To Be Initiated By The Supervisor For Impaired Employees

Because this company recognizes the tragic effect that substance abuse can have on the productive work life of the employee, his co-workers and his personal life, it is committed to early identification and referral for professional medical treatment of substance abusers. However, its commitment to personal assistance does not waive any disciplinary procedures invoked by the behavior of an employee, particularly when the employee does not first come forward voluntarily to management with his/her substance abuse problem.

Supervisors will be trained to:
1. Detect and document any job performance or work behaviors that indicate personal problems;
2. Identify on-the-job use or impairment of drugs or alcohol;
3. Initiate the process of mandatory referral for impaired employees for medical assessment;
4. Require testing for employees who are suspected of drug or alcohol impairment on the job;
5. Utilize confrontation techniques to establish a violation of company policy;
6. Understand the drug testing procedures and technology;
7. Know when random testing is appropriate,
8. Be responsible for detecting substance abuse problems in their work area;
9. Encourage voluntary referral to the company's Employee Assistance Program;
10. Know the procedure for conducting workplace inspections, and will be informed about the employee's right to privacy.

## III. Authorized Use Of Prescribed Medicine

When employees are taking a medically prescribed drug that can alter behavior, physical ability or mental function, they must report the use of this drug to the personnel department, which will determine whether temporary job reassignment/medical leave is warranted until the treatment is finished. Employees must keep all prescribed medications in the original container, which identifies the drug, dosage, date or prescription and prescribing physician.

## IV. Arrest or Conviction Under Criminal Drug Statute

Employees must notify, in writing, the director of personnel within five days of any arrest or conviction of a criminal drug statute. This requirement is set forth to comply with the Federal contractor Drug-Free Workplace Act.

## V. Policy Violations

XYZ Company specifically prohibits the following and will routinely discipline an employee up to and including discharge for any of the following:

1. Use, possession, manufacture, distribution, dispensation or sale of:
   a) Illegal drugs or drug paraphernalia;
   b) Unauthorized controlled substances; or
   c) Alcohol on company remises or company business; in company supplies vehicles, or during working hours.
2. Storing in a locker, desk, automobile or other repository on company premises any illegal drug, drug paraphernalia, any controlled substance whose use is unauthorized, or any alcohol.
3. Being under the influence of an unauthorized controlled substance, illegal drug or alcohol on company premises or company business, in company supplied vehicles, or during working hours. The term "being under the influence" of alcohol is defined as blood alcohol level of 0.04. The definition of "being under the influence" of unauthorized controlled substances or illegal drugs is testing positive at a specified mg/dl level.
4. Use of alcohol off company property that adversely affects the employee's work performance, his or other's safety at work or the company's reputation in the community.
5. Possession, use, manufacture, distribution, dispensation or sale of illegal drugs off company property that adversely affects the employee's work performance, his/her own or others' safety at work of the company's reputation in the community.
6. Switching or altering any urine sample submitted for drug or alcohol testing.
7. Refusing to consent to testing or to submit a breath, saliva, urine or blood sample for testing when requested by management.
8. Refusing to submit to an inspection that is requested by management.
9. Conviction under any criminal drug statute.
10. Arrest under any criminal drug statute under circumstances which adversely affect the company's reputation in the community.
11. Failure to notify the company of any arrest or conviction under any criminal drug statute within five days of the arrest or conviction.
12. Failure to report to the personnel department the use of a prescribed medication which may alter behavior, physical ability or mental functions of the employee.
13. Failure to keep prescribed medications in its original container with a label that states the name of the drug, the frequency of dosage, the date prescribed and the name of the prescribing physician.
14. Refusing to sign a statement to comply with the company's drug and alcohol abuse policy.

15. Refusing to complete a medical questionnaire and consent form prior to testing.

16. Refusal to complete the toxicology chain of custody form after submission of a urine or blood specimen.

## VI. Other Testing

If XYZ Company suspects that an employee's on-the-job performance may have been adversely affected in any way by drugs or alcohol, of that an employee has otherwise violated this policy, it may require the employee to submit a breath, saliva, urine, and/or blood sample for alcohol or drug testing. The employee will be in violation of this policy, if he/she tests positive for alcohol or drugs during this testing.

Whenever this company requires a standard physical examination, that examination will include a breath, saliva, urine and/or blood test for alcohol and drugs. A positive test for alcohol or drugs during this testing will be a violation of this policy.

Employees who transport company products and materials on interstate highways will be subject to the random testing requirements established by the Federal Department of Transportation (Note: We do not recommend random testing for employees other than that required by state and federal regulations.) An employee who tests positive for alcohol or drugs will be in violation of this policy.

Whenever an employee is involved in an accident involving fatality, serious bodily injury, or substantial property damage, the company may require the employee to submit a breath, saliva, urine and/or blood specimen for alcohol of drug testing. The employee will be in violation of this policy if tests for drugs or alcohol are positive.

Prior to testing of applicants and employees, the company will allow the person to list all prescriptions and non-prescription drugs taken within thirty days, and to provide an explanation for the use of these drugs.

Before testing, all applicants and employees must sign an approved from consenting to the testing and the release of test results to the company's personnel department.

If an employee tests positive for alcohol or drugs, he/she will be given the opportunity to explain the test results before any action is taken.

## VII. Inspections

Whenever the company suspects that an employee's work performance or on-the-job behavior may have been affected in any way by alcohol or drugs, or if the company suspects that the employee has sold, purchased, used or possessed alcohol, drugs or drug paraphernalia on company property, the company may inspect the employee, the employee's locker, desk or other company property under the control of the employee, as well as the employee's personal effects or automobile on the company property.

The company will post he following "Right to Inspect" notice at or near each entrance to company property:

### Right to Inspect
*XYZ Company reserves the right inspect the property and person of any individual or vehicle on company property. This right includes, but is not limited to, the inspection of the employee's vehicle, parcels, packages, purses, lunch boxes, briefcases, lockers, workstations and desks*

## VIII. Condition Of Employment

Compliance with XYZ's Company substance abuse policy is a condition for employment. The failure or refusal of an employee to cooperate full, sign any required document or submit to any inspection or test will be grounds for termination.

## IX. Reservation of Rights

XYZ Company reserves the right to interpret, change, rescind or depart from this policy in whole or in part without notice. Nothing in this policy alters an employee's status. The company hopes each employment relationship will be happy, productive and enduring. Nevertheless, employees remain free to resign their employment at any given time, for any reason or no reason without notice. Similarly, XYZ Company retains the right to terminate any employee at any time, for any or no reason, without notice.

## X. Applicant Testing

Applicants will be required to complete the Applicant's Certification and Agreement form as a part of the routine application process. (A sample is available from *Employee Law Update*, Box 15250, Evansville, IN. 47716, 812-476-4520) They will then be tested for drugs and alcohol as a part of the application process.

Note: An employer does not have any legal obligation to tell the applicant the reason for rejection of employment. If an applicant is rejected for failing a drug teat, it may be advisable not to give this reason for not hiring the applicant. The employer can simply state to the applicant that not being hired was the result of failing the total interview process covering hiring requirements. This should also aid in avoiding lawsuits for defamation, based on a claim that the employer labeled the applicant as a "drug user."

## XI. Employee Drug Testing

1. The employee will be asked to list all drugs consumed during the past thirty days, and will have the opportunity to explain the use of each one.
2. The employee will complete a consent or alcohol and testing form. The refusal to do so will be considered a violation of company policy, and the employee will be terminated.

3. Test results will be returned to the personnel director for review with the employee, and a copy of the test results will be place in the employee's personnel file. All positive results will be given a second verification test.
4. If an employee tests positive after the second verification test, he/she will be disciplined up to and including discharge for violation of company policy. The termination of an employee or use of an employee assistance program will be the decision of management, depending on the circumstances in the judgment of management. All disciplinary action will be controlled by management.

---

Author's note: We are grateful to Rutkowski and Associates, publishers of *Employment Law Update,* for granting permission to reprint the **Alcohol and Drug Abuse Policy**. The terms in the policy were developed by Rutkowski and Associates and do not reflect the opinions or advice of the authors or publisher. The authors, the publisher and Rutkowski and Associates do no intend to render legal advice in providing this example company policy. It is presented here as an example only. Each company's situation, work force and needs are different and the company policy should be carefully tailored to fit the company's unique situation and state laws, especially as they pertain to privacy rights. The reader should employ legal counsel to determine the applicability of the material reprinted from *Employment Law Update* to their particular circumstances.

# Procedure To Be Followed For Employee Who Is Under The Influence

Procedure to be followed in situations (particularly employers that have unions) where there is an employee who appears to be under the influence of alcohol, drugs or controlled substances or both. In an effort to establish if a violation of Company rules and regulations occurred, all inquires should be made according to the following procedure.

1. Determine if an employee "appears" to be under the influence of an alcohol beverage, drugs, including controlled substances and prescriptions, or both.
2. If available, get another supervisor or management representative to personally escort the employee to the supervisor's office.
3. Bring in a union representative (or any other representative the employee chooses) to be present during the investigation (*in this situation*).
4. Ask the questions indicated in "Questions for Suspected Alcoholic or Substances Users."
5. During the investigation, with the employee and union representative still present, complete the "Observation Checklist."
6. If the employee has previously agreed, have the employee take the "Basic On-Site Coordination Examination."

7. Complete the "Opinion Based on Observations Checklist."
8. If you conclude that the employee does not appear to be under the influence of alcohol or drugs, including controlled substances and prescription drugs, and he is able to perform his work duties, then have the employee return to his work station.
9. If you conclude that the employee *is* under the influence of alcohol, drugs, or both, then suspend the employee pending final determination, in the presence of his union representative, and advise him of the Company rule(s) that he violated.
10. Make the necessary arrangements to have the employee taken home. Do not permit him to go home or drive by himself. If the employee refuses any assistance, such as by his union representative, then make sure the union representative and your company representative *can* verify that the *employee refused such assistance.* However, if and employee cannot control his action, then under *no* circumstances should he be allowed to leave without assistance. You must call the local police chief or sheriff to warn them of the grievant's condition and refusal of assistance before the employee is allowed to leave the plant. Tell the law enforcement officials the employee's name and make of car.

Note: The reason for calling the local law enforcement authorities and providing assistance before the employee leaves the plant, is based on the Texas case of *Otis Engineering Corp. v. Clark,* 668 s.w. 2d 307 (Tex. 1983). In this case, an employee who was clearly under the influence while at the plant was ordered to punch out by his immediate supervisor. While attempting to drive home, the drunk employee killed two individuals in a traffic accident. The Texas Supreme Court found that the decedents' family could bring a wrongful death action against the employer holding:

*"When, because of an employee's incapacity, an employer exercises control over the employee, the employer has a duty to take action as a reasonably prudent employer under the same or similar circumstances would take to prevent the employee from causing an unreasonable risk of harm to others. Such a duty may be analogized to cases in which a defendant can exercise some measure of control over a dangerous person when there is a recognizable great danger of harm to third persons. Thus, you do all that you can to prevent an obviously intoxicated employee from driving home alone."*

11. Whenever possible, have a *management representative present throughout* the *entire proceedings* with appropriate *notes* being taken for future reference and supporting documentation.

Note: Review the procedure and questions with all your supervisors and other appropriate personnel.

# Basic On-Site Coordination Examination

**1. Balance:**
__Fair __Falling __Swaying __Staggering
__Sagging Knees (eyes closed, one foot and head back, etc.)

**2. Walking and Turning:**
__Fair __Swaying __Stumbling __
Arms extended for balance __Falling
__Sure footed __Reaching for support.

**3. Finger to Nose:**
Right. __Sure __Uncertain
Left. __Sure __Uncertain

**4. Speech:**
__Fair __Slurred __Incoherent
__Confused __Silent __Whispering

**5. Awareness:**
__Fair __Confused __Bewildered
__Sleepy __Alert

# Observation Checklist

*Directions:* Check pertinent items

| | |
|---|---|
| **1. Walking:** | __Stumbling __Swaggering __Falling<br>__Unable to __Swaying __Holding on |
| **2. Standing:** | __Swaying __Rigid __Unable to stand<br>__Feet wide apart __Staggering<br>__Sagging at knees |
| **3. Speech:** | __Shouting __Silent __Whispering<br>__Slow __Rambling __Mute __Slurred<br>__Slobbering __Incoherent |
| **4. Demeanor:** | __Cooperative __Polite __Calm<br>__Sleepy __Crying __Silent __Talkative<br>__Excited __Sarcastic __Fighting |

5. Actions: __Resisting communications __Fighting __Threatening __Calm __Drowsy __Profanity __Hyperactive __Hostile __Erratic

6. Eyes: __Bloodshot __Watery __Dilated __Glassy __Droopy __Closed

7. Face: __Flushed __Pale __Sweaty

8. Appearance & Clothing: __Unruly __Messy __Dirty __Partially dressed __Neat __Having odor __Stains on clothing __Bodily excrement stains

9. Breath: __Alcoholic Odor __Faint Alcohic odor __No alcoholic odor

10. Movements: __Fumbling __Jerky __Slow __Normal __Nervous __Hyperactive

11. Eating: __Gum __Candy __Mints __Other, specify_____

12. Otherobservations: _____.

# Opinion Based on Observations

A. Under influence of alcohol_____

B. Under influence of drugs_____

C. When not sure, which one of either alcohol or drugs or both_____

D. Unfit to operate machinery or to perform safely in workplace_____

E. Unfit for work for other reason (List)_____

F. Recommended for physical examination_____

G. Does not appear to be under influence of alcohol_____

H. Does not appear to be under influence of drugs_____

Remarks: _____

Signed_____ Date_____
Witnessed by: _____ Date_____

# STATEMENT

### Voluntary Submission for Physical Examination of Drug/Alcohol Testing and the Release of Findings and Information

I, _____, voluntarily agree to take a physical examination which may include blood, breath, saliva, and/or urine analysis by a physician, medical center, hospital, or medically qualified personnel. Furthermore, I authorize the release of these tests and examination results to _____Company or any of its representatives. By this authorization, I do hereby release any physician, medical personnel, hospital, medical center, clinic, etc., _____Company, or any of its representatives from any and all liabilities arising from  the release or use of the information derived from or contained in my physical examination and test results.

| | |
|---|---|
| _____ | _____ |
| Witness | Employee |
| _____ | _____ |
| Witness | Date |

# Inspection and Waiver Agreement

*To be signed by job applicant in consideration of being employed*

I hereby acknowledge assignment from _____Company of locker number _____, receipt of one lock serial number _____, and _____ keys which have been provided to me for use only on the assigned locker. The locker, lock and keys have been provided to me without charge. I understand that no keys have been retained by the Company and that it will be my responsibility to return the keys, lock and locker in normal working condition, or to replace them of equal value upon termination of my employment. If I fail to do so, I hereby authorize _____Company to deduct the replacement cost from my last pay check.

In consideration of being hired, I have the Company's permission to use a Company locker and to receive a lock for use thereon. I agree that I will not use the locker for any purpose that would constitute a violation of any Company rule. I further agree to permit the Company in the exercise of its discretion to search my vehicle, lunch box, purse, parcels, packages, briefcase, desk or work station or to open the locker and search the contents thereof.

| | |
|---|---|
| _____ | _____ |
| Employee | Company Representative |
| _____ | |
| Date | |

# Conditional Reinstatement Agreement
## Employee Assistance Program

*The conditional reinstatement agreement was designed to provide a worthy employee the opportunity to go through rehabilitation without undue costs of repeated inpatient rehabilitation stays to the company, since the acute treatment of alcohol or drug withdrawal can cost from $10,000 to $20,000 depending on what is needed and the region of the country. Most employees eligible for this program would be those who sought voluntary help. Thus, there may be some instance where an impaired employee is removed from the job and then offered this program in lieu of being terminated. Circumstances for such company leniency would include willingness of the employee to seek help, evidence that this employee has been a good worker and could be valuable again if the substance abuse problem was corrected, and lack of evidence of any harm or damage to other persons or property during the incident where the employee was identified as having a problem.*

# Conditional Reinstatement Agreement

The undersigned parties hereby agree as follows:

1. That (*employee's name*) recognizes that the Company was lenient in working with him/her due to (*employee's name*) unexcused absence(s) because of alcohol/drug abuse and letting him/her go through its employee assistance/rehabilitation program to help (*employee's name*) deal with his/her drug/alcohol addiction problem.

2. That the Company will conditionally reinstate (*employee's name*) after he/she successfully completes his/her rehabilitation stay at (*hospital name*). (*Employee's name*) will be conditionally reinstated provided he/she agrees to and performs the following:

*Here insert conditions applying to drug rehabilitation treatment*

Examples of Alcohol Rehabilitation Program:
a) Daily use of antabuse 250 mg. h. s.
b) A minimum of two (2) AA Meetings per week.
c) Requirements of state board for licensed personnel.

3. If within the next three (3) years, (*employee's name*) is unable to perform his job duties due to alcohol/drug abuse or fails to continue this alcohol/drug rehabilitation program and the conditions set forth above as outlined in Item 2 and as required by (*employer's name*), alcohol/drug counselor or physician, he or she will be terminated.

4. (*Employee's name*) understands and agrees that if he has to be admitted to a hospital or rehabilitation center again within the next three (3) years he/she will be terminated.

5. *Statement of Agreement.* This agreement is not an employment contract. The company is not guaranteeing employment to an employee for any term of employment, and may terminate the employee at any time without notice. Likewise, the employee may terminate his/her employment with the company at any time without explanation. Where there is a job available and the employee complies with the terms of the employee assistance program, the employee will be conditionally reinstated for an indefinite term, as long as that reinstatement is consistent with the business needs of the company.

| Union Representative (if applicable) | Employee | Company Representative |
| --- | --- | --- |

Appendix B, **Sample Alcohol and Drug Policy** is reprinted, with permission, from *Employment Lay Update* Copyright © 1989, Rutkowski and Associates, Inc. *Employment Law Update* is a monthly newsletter available from *Employment Law Update*, Box 15250, Evansville, IN. 47716-0250, 812-476-4520.

**Arthur D. Rutkowski, J.D.,** Legal Editor of *Employment Law Update* is a partner in the law firm of Bowers, Harrison, Kent and Miller. He has represented management in labor and employment law for over 20 years and has successfully directed hundreds of union organizing and decertification campaigns and collective bargaining negotiations for management in the USA and Canada. He is a member of the American Bar Association Labor Law Committee on Labor Arbitration and Collective Bargaining.

**Barbara Lang Rutkowski, Ed.D.,** Managing Editor of *Employment Law Update,* Specializes in management consulting, management seminar development and labor relations/employment law. Dr. Rutkowski has been on the faculty of the University of Florida and a manager at the University of Florida and Miami Children's hospital.

# Sample Policy For State Employers

## Pre-Employment Screening

The Personnel Board has both constitutional and statutory authority for administering the State's Civil Service Merit Selection System. This includes determining what tests of fitness are appropriate to evaluate applicants for State positions. Since drug-induced behavior has the potential to seriously impact job performance, drug screening may be appropriate for applicants for some classifications. The Personnel Board is the agency responsible for regulating such drug testing.

In 1986, the Governor issued and Executive Order directing the Personnel Board to cooperate with the Department of Personnel Administration to develop policies and procedures to help bring about a drug-free State workplace. To achieve this end, the Board held five public hearings before adopting regulations and developing rules governing drug screening.

In developing the regulations, the Board attempted to craft them in a way that would address the major concerns about drug testing, such as credibility of test result, the confidentiality of test result and applicants rights and due process.

The salient features of the regulations are summarized here to illustrate the balance between employer needs and applicant rights.

The regulations do not mandate drug screening of applicant for any classification in State service. Rather, they set forward a framework within which a department may come forward and request to institute an applicant screening program, and they regulate such testing.

The rules only regulate drug screening of applicants at initial entry into a sensitive position and do not apply to applicant for promotion who are already in a sensitive position and they do not apply to testing of current employees for assessing their ability to carry out their jobs safely. These are the purview of the Department of Personnel Administration.

Drug Screening of applicant would only be permissible under regulations of jobs where there is a high risk to health and safety as a result of drug-induced behavior. Legal advice indicated that the Board must carefully lay a record that shows that it is not arbitrarily and capriciously identifying a position as sensitive and therefore, as one for which drug testing is job-related. Having departments come in and lay out evidence that proves the position is sensitive is a pro-active measure to minimize exposure to being sued.

Whether a job is sensitive would be determined in a hearing before the Board, a public hearing, at which a department would need to present documentation as to:

(1) The nature of the duties,
(2) The risks to health and safety, and
(3) he sensitivity to drug-induced behavior.

Other parties who are interested should have an opportunity to input, and if the Board concurs that drug testing is in fact job related, then drug screening of applicants would become a requirement in future examinations for that classification. In short, drug screening of applicants for State positions is not universal, but is selective.

The regulations provide for full disclosure to applicant, both beforehand, when they're told when a drug screening test will be required, and afterward, when they're entitled to know the results of their individual drug test.

The regulations also set forth standards for the testing laboratories. Only laboratories that are certified by the National Institute on Drug Abuse, or accredited by the College of American Pathologists and who participate in a quality assurance program may participate in a drug testing for the State.

In order to fail the drug test, a sample must fail two separate tests utilizing different methodology. The first, or screening test, must use a form of immunoassay tests, the second or confirmatory test uses gas chromatography/mass spectrometry. Forensic experts in the field have testified before the Board that this represents the "gold standard" in terms of drug testing, drug screening, and is the most defensible way to proceed.

Regulations also require that a department follow strict chain of custody procedures so that samples are not misidentified. Applicants are also required to disclose medications that they have taken during the two weeks prior to the test. This is a protection for applicants against inappropriate disqualification based on a positive drug test that might result from ingesting a legally obtained and legally used substance.

Applicant appeal rights are specified, as is the right of the applicant to have his of her sample retested if they choose to do so at their own cost.

Confidentiality of test results is assured by limiting access severely to test results and ensuring that the test results are used only for the purpose of administering these rules; that is, to determine an individual's eligibility to take State exams where drug testing is required.

Finally, the regulations specify the consequences of failing a drug test. An individual is obviously disqualified for the examination that they're taking. In addition, they're prohibited for a period of one year from competing in any other State examination for which drug testing is required.

In addition, if they test positive for a hard drug — a drug the possession of which would constitute a felony offense — they are prohibited for a period of ten years from competing in any State peace officer examination.

Failing a drug test would not impact an individual's ability to take any other examination for which drug testing has not been deemed job-related.

Extrapolated from testimony of Duane Morford
Chief, Policy Division, Personnel Board, State of California
Senate Select Committee on Substance Abuse
Senator John Seymour, Chairman
October 25, 1988

## 213. Pre-Employment Testing for Drug Usage.

An appointing power may conduct drug testing of applicants for a class only when:

(a) The appointing power has documented the sensitivity of the class and the consequences of drug-related behavior by showing that:

(1) The duties involve a greater than normal level of trust for, reponsibility for or impact on the health and safety of others, and
(2) Errors in judgement, inattentiveness of diminished coordination, dexterity of composure while perfoming their duties could clearly result in mistakes that would endanger the health nad safety of others; and
(3) Employees in these positions work with such independence, or, perform such tasks that it cannot be safely assumed that mistakes such as those described in (2) could be prevented by a supervisor or another employee.

(b) The board concludes after a public hearing that the appointing power has adequetely documented the sensitivity of the class and the consequences of drug-related behavior and that drug testing is, therefore, job related for the class; and
(c) As a result of (a) and (b) above, the board approves the inclusion of a requirement for drug testing in the minimum qualifications for the class.

## 213.1 Notice of Drug Testing in Examination Announcements

Any examination that includes drug testing as provided by Rule 213 shall specify in the examination announcement the type of specimen to be collected and the consequences of failing the drug test.

## 213.2 Drug Testing of Current Employees and Individuals Reinstating

An applicant or transferee to a class for which drug testing is required pursuant to Rule 213 who is a current employee or a former permanent or probationary employee with a break in service as defined in Rule 6.4 shall be subject to drug testing pusuant to Rule 312, except that if such employee has a current appointment to a class for which drug testing is required pusuant to Rule 213, he or she shall not be tested. A current or former employee subject to testing under this rule is deemed to be an applicant for purposes of Rules 213.4, 213.5, and 213.6.

## 213.3 Laboratories Authorized to Conduct Drug Testing

Drug test samples shall be analyzed by:

(a) A commercial laboratory meeting standards that are the same as those used by the Department of Health and Human Services (DHHS)/National Institute on Drug Abuse (NIDA) to certify laboratories engaged in urine drug testing for Federal agencies (Mandatory Guidelines for Federal Workplace Drug Testing Program, Federal Register, Vol.53, No.69) or those standards used by the College of American Pathologists (CAP) to accredit laboratories for forensic urine drug testing (Standards for Accreditation, Forensic Drug Testing Laboratories, College of American Pathologists); and

(1) Is capable of same site initial screening and confirmatory test,

(2) Utilizes FDA-approved immunoassay tests, and

(3) Participates in a laboratory proficiency testing program, and

(b) A laboratory which is not a component organization of a State department.

## 213.4 Required Components for Drug Testing.

Any drug testing or retesting procedure conducted pursuant to Rule 213 or 213.2 must be approved by the executive officer and shall include all of the following:

(a) The drug screening methodology to be used, which shall be a type of immunoassay, except that another may be used if a department can demonstrate that it is equally reliable as immunoassay;

(b) The drugs to be tested which shall include at least the following drugs of abuse:

(1) Amphetamines and Methamphetamines

(2) Cocaine

(3) Marijuana/ Cannabinoids (THC)

(4) Opiates (narcotics)

(5) Phenocyclidine (PCP)

(c) Cut-off levels for screening tests that will identify positive sample while minimizing false positive results;

(d) An authorization to test forms which shall include at least the following:

(1) A list of the specific drugs to be tested for, and a description of the consequences of failing, the drug test as specified in Rule 213.5;

(2) A signature block, to be signed by the applicant before the drug test begins, authorizing the test to proceed and authorizing the necessary disclosure of medical information pursuant to Rule 213.4.

(3) A statement that applicants who decline to sign the form of decline to be tested will be disqualified from the examination.

(e)

(1) A requirement that the applicant disclose on a form, separate from the authorization to test form, all drugs and other medications taken whether prescribed or not, within the 14 days prior to testing. This information shall be examined only by the appointing power and only if the applicant has a positive confirmatory drug test, except that for purposes of administering Rule 213.6, this information may be examined by the board and staff authorized to investigate and/or hear appeals.

(2) A requirement that the appointing power utilize a Medical Review Officer, who shall be a licensed physician with knowledge of substance abuse, to review and interpret positive results of confirmatory tests and the information submitted by the applicant pursuant to Rule 213.4(e)(1), determine whether the result may have been caused for any medically acceptable reason, such as prescribed or over the counter medications, and report to the appointing power his/her opinion as to the cause of the positive drug test. In the process of making this decision, the Medical Review Officer may request the applicant to provide additional information regarding all drugs and other medications taken.

(f) Specimen chain of custody provisions which shall include at least the following:

(1) A procedure to assure that a valid specimen is acquired, the donor is properly identified, and that no tampering or mishandling of the specimen occurs from the initial collection to final disposition.

(2) A written log in which is recorded the name, signature, time of receipt, and time of release of each person handling, testing or storing each specimen, and reporting teat results.

(3) Collection of specimen samples in a clinical setting such as a laboratory collection station, doctor's office, hospital or clinic, or in another setting approved by the executive officer on the basis that it provides an equally secure and professional collection process.

(g) Procedure for confirmation of positive screening test results utilizing gas chromatography/mass spectrometry (GS/MS);

(h) Notes to the applicant which shall be written and based on the following:

(1) If the screening test result is negative, the test is concluded and the applicant has passed the drug test.

(2) If the necessary confirmatory test result is negative, the test is concluded and the applicant has passed the drug test.

(3) If both the screening test and the confirmatory test results are positive and the Medical Review Officer's opinion is that he positive test results are not because of prescribed or over the counter medication or for any other medically acceptable reasons, the applicant has failed the drug test.

(i) Specimen retention and retesting procedure which shall include at least the following:

(1) Retention of all confirmed positive specimens and related records by the testing laboratory in secure frozen storage for at least one year following the test or until all appeals of litigation are concluded, whichever is longer.

(2) Provisions for retesting of confirmed positive specimens by any laboratory authorized to conduct drug testing pursuant to Rule 213.3, at the request of an applicant and at the applicant's expense, provided that the request is received within 30 day of notifying the applicant of his/her disqualification. Retesting shall correspond exactly with the initial methods and procedures.

(j) Provisions for maintaining the confidentiality of test results, which shall include at least the following:

(1) The results of any test conducted pursuant to Rules 213, 213.2 or 213.4(i) (2) shall be given power or the executive officer, and cannot be revealed to any other party without the written authorization of the applicant except for the purposes of administering

(A) Rule 213.5, the executive officer shall reveal a failed drug test to other State appointing powers who administer an examination for which drug testing is required and for which the individual is an applicant; or

(B) Rule 213.6, the executive officer may reveal a failed drug test and other relevant information to the board and staff authorized to investigate and/or hear appeals.

(2) The results of any test conducted pursuant to Rule 213.2 shall not be used in any adverse action proceedings.

(3) The information disclosed by the applicant pursuant to Rule 213.4(e) (1) shall be examined only by the appointing power and only if the applicant has a positive confirmatory drug test, except that for purposes of administering Rule 213.6, this information may be examined by the board and staff authorized to investigate and/or hear appeals.

(4) Drug test results which are positive shall be purged from all records one year from the date the drug test specimen is given except as follows:

(A) The retention period for drug test results which are positive for a drug as specified in Rule 213.5 (b) shall be ten years from the date the drug test specimen is given;

(B) If a disqualification from an examination as the result of a positive test is appealed of litigated, the drug test results shall be retained until the appeal or litigation is removed.

## 213.5 Consequences of Failing the Drug Test

(a) Applicant who fail the drug test pursuant to Rule 213.4(h), will be disqualified from the examination in which they are competing and, except as provided by Rule 213.5(d), shall not be eligible to take any State civil service examination for a class for which drug testing is required until one year has elapsed from the date the drug test specimen is given.

(b) Except as provided by Rule 213.5(d), applicants who fail the drug test because of a drug for which possession would constitute a felony offense under Health and Safety Code Section 11350 shall not be eligible to take any State civil service examination for a peace officer until ten years have elapsed from the date the drug test specimen is given.

(c) Any applicant for a State civil service examination for a peace officer class who discloses or whose background investigation reveals use of a drug for which possession would constitute a felony offense under Health and Safety Code Section 11350, subsequent to his or her eighteenth birthday shall be disqualified from the examination in which he or she is competing unless 10 years have elapsed from the date of the disclosed use of the drug; and shall not be eligible to take any State civil service examination for a peace officer class until 10 years have elapsed from the date of the disclosed use.

(d) Any applicant who is disqualified from taking any subsequent examination as specified in this rule may, upon request and with the consent of the executive officer, be permitted to take the specified examination. In acting on the request, the executive officer shall consider evidence submitted by the person of rehabilitation from drug abuse and/or extenuating circumstances regarding the drug use.

Persons denied permission to take a subsequent examination within the specified one- and ten-year periods may appeal in writing to the Board within 30 days of notification.

## 213.6 Appeal of a Disqualification Resulting From a Failed Drug Test of Background Investigation Report

(a) This rule pertains to and outlines administrative appeal rights only. An applicant appealing under this rule shall follow the procedures in Rules 63 through 74, inclusive.

(b) An applicant disqualified as the result of failing the drug test may only appeal the disqualification on the grounds that the drug was obtained legally, or there has been a violation of test protocol or chain of custody procedures, or other irregularity that invalidates the test result. A disqualified applicant may have his/her drug test specimen retested at his/her own expense as provided in Rule 213.4(1)(2) and include the results of the retesting in his/her appeal.

(c) An applicant disqualified or withheld from certification as a result of disclosure of drug use or whose background investigation reveals use of a drug pursuant to Rule 213.5(c) may appeal the disqualification of the withholding from certification on any grounds allowable by law.

(d) An applicant who prevails upon appeal under this rule will be restored eligibility in the examination from which disqualified or restored to the eligible list from which withheld.

California State Personnel Board, Title 2, Register 89, no. 18, 5-6-89

# Substance Abuse Policy

## Introduction

The State Department of Personnel is charged with implementing the Governor's Executive Order D-58-86, which calls for a drug-free State workplace.

To achieve this the Department of Personnel Administration Established a program under which employees serving in sensitive positions in State service are subject to drug and/or alcohol testing when there is reasonable suspicion that they are under the influence while at work or on standby.

The program supplements measures previously in place to deal with employee substance abuse, such as employee assistance and discipline programs.

Employee constitutional privacy rights much be considered before implementing substance testing. The State's need to test must be balanced with the employee's normal entitlement to be protected from such action under search and seizure and privacy provisions. This end is achieved by focusing testing on sensitive positions in which:

(1) Impaired performance could clearly endanger the health and safety of others; and

(2) Less intrusive measures could not reliably deal with this problem.

Sensitive positions were specifically identified in such fields as law enforcement, corrections, fire fighting, health care, and heavy truck and equipment operations, among others.

Whether testing should be random, periodic, or for cause was considered. Again, there was a need to balance the State's interests with employee rights. Legal advice indicated that random is still in some legal dispute, where there is solid legal support for testing based on reasonable suspicion.

A review of State agencies indicated that the majority of State employees perform their work without being under the influence of drugs or alcohol. In view of this, testing based on reasonable suspicion was elected.

With these policy issues decided, the issues surrounding the technical accuracy of drug testing was considered. Extensive technical safeguards were included to avoid the pitfalls of high error rates, questionable sample collection practices, easy ways to beat the tests, and improper interpretation of test results.

Employees expressed apprehension concerning supervisor harassment, test accuracy, invasion of privacy, and due process. In response, the following employee rights were included in the provisions:

(1) Employees and unions are notified and given an opportunity to respond before positions are designated sensitive and become subject to the policy;

(2) Before and employee can be sent for a drug test, the initial determination of reasonable suspicion must be confirmed by second supervisor or manager who is specifically trained in the testing policy and the detection of reasonable suspicion;

(3) Employees have the right to representation in any interviews that could lead to a decision to take action against them;

(4) At their own expense, employees have the opportunity to have their sample retested at a lab of their choice;

(5) Employees receive copies of all test results and related documentation;

(6) Confidentiality is maintained with test results being released only on a need-to-know basis;

(7) A licensed physician reviews all positive results and considers any medical reasons provided by employees for any positive results that may come back on them.

Input was solicited from employee unions concerning the policy and how it could impact on their employees. The impact the policies have upon employees is subject to collective bargaining.

Extrapolated from testimony
Peter Strom, Manager, Policy Development Section
Department of Personnel Administration, State of California,
Senate Select Committee on Substance Abuse,
Senator John Seymour, Chairman, October 25, 1988

# 599.960 General Policy

(a) It is the purpose of this article to help ensure that the State workplace is free from the effects of drug and alcohol abuse. These provisions shall be in addition to and shall not be construed as a required prerequisite to or as replacing, limiting or setting standards for any other types of provisions available under law to serve this purpose, including employee assistance, adverse action and medical examination.

(b) Consistent with Government Code Section 19572 and Governor's Executive Order D-58-86, no State employee who is on duty or on standby for duty shall:

(1)Use, possess, or be under the influence of illegal or unauthorized drugs or other illegal mind-altering substances; or

(2) Be under the influence of alcohol to any extent that would impede the employee's ability to perform his or her duties safely and effectively.

(c) Employees serving in sensitive positions shall be subject to drug and alcohol testing, hereinafter referred to as substance testing, as provided in this Article when there is reasonable suspicion that the employee has already been found in violation of subsection (b) through the adverse action or medical examination processes under the Civil Service Act (Government Code Section 19253.5; Government Code Sections 19570-19593), as a result of substance testing under this article, or by the employee's own admission, the employee may be required to submit periodic substance testing as a condition of remaining in or returning to State employment. Unless otherwise provided in the settlement of an adverse action the period for this testing shall not exceed one year.

(d) No employee shall perform duties which, because of drugs taken under a legal prescription, the employee cannot perform without posing a threat to the health and safety of the employee or others. Employees whose job performance is so restricted may be subject to reassignment, medical examinations or other actions specified by applicable statues and regulations.

## 599.961 Sensitive Positions

(a) For the purposes of this Article, sensitive positions are peace officer positions, as defined by Section 830 of the Penal Code, and other positions in which drug or alcohol affected performance could clearly endanger the health and safety of others. These other positions have the following general characteristics:

(1) Their duties involve a greater than normal level of trust, responsibility for or impact on the health and safety of others; and

(2) Errors in judgment, inattentiveness or diminished coordination, dexterity or composure while performing their duties could clearly result in mistakes that would endanger the health and safety of others; and

(3) Employees in these positions work with such independence, or, perform such tasks that it cannot be safely assumed that mistakes such as those described in (2) could be prevented by a supervisor or another employee.

(b) Filled positions shall be identified as sensitive through the following process:

(1) Subject to Department of Personnel Administration approval, each appointing power shall identify the positions under his/her jurisdiction that meet the standards in (a).

(2) The employees serving in the identified positions and, where applicable, their union representative, shall receive an initial notice that the position has been identified as sensitive and shall be given 30 days to respond.

(3) After considering responses to the initial notice and meeting with employee representatives as required by the Ralph C. Dills Act (Government Code Sections 3512-3524), the Department of Personnel Administration shall issue a final notice to the employees serving in the positions that have been identified as sensitive. This notice shall include a description of the provisions of this Article. Existing practices in this area shall not change for any positions until 60 days after the final notice concerning it is issued.

(c) Vacant positions shall be identified as sensitive through the procedures specified in (b), including those procedures involving employee organizations, except that the employee notification provisions as stated in (b) (2) and (b) (3) shall not apply.

(d) Once a position has been designated sensitive, the appointing power shall take measures to reasonably and likely ensure that future appointees to it are aware that it is sensitive and are informed of the provisions of this Article.

## 599.962 Reasonable Suspicion

(a) Reasonable suspicion is the good faith belief based on specific articulable facts of evidence that an employee may have violated the policy prescribed in section 599.960(b) and that substance testing could reveal evidence related to that violation.

(b) For the purposes of this Article, reasonable suspicion will exist only after the appointing power or his/her designee has considered the fact and/or evidence in the particular case and agreed that they constitute a finding of reasonable suspicion. The designee shall be a person who is authorized to act for the appointing power in carrying out this Article and who is thoroughly familiar with its provisions and procedures.

(c) After it has been confirmed by the designee the facts and/or evidence upon which the reasonable suspicion is based shall be documented in writing. A copy of this shall be given to the affected employee.

## 599.963 Testing Process and Standards

Substance testing under this Article shall comply with the following standards and procedures.

(a) The drug testing process shall be one that is scientifically proven to be at least as accurate and valid a urinalysis using an immunoassay screening test, with all positive screening results being confirmed utilizing gas chromatography/mass spectrometry before a sample is considered positive. The alcohol testing process shall be one that is scientifically proven to be at least accurate and valid as

(1) Urinalysis using enzymatic assay screening test, with all positive screening results being confirmed using gas chromatography before a sample is considered positive or

(2) Breath sample testing using breath alcohol analyzing instruments which meet the State Department of Health Service standard specified in Title 17, Group 8, Article 7 of the California Code of Regulations.

(b) Substances to be tested for shall include the following:

(1) Amphetamines and Methamphetamines
(2) Cocaine
(3) Marijuana/Cannabinoids (THC))
(4) Opiates
(5) Phencyclidine (PCP)
(6) Barbiturates
(7) Benzodiazepines
(8) Methaqualone
(9) Alcohol
(10) In addition, with the approval of the department testing may be conducted for other controlled substances when the appointing power reasonably suspects the use of other substances.

(c) After consulting with expert staff of the laboratory of laboratories selected to perform the testing under this Article, the department shall set test cutoff level that will identify positive test samples while minimizing false positive test results.

(d) Test samples will be collected in a clinical setting such as a laboratory collection station, doctor's office, hospital or clinic or in another setting approved by the department on the basis that it provides for at least an equally secure and professional collection process. The department shall specify procedures to ensure that true samples are obtained.

(e) The department shall specify measures to ensure that a strict chain of custody is maintained for the sample from the time it is taken, throughout the testing process, to its final disposition.

(f) Drug tests shall be performed by a commercial laboratory selected based on its meeting standards that are the same as those used by the National Institute on Drug Abuse (NIDA) to certify laboratories engaged in urine drug testing for Federal agencies (Mandatory Guidelines for Federal Workplace Drug Testing Program, Federal Register, Vol. 53, No. 69) or those used by the

College of American Pathologists (CAP) to accredit laboratories for forensic urine drug testing (Standards for Accreditation, Forensic Drug Testing Laboratories, College of American Pathologists)

# 599.964 Employee Rights

(a) Employees suspected of violating the policy prescribed in section 559.960 shall be entitled to representation during any interrogative interviews with the affected employee that could lead to a decision by the appointing power to take adverse action against the employee, regardless of whether these interviews occur before of after the sample is taken. Employees shall also be entitled to representation in any discussions with the Medical Review Officer that occur under section 599.965.

(b) The sample collection process shall include the opportunity for the employee to provide legally prescribed medication, that could cause a positive test result. At the employee's option, this information may be submitted in a sealed envelope to be opened only by the Medical Review Officer if the test results is positive.

(c) The employee shall receive a full copy of any test results and related documentation of the testing process.

(d) All confirmed positive samples shall be retained by the testing laboratory in secure frozen storage for one year following the test or until the sample is no longer needed for appeal proceeding litigation, whichever is longer. At employee's request and expense the sample may be retested by that laboratory of another laboratory of the employee's choice.

# 599.965 Medical Review Officer

Each appointing power shall designate one or more Medical Review Officers, who shall be licensed physicians, to receive test results from the laboratory. Upon receiving results, the Medical Review Officer shall:

(a) Review the results and determine if the standards and procedures required by this Article have been followed.

(b) For positive results, interview the affected employee to determine if factors other than illegal drug use may have caused the result.

(c) Consider any assertions by the affected employee of irregularities in the sample collection and testing process.

(d) Based on the above, provide a written explanation of the test results to the appointing power or his/her designee. The employee shall also receive a copy of the explanation.

## 599.966 Records; Confidentiality

As prescribed by the director, each appointing power shall maintain records of the circumstances and results of any employee under this Article. These records, and any other information pertaining to an employee's drug or alcohol test, shall be considered confidential and shall be released only to:

(a) The employee who has tested or other individuals designated in writing by that employee.
(b) The appointing power's Medical Review Officer.
(c) The Department of Personnel Administration as needed for the effective administration of the Article.
(d) Individuals who need the records or information to:

(1) Properly supervise assign employee.
(2) Determine, or assist in determining, what action the appointing power should take in response to the test results.
(3) Respond to appeals or litigation arising from the drug test or related actions.

Department of Personnel, State of California
Title 2, Register 89, No. 37

# Bargaining Unit Agreement

Agreement between International Union of Operating Engineers and The State of California for Maintenance Employees

## Commercial Drivers License
## Drug And Alcohol Agreement

Federal Regulations 49 Code of Federal Regulations (CFR) Parts 382, et. al. and 40 CFR Part 40 require the State of California (State) to test its commercial drivers for controlled substances and alcohol. As specified below, this requirement covers certain employees in Bargaining Unit 12. Having met and conferred, the State and the International Union of Operating Engineers (IUOE), agree to the following regarding the impact of this testing on employees in Unit 12.

### 1. Authority And Purpose

A.. The State will conduct drug and alcohol testing of commercial drivers in Bargaining Unit 12, as specified in Federal Regulations 49 CFR Parts 382, et al. and 49 CFR Part 40. This is in addition to and separate from other State drug and alcohol testing provisions (Department of Personnel Administration [DPA] Rules 599.960-599.966 and State Personnel Board Rules 213-213.6).

B. The State will apply this Agreement to all employees in Bargaining Unit 12, other than those in the Department of Transportation, who meet the criteria for testing required by 40 CFR Part 382 et al. This includes employees who:

1. Are in a classification that requires the possession of a Commercial Drivers License (CDL); or who

2. Possess a CDL and drive a motor vehicle for the State of California that:

a) Has a gross combination weight rating or gross combination weight of 26,001 or more pounds inclusive of a towed unit with a gross vehicle weight rating or gross vehicle weight of more than 10,000 pounds; or
b) Has a gross vehicle weight rating or gross vehicle weight of 26,001 or more pounds; or
c) Is designed to transport 16 or more passengers, including the driver; or
d) Is of any size and is used in the transportation of materials found to be hazardous for the purposes of the Hazardous Materials Transportation Act and which require the motor vehicle to be placarded under the Hazardous Materials Regulations (49 CFR Part 172, Subpart F).

3. Possess a CDL, periodically drive a commercial vehicle (as described in subsection 2, above) for the State, and elect to remain in the Federal testing program during their non-driving periods; provided that the State determines that it is feasible and beneficial to the State to have them remain.

C. This Agreement restates and describes certain of the Federal testing provisions and requirements. However, the State and the IUOE agree that the applicable Federal regulations shall be applied in their entirety, and as they are specifically set forth in the CFR.

## II. DPA Consortium
DPA will serve as the administrator for the consortium that will provide drug/alcohol testing services for the Federal testing program to State departments, other than the Department of Transportation.

## III. Types of Testing

A. Random Testing: Each year, a number of drug tests that equals 50 percent of the employees in the DPA consortium will be conducted on employees who are randomly selected from the consortium. In addition, a number of alcohol tests that equals 25 percent of the number of employees in the DPA consortium will be conducted on employees who are randomly selected form the consortium. DPA will randomly select employee names using the HEIDI computer software program.

Employees will usually provide urine specimens (for drug tests) and take breath alcohol tests for the random testing program during normal work hours. Employees whose regularly scheduled work shift occurs outside of the designated collection sites' normal hours of operation may be held after shift to be tested, or the employing department may make arrangements to have them tested during their shift.

In no event shall an employee be called in for the purpose of participating in a random test while the employee is on vacation, regular days off, sick leave, compensating time off, or other leave status.

B. Reasonable Suspicion: Employees will be required to submit to a reasonable suspicion drug test and/or a breath alcohol test if the supervisor has reasonable suspicion to believe that the driver has violated the Federal requirements on the use of controlled substances and/or alcohol. A finding of reasonable suspicion must be based on specific, contemporaneous, articulable observations concerning the appearance, behavior, speech, or body odors of the driver. The observations may include indications of the chronic and withdrawal effects of controlled substances.

Supervisors who make a determination of reasonable suspicion must receive: 1) at least 60 minutes of training on alcohol misuse; and 2) at least an additional 60 minutes of training on controlled substances use. The training shall cover the physical, behavioral, speech, and performance indicators of probable alcohol misuse and use of controlled substances.

A CDL holder covered by this testing program is subject to reasonable suspicion testing for alcohol anytime the CDL holder is ready to perform, is immediately available to perform, is performing, or has just performed a safety-sensitive function. A CDL holder covered by this testing program is subject to reasonable suspicion tests for drugs anytime the CDL holder is on duty.

The basis for all reasonable suspicion determinations shall be documented as follows:

1) Preliminary documentation. Before the employee is sent to provide a urine specimen and/or take an alcohol breath test, the employee shall be given a preliminary, informal written statement that indicates why the employee is being sent to testing. The purpose of this is to give the employee a specific but concise summary of why he/she is being sent to testing. Because of the need to act quickly in these situations, these statements nay not contain a complete narration of the observations and circumstances surrounding the decision to initiate a reasonable suspicion test.

2) Official reasonable suspicion documentation will be completed and made available to the employee within two working days after being asked to submit to testing. This will be a specific, written description of the observations concerning the employee's appearance, behavior, speech, or body odor that led to the decision to test. It will also list the dates, times and places of these observations, as well as the names of the observers. While the State intends to develop and use standard forms for this purpose, an official documentation will not be deemed to be out of compliance with these requirements simply because it is not presented on a standard form.

3) Differences between the preliminary and official documentation will not, in and of themselves, compromise the integrity of an otherwise valid order to go for a reasonable suspicion drug test.

C. Post Accident: A driver who is in an accident involving a commercial vehicle shall be tested for alcohol and controlled substances if the following conditions exist:

1) The driver was performing safety-sensitive functions with respect to the vehicle, and the accident involved the loss of human life; or

2) The driver received a citation under State of local law for a moving traffic violation arising from the accident, and the accident involved bodily injury requiring treatment away from the scene and/or resulted in damage to any vehicle that required the vehicle to be towed/transported away.

D. Pre-Employment/Pre-Duty Testing: A pre-employment/pre-duty controlled substance and alcohol test must be conducted before the first time a driver performs a safety-sensitive function for the State. A driver must also take a pre-duty controlled substances and alcohol test when he/she transfers from a position not performing safety-sensitive functions to a position performing safety-sensitive functions. This also applies to a driver returning form a leave of absence for more than 30 days due to illness, lay-off, injury, extended leave, (paid or unpaid) etc., who has not remained in the controlled substances and alcohol testing program and, therefore, has not been subject to the random testing process. A negative test result is required prior to performing safety-sensitive functions.

A driver may be exempted from pre-employment/pre-duty testing if the State verifies his/her participation in and compliance with a Federal testing program under a prior employer, as specified in the Federal regulations.

E. Return-To-Duty Testing: Employees who have engaged in prohibited conduct under the Federal regulations must submit to and pass a return-to-duty test prior to performing safety-sensitive duties again.

F. Follow-Up Testing: Following the Substance Abuse Professional's (SAP) determination that the employee has properly followed the SAP's recommendation for rehabilitation, the employee will be subject to a minimum of 6 unannounced follow-up alcohol and/or drug tests during the first 12 months following his/her return to work. Any additional testing or other requirements will be specified in the employee's last chance agreement.

## IV. Testing Process

### A. Drug Testing

Following are the controlled substances (drugs) included in the Federal testing program, and the cut-off levels used in the tests for each of them. This information was current when this Agreement was signed but is subject to change by the Federal government.

| Confirmatory Substance | Cut-Off | Cut-Off |
| --- | --- | --- |
| Amphetamines/ Methamphetamine | 1,000 nanograms per milliliter | 500 nanograms per milliliter |
| Cannabinoids | 50 nanograms per milliliter | 15 nanograms per milliliter |
| Cocaine (Bensoylecogonine) | 300 nanograms per milliliter | 150 nanograms per milliliter |
| Opiates | 300 nanograms per milliliter | 300 nanograms per milliliter |
| Phencyclidine (PCP) | 25 nanograms per milliliter | 25 nanograms per milliliter |

Drug testing shall be performed on a urine sample using an immunoassay screening test and gas chromatography/mass spectrometry confirmatory test for positive tests. The State shall use a SAMSHA-approved laboratory for these tests.

### B. Alcohol Testing

Alcohol testing will be performed by certified Breath Alcohol Technicians (BATs) using Federally-approved (NHTSA) evidential breath testing devices. For a positive test result with an alcohol level of 0.02 to 0.039, the employee may not be assigned to perform safety-sensitive functions for a period of 24 hours. For a positive test result with an alcohol level of 0.040 and above, the employee has violated 49 CFR.

c, Urine Collection/Breath Testing Process

Urine collection/breath alcohol testing services will generally be conducted in private clinical facilities. In addition, the State will utilize on-site (mobile) urine collection/breath alcohol testing services provided by private contractors. The State will specifically inform IUOE of any situations in which State agencies plan to use their own staff and facilities to collect urine samples.

Time that is required for the employee to provide urine samples and take breath tests for the random, reasonable suspicion, post-accident, and follow-up testing programs shall be considered State work time. This shall be the time required to travel to the collection/testing site, the time involved in waiting for and completing the collection/testing process, and travel back to the employee's headquarters. If the employee returns to his/her home after the collection/testing process, that travel time, minus the employee's normal commute time from home to headquarters, shall also be work time. Pre-duty testing that is required because of the State-initiated assignment of commercial driving duties to an employee shall also be covered by this provision.

If urine collection/breath testing is not completed until after the completion of the employee's scheduled work day, of if the employee is to remain away fro the worksite pending the outcome of the tests, the employing State agency shall ensure that the employee has a safe and reasonable way to get home.

D. Re-Tests

For controlled substance tests, employees may request that a re-test, using the second portion of their split-sample urine specimen, be conducted at a NIDA-certified laboratory of their choice, provided they do it through the Medical Review Officer (MRO) who reviewed their laboratory results and make their request within 72 hours of receiving notice of the MRO's determination regarding the results of the first drug test. If the second test confirms the results of the first drug test, the employee will pay for the costs of the second test. If the re-test is done at the laboratory that is under contract with the State consortium, the cost will be equal to the rate specified in the contract with the laboratory for re-tests. If the second test indicates that the first test results were erroneous, the State will pay for the second test.

## E. Medical Review Officer Services

All drug test results will be reviewed by a MRO, who, in turn, will report his/her finding to the State agency. MRO services will be provided by a licensed physician (medical doctor or doctor of osteopathy) who has knowledge of substance abuse disorders and has appropriate medical training to interpret and evaluate drug test results.

## F. Substance Abuse Professional Services

In accordance with Section IX, all employees who test positive for drugs or alcohol will be referred to a SAP for evaluation. SAP services will be provided by a licensed physician (medical doctor or doctor of osteopathy), or a licensed or certified psychologist, social worker, employee assistance professional, or addiction counselor (certified by the National Association of Alcoholism and Drug Abuse Counselors Certification Commission), with knowledge of and clinical experience in the diagnosis and treatment of drug and alcohol-related disorders. DPA will provide a statewide network of SAPs. The State will pay for the State-provided SAP services. Any prescribed rehabilitation will be on the employee's own time and expense (except as any of these expenses may be covered by the employee's State health insurance plan).

G. All procedures used for urine collection (including that involving State staff and/or facilities), breath alcohol testing, laboratory analysis of urine specimens, medical review of test results, and SAP evaluations shall be in conformance with 49 CFR Part 40 and 40 CFR Part 382, et al. as they now exist, or may exist in the future.

# V. Employee Rights And Representation

A. The collection of a urine specimen and the administration of a breath test are not, in themselves, investigative interviews that would trigger an employee right to representation. However, the State agrees to make reasonable effort to grant employee requests for representation during the urine sample and breath alcohol testing process, provided that this can be done without delaying the testing process or causing operational difficulties for the State.

B. In addition, employees have the right to representation at any investigative interview that could lead to a decision by the State to take adverse action. Notwithstanding subsection A, this includes any such interviews that occur in conjunction with the urine sample collection/breath testing process.

C. Employees also have the right to representation in any discussion with the MRO except that the inability of the employee to arrange for such representation may not delay the conversation beyond 5 days after the earliest of the following: a) being contracted by the MRO; or b) being contracted by the State and ordered to contact the MRO; or c) not being available for employer contact after a good faith effort on the employer's part. If the employee fails to arrange for representation, the employee may either discuss the findings of the lab results with the MRO or decline to do so; in either case, the MRO will proceed to issue a determination regarding the results of the drug test. Conversations between the MRO and the tested employee will be by telephone in all or nearly all cases. In no case, shall the testing and review process be delayed.

## VII. Records And Reports

A. the State will keep all drug testing records (in its possession) that identify or pertain to individual employees confidential, releasing information only according to Federal regulations, State rule, or as expressly authorized by the employee in writing.

B. Employees will receive a copy of the custody and control form certified by the MRO as to the results of all drug tests ordered by the State. Upon written request to the State, the State will send the employee copies of any and all documents that the State has in its possession and that relate to the employee's drug test, including laboratory results, reasonable suspicion documentation, MRO reports, and disciplinary reports. This material will be released to the employee's representative only upon written request of the employee.

C. Statistical information about the drug testing program that cannot be used to identify particular individuals is not confidential.

D. Drug testing records are not confidential, even though they may contain the names of employees who have attended drug-related training sessions.

## VII. Employee Conformance With Federal Requirements

A. All commercial drivers in Unit 12 are expected to comply with the requirements set forth in 49 CFR Parts 40 and 382 et al. Failure to provide a breath sample, refusing to take a required drug test, or engaging in any other conduct that obstructs the testing process shall be considered as insubordination. Any violation of the Federal requirements including but not limited to testing positive may be the basis for adverse action, up to and including dismissal.

B. It is the State's general policy to respond to an employee's first violation of the Federal requirements or any other substance abuse provisions with a "last chance" approach, under which the employee is allowed to retain his/her job, subject to future compliance with these requirements and provisions, successful completion of rehabilitation, follow-up testing, etc. However, each case will be reviewed individually to determine the appropriateness of this approach, realizing that there will be cases in which the severity of the employee's offense, his/her past history, or the particularly sensitive nature of his/her required job duties (e.g., close contact with prisoners or wards) may rule out a "last chance" approach. Adverse action may be included with the last chance agreement.

C. Employees who use prescription medications or over-the-counter medications, which may render them unable to perform their regularly assigned duties safely, must report such use to their supervisor. In such instances, the State may reassign the employee to nonsafety-sensitive duties.

## VIII. Temporary Loss Of A Commercial Drivers License

Employees whose CDL had been revoked, suspended, restricted, or affected by any other action that would limit or restrict the employee's ability to drive a commercial vehicle shall report such loss to their supervisor their first day of work after losing the license.

## IX. Substance Abuse Professional Network

A. If the State contracts with a private provider of the provision of SAP services, as provided in Section IV - F, the State agrees to meet with IUOE to discuss how these services will be provided after October 1, 1997. these discussions will begin by January 1, a997. If the contract for SAP services is terminated prior to January 1, a997 for any reason, these discussion will commence immediately upon that termination.

B. If the State elects not to contract for a SAP network, as provided in Sections IV - F, the following will occur:

1. The State will establish a system under which employees will select their own SAP and either: a) the employee will pay the SAP and will be reimbursed by State for up to $350 of this expense, based on the SAP's normal and customary charges; or b) the SAP will bill the State for up to $350, based on his/her normal and customary charges.

2. The State will be available for informal discussions with IUOE regarding alternative methods of providing SAP services, and agrees to meet with IUOE to discuss this issue beginning on or after June 1 1996.

## X. Conflict Resolution

Any disputes arising from the interpretation of application of Federal Regulations 49 CFR Part 382, et al. and 40 CFR Part 40 shall not be subject to the grievance and arbitration process.

A. when IUOE believes that the CFR provisions are being improperly interpreted or applied by a State agency having commercial drivers, it may provide written notice of this to DPA. Within 30 days of receiving such a notice, DPA shall investigate the alleged improper interpretations or allegations and shall report its findings and any actions back to IUOE.

B. In any conflict between the CFR and this Agreement, the CFR shall prevail. When such a conflict arises, DPA shall do all of the following:

1. Provide written notice to IUOE, describing the conflict and referencing the specific CFR sections(s) from which it arises.

2. Upon written request of IUOE, DPA shall seek a written interpretation form the Federal government regarding any of the referenced CFR provisions that cannot be readily interpreted on their face. This shall not suspend or delay testing, or related practices, that the State believes are necessary to comply with the CFR.

3. when DPA receives such written interpretations from the Federal government, it will share them with IUOE and change its testing practices as necessary, to conform with the Federal interpretation.

C. Should any Federal rule or regulation be enacted, altered, or formally interpreted by the Federal Department of Transportation which creates a conflict with the terms of conditions of this Agreement, the remainder of this Agreement will remain in force. Upon occurrence of such an event, DPA shall provide written notice to IUOE describing the conflict and referencing the specific CFR sections(s) from which it arises and the sections of this Agreement with which it conflicts. Upon occurrence of such an event, the parties will meet and confer as soon as practical to renegotiate the invalidated provisions and/or their impact on the unit members.

This prevision was signed by the Business Representative and three Coordinators of the International Union of Operating Engineers and the following officers of the State of California Department of Personnel Administration, Labor Relations Officer, the Assistant Chief of the Policy Development Office, and the Substance Abuse Program Administrator.

Provided by Policy Development Office
Department of Personnel Administration
State of California.

# Drug Testing Web Sites

Addiction Research Foundation Toronto, Ontario, Canada, www.arf.org
American Council for Drug Education, www.acde.org/
Campaign Drug Free sponsored by the U.S. Naval Reserves
    www.nct.navy.mil/navresfor/cdf/drugfree.html
Candian Centre on Substance Abuse, www.ccsa.ca
Center for Substance Abuse Research, www.bsos.umd.edu/cesar/cesar.html
Centers for Disease Control and Prevention, www.cdc.gov
Community Epidemiology Work Group (CEWG)
    www.cdmgroup.com/CEWG/
Drug Enforcement Administration (DEA), www.usdoj.gov/dea/
Elks Drug Awareness Program, www.elks.org/drugs
European Monitoring Centre for Drugs and Drug Addiction (EMCDDA)
    www.emcdda.org
The Higher Education Center for Alcohol and Other Drug Prevention
    www.edc.org/hec/
High Intensity Drug Trafficking Area Program, www.drugs.hidta.org/
The Indiana Prevention Resource Center, www.drugs.indiana.edu/
Institute for a Drug-Free Workplace, www.drugfreeworkplace.org
International Narcotics Control Strategy Report
    www.state.gov/www/global/narcotics_law/
Join Together, www.jointogether.org/jto/
National Association of State Alcohol and Drug Abuse Directors
    www.hasada.org/
National Center on Addiction and Substance Abuse at Columbia
    University (CASA), www.casacolumbia.org
National Clearinghouse for Alcohol and Drug Information,www.health.org
National Drug Intelligence Center, www.usdoj.gov/ndic/
National Families in Action, www.emory.edu/NFIA

National Inhalant Prevention Coalition (NIPC), www.inhalants.org/
National Institute on Drug Abuse, www.nida.nih.gov
OAS Inter-American Drug Abuse Control Commissin
    www.oas.org/EN/PROG/w3/index.htm
Patnership for a Drug-Free America, www.drugfreeamerica.org/
Project funding from HUD to foster Drug Elimination in Public
    and Assisted Housing, www.hud.gov/nofa/suprnofa/supnofa/
    pihdrug.html
RAND Drug Policy Research Center, www.rand.org/centers/dprc
SAMHSA CSAT/TIPs—Treatment Inprovement Protocols
    www.nlm.nih.gov/ftrs/dbaccess/tip
Substance Abuse and Mental Health Services Administration (SAMHSA)
    www.samhsa.gov
Substance Abuse Information Database
    gatekeeper.dol.gov/dol/asp/public/programs/drugs/main.htm
United Nations International Drug Control Programme, www.undcp.org
United Stated Code Chapter 13: Drug Abuse Prevention and Control
    www.law.cornall.edu/uscode/21/ch13.html
Web of Addictions, www.well.com/user/woa/

*Compiled by the National Criminal Justice Reference Service.*

# BIBLIOGRAPHY

— *Urine Specimen Collection Handbook for Ferderal Workplace Drug Testing Program,* CSAP Technical Report 12, DHHS Publications No (SMA) 96-3114, 1996.

Abercrombie, Marsh L., and John S. Jewell, Evaluation of EMIT and RIA High Volume Test Procedures for THC Metabolites in Urine Utilizing GC/Ms Confirmation, *J. Analytical Toxicology,* Sept./Oct. 1986, v. 10, pg. 178-180.

Adams, Marilyn, Drug Tests in View for Truckers, *USA Today,* Jun. 15, 1988.

Adams, William F., and Cynthia L. Remmers, Drugs and Alcohol in the Workplace: Technology, Law and Policy, Santa Clara Computer and High- *Technology Law Journal,* Apr. 1986, v. 2, no. 2.

Adams, William F., and David D. Rosenbloodm, Developments in Drug Testing: the New Federal Standards, *Labor and Employment Law Update,* Apr. 24, 1989, no. 89-4, pg. 1-6, Orrick, Herrington & Sutcliffe, San Francisoc.

Adams, William F., Controlling Drug and Alcohol in the Workplace: Summary of Drug Testing Law and Legislation and Guide to Corporate Policy Development, Institute for Applied Management and Law, San Francisco, Oct. 28, 1988.

Adler, Jerry, Pamela Abramson, Susan Katz, and Mary Hager, Getting High on "Ecstasy," *Newsweek,* Apr. 15, 1985, pg. 96.

Alrazi, J., M. Lehrer, S. J. Mule, and K. Verebey, One Hundred EMIT Positive Cannabinoid Urine Samples Cofirmed by BPA/TLC, RIA, and GC/Ms, *J. Analytical Toxicology,* Mar./Apr. 1986, v. 10, pg. 79.

American Civil Liberies Union, What ACLU Has to Say About ... Drug Testing in the Workplace, American Civil Liberies Union, New York, 1986.

American Civil Liberties Union, Drug Tests Halted, *ACLU News,* Oct./Nov. 1986.

Anagarola, Robert T., and Judith R. Brunton, Legal Implications for Corporate Actions, *Substance Abuse in the Workplace,* Haight-Ashbury Publications, San Francisco: April 1985, pg. 35-42.

Angarola, Robert A., Drug Detection Programs in Industry, *PharmChem Newsletter,* Jul./Aug. 1984, v. 13, no. 4, pg. 4.

Armbrister, Trevor, We Can Conquer Cocaine, *Reader's Digest,* Feb. 1987, pg. 63-68.

Associated Press Staff Writers, THC in Pot Eats Away at Brain Cells, Study Says, *San Francisco Examiner,* Sep. 25, 1986, pg. A-11.

Baselt, R. C., Stability of Cocaine in Biological Fluids, *J. Chromatography,* 1983, v. 268, no. 3, pg. 502-505.

Baumgartner, W. A., Hill, V. A., and W. H. Blahd. Hair Analysis for Drugs of Abuse, J. of Forensic Science, 1989, vol. 34, pp. 1433-53.

Beggs, Charles E., Move to Legalize Pot on Oregon Ballot, Associated Press, 1986.

Bennett, John, Tests for Drug Use Predicted to Spread Through Federal Workforce, *Rocky Mountain News,* Mar. 4, 1986.

Bennett, William, *National Drug Control Strategy,* U.S. Governement Printing Office, Sep. 1989.

Berger, Gilda, *Drug Testing,* Impact Books, NY: 1987.

Blanck, D. L., and D. A. Kidwell. External Contamination of Hair by Cocaine: An Issue In Forensic Interpretation. Forensic Science International, 1993, vol. 63, pp. 145-56.

Bloch, Jeff, So What?, Everbody's Doing It, *Forbes,* Aug. 11, 1986, pg. 102.

Bodovitz, Kathy, Refinery Workers Ask for Drug Test Ban, *San Francisco Chronicle,* Jan. 17, 1987.

Bogdanich, Walt, Labs Offering Workplace Drug Screens in New York Have Higher Error Rate, *The Wall Street Jounal,* Feb. 2, 1987.

Bogdanich, Walt, Medical Labs, Trusted as Largely Error-Free, are Far From Infallible, *The Wall Street Journal,* Feb. 2, 1987.

Boone, Joe, Obtaining and Maintaining Reliable Drug Testing Services, Centers for Disease Control, Public Health Service, U.S. Dept. of Health and Human Services, pg. 1-8.

Brinkley, Joel, U.S. Illegal Drugs at Record Levels, *Oakland Tribune,* Jun. 2, 1986, pg. A-1.

Burmaster, David R., EmployeeDrug Use Creates Losses But Proper Polices Can Control It, *Occupational Health and Safety,* Dec. 1985, pg. 39.

Burrough, Bryan, HOw GM Began Using Private Eyes in Plants to Fights Drugs, Crime, *The Wall Street Journal,* Feb. 27, 1986.

Burton, Ann, and Syva Company, Syva Product Literature Syva Company, Palo Alto, CA., August 30, 1983.

Cais, M., S. Dani, and M. Shimoni, A Novel Non-Centrifugation Radioimmunoassay for Cannabinoids, *Isr. Arch. Toxicology,* 1983, v. 53, suppl. 6, pg. 105-113.

California Government Code, Dept. of Personnel Administration, Title 2, Article 29, Substance Abuse, Register 89, No. 37, Sep. 16, 1989.

California Government Code, State Personnel Board, Title 2, 213, Register 89, No. 18, May 6, 1989.

Callen, Kate, How Cocaine Kills - Even in Tiny Doses, *San Francisco Examiner,* Sep. 25, 1986, pg. A-12.

Carlseen, William, Trucker Fights "Zero Tolerance" Seizure of Rig, *San Francisco Chronicle,* Jul. 1988.

Castro, Janice, Telltale Hair, *Time Magazine,* Mar. 17, 1986, pg. 55.

Castro, Janice, Telltale Hair, *Time,* Mar. 17, 1986, pg. 55.

Center for Disease Control, The Results of Unregulated Testing, JAMA, Apr, 26, 1985.

Chen, Edward, M., and John M. Ture, III, Recent Developments in Employment Drug Testing, *Civil rights and Attorney's Fee Annual Handbook,* 1989, Vol. 4.

Christophersen, Asbjorg S., Tetrahydrocannabinal Stability in Whole Blood: Plastic Versus Glass Containers, *J. Analytical Toxicology,* Jul./Aug. 1986, v. 10, pg. 129-131.

Clare, Anthony W., Drugs Are Big Business, *World Health,* June 1986, pg. 18-19.

Clark, Matt, and Karen Springen, Docs and Drugs, *Newsweek,* Oct. 6, 1986, pg. 28

Cody, J. T. and R. H. Schwarzhoff. Impact of Adulterants of RIA Analysis of Urine for Drugs of Abuse. J. of Analytical Toxicology, 1989, vol. 13, pp. 277-84.

Collins, Robert, U. S. District Judge, Perspectives Quote, *Newsweek,* Nov. 24, 1986, pg. 29.

Collins, William C., Urine Testing and the Workplace: Some Legal Considerations, Syva Company, Palo Alto, CA, 1986, pg. 1-20.

Cone, E. J. Marijuana Effects and Urinalysis After Passive Inhalation and Oral Ingestion. Laboratory of Chemical and Drug Metabolism, NIDA, Research Monograph, 1990, Vol. 99, Pp. 88-96.

Cone, E. J. Testing human hair for drugs of abuse: Individual does and time profiles of morphine and codeine in plasma, saliva, urine, and beard compared to drug-induced effects on pupils and behaivor. Journal of American Toxicology 14:1-7, 1990.

Cone, E. J., et al., Passive Inhalation of Marijuana Smoke: Urinealysis and Room Air Levels of Delta-9-Tetrahydrocannabinol. J. Anal. Toxicol. 11:89-96(1987)

Cone, E. J., Johnson, R.e., Darwin, W. D., Yousefnejad, D., Mell, L.D., Paul, B. D., and J. Mithcell. Passive Inhalation of Marijuana Smoke: Urinalysis and Room Levels of Delta-9-Tetrahydrocannabinol. J. of Analytical Toxicology, 1987, Vol. 11, pp. 89-95.

Cone, E.J., Hillsgrove, M.J., Jenkins, A.J., Keenan, R. M., and Darwin, W.D. Sweat testing for heroin, cocaine, and metabolites. Journal of Analytical Toxicology 18:298-305, 1994.

Cook, Stephen C., Cocaine Crack; Quick, Convenient — and Deadly, San Francisco Examiner, Jul. 6, 1986, pg. A-1.

Crane, Richard, Legal Issues in Employee Drug Detection Programs, Syva Product Literature, Syva Co., Palo Alto, CA., 1987.

Danner, Mark D., M. Kleiman, A. Revach, R. Stutman, R. Giulani, L. Garcia, L. Grinspoon, E. Van Den Haag, and H. London, What is America's Drug Problem?, Harper's Magazine, Dec. 1985, pg. 39.

de Bernardo, Mark A., and Nancy N. Delogu, 1997-1998 Guide to State and Federal Drug-Testing Laws, Sixth Edition, Institute for a Drug-Free Workplace (800/842-7400), Washington, D.C.

de Bernardo, Mark A., Drug & Alcohol Abuse Prevention and the ADA: An Employer's Guide, The Institute for a Drug-Free Workplace, Washington D.C., 1992.

Decresce, Robert P., and Mark S. Lifshits, Drug Testing in The Workplace, American Society of Clinical Pathologists Press and The Bureau of National Affairs Books, 1989.

Denniston, Lyle, U.S. Issues Guidelines for Fighting Jar Wars, San Francisco Examiner, Feb. 20, 1987.

Dezelsky, T.L., J.V. Toohey, and R.S. Shaw, Non-Medical Drug Use Behaviour ar Five United States Universities: A 15-year Study, Bulletin on Marcotics, 1985, v. 37, no. 2-3, pg. 49-53.

Dickey, Glenn, NCAA Should Just Say No to Drug Testing, San Francisco Chronicle, Mar. 30, 1987, pg. 25.

Didson, Marcida, Drug Testing Comes Home, San Francisco Chronicle, Jun. 6, 1989, pg. B-6.

Diegelman, Robert, Substance Abuse: The Business Approach, Substance Abuse in the Workplace, Haight-Ashbury Publications, San Francisco: April 1985, pg. 57-75.

DuPont, Robert L., Awash in Alcohol, Listen, Oct. 1983, pg. 11.

DuPont, Robert L., Marijuana, Alcohol, and Adolescence: A Malignant Synergism, Seminars in Adolescent Medicine, Dec. 1985, v. 1, no. 4, pg. 311.

DuPont, Robert L., Substance Abuse, JAMA, Oct. 25, 1985, v. 254, no. 16, pg. 2335.

DuPont, Robert L., Testimony by Robert L. DuPont, M.D. Before the Subcommittee on Health and Safety, Commitee on Education and Labor, U.S. House of Rep., Oct. 31, 1985.

DuPont, Robert L., The Drug Epidemic and Related Disasters Getting Tough on Gateway Drugs, AMA: 1988.

DuPont, Robert L., The Treatment and Prevention of Substance Abuse in Adolescents, *Directions in Psychiatry,* 1984, v. 4, lesson 33, pg. 1-8.

DuPont, Robert L., The Treatment and Prevention of Substance Abuse in Adolescents, *Directions in Psychiatry,* 1984, v. 4, lesson 33, pg. 1-8.

DuPont, Robert L., Urine Testing in the Workplace, *The U.S. J. Drug and Alcohol Dependence,* Jan. 27, 1986.

Dutt, M. C., Laboratory Diagnosis of Opiate Drugs, *Ann. Acad. Med. Singapore,* 1984, v. 13, no. 1, pg. 53-65.

E.D. Wish and B. Gropper, 1990. "Drug testing by the criminal justice system." In Drugs and Crime, ed. Michael Tonry and James Q. Wilson, vol. 13 of Crime and Justice: A Review of Research. Chicago, University of Chicago Press.

Editorial Staff, City's Landmark Privacy Ordinance, *Marin Independent Journal,* Dec. 2, 1985.

Editorial Staff, Drug Tests Aren't the American Way, *Marin Independent Journal,* Mar. 8, 1986.

Editorial Staff, Exclusive Report: Drug Abuse in the Printing Industries, *Printing Impressions,* Aug. 1986, pg. 6.

Elahi, Nasik, Encapsulated XAD-2 Extraction Technique for a Rapid Screening of Drugs of Abuse in Urine, *J. Analytical Toxicology,* Jan./Feb. 1980, v. 4, pg. 26-30.

Erickson, P. G., Cannabis Legislation Reforms in the USA, an Unfinished Job, *Psychotropes,* 1985, v. 2, no. 1, pg. 96-98.

Ferslew, K. E., J. E. Manno, and B. R. Manno, Determination of Urinary Cannabinoid Metabolites Following Incidental Exposure to Marijuana Smoke, *Res. Common. Substance Abuse,* 1983, v. 4, no. 4, pg. 289-300.

Findlay, Steven, Kids May Be Catching Adults' Cocaine Habit *USA Today,* May 23, 1986.

Flinn, John "Ecstasy" Causes Agony for Doctors, Government, *San Francisco Examiner,* May 1985, pg. A3.

Frank, James F., and Theodore E. Anderson, Feasibility Assessment of Chemical Testing for Drug-Impaired Driving, National Technical Information Service, Springfield, VA, Sep. 1985.

Freeman, Robert, How to "Beat" a Drug Test, *High Times,* Aug. 1988, no. 156, pg. 19.

Garner, Joe, New Railroad Rules on Drugs Take Effect, *Rocky Mountain News,* Jan. 28, 1986.

Gieringer, Dale, (ed.) Drug Testing Advice, *California NORML Reports,* Feb. 1988, v. 12, no. 1.

Gold, M.D., Mark S., and Charles A. Dackis, M.D., Role of the Laboratory in the Evaluation of Suspected Drug Abuse, *J. Clinical Psychiatry,* Jan. 1986, v. 47, no.1, pg. 17-23.

Goldberg, Jeff, and Dean Latimer, Future Drugs - They're All in Your Head, *High Times,* October, 1987.

Goldstein, Richard, Getting Real About Getting High, *Voice,* Sep. 30, 1986, pg.21.

Goodman, Richard A., Alcohol Use and Homicide, *PharmChem Newsletter,* Mar./Apr. 1986, v. 15, no. 2, pg. 1-9.

Gordon, Bill, Judge Halts Drug Tests at East Bay Refinery, *San Francisco Chronicle.*

Gottheil, Edward, Glenn R. Caddy, Ph.D., and Deborah L. Austin, Fallibility of Urine Drug Screens in Monitoring Methadone Programs, *JAMA,* Aug. 30, 1976, V. 236, no. 9, pg, 1035-1038.

Greenhouse, Linda, Court Backs Tests of Some Workers to Deter Drug Use, *The New York Times,* Mar. 22, 1989.

Greenhouse, Linda, Justice Hearn Thornburgh Defend Drug-Testing Plan, *The New York Times*, Nov. 3, 1988, pg. A-10.

Guinn, Bobby, Job Satisfaction, Counterproductive Behavior and Circumstantial Drug Use Among Long-Distance Truckers, *J. Psychoactive Drugs*, Jul./Sep. 1983, v. 15, no. 3, pg. 185-188.

Gupta, R. N., Drug Level Monitoring: Sedative Hypnotics, *J. Chromatogr. Biomed. Appl.*, 1986, v. 340, pg. 139-172.

Hanners, David, Powdered Urine Seen as Million Dollar Idea, *The Dallas Morning News*, Dec. 14, 1986.

Hansen, H. J., S. P. Caudill, and D. J. Boone, Crisis in Drug Testing, *JAMA*, 1985, v. 253, no. 16, pg. 2382-2387.

Henderson, G. L., Harkey, M.R., and C. Zhou. Incorporation of Isotopically Labeled Cocaine and Metabolites Into Human Hair: 1 Dose-Response Relationships, J. of Analytical Toxicology, 1996, vol. 20, pp. 1-11.

Hennegerg, M., I. Wozniak, D. Brodzinska, and K. Wencel, An Original 'Street Test' for Urine Screening for Morphine and Its Evaluation, Med. Cent. Grad. Educ., Bydgoszcz Pol, *Alcohol Alcohol*, 1984, v. 19, no. 4, pg. 311-317.

Herzfeld, John, Brain Scans on the Job? *American Health*, Jul./Aug. 1986, pg. 72.

Hoffman, Abbie, with Jonathan Silvers, *Steal This Urine Test*, Penquin Books, 1987.

Hoffman, Joan W., and Ken Jennings, Will Drug Testing in Sports Play for Industry? *Personnel J.*, May 1987, pg. 52.

Holtorf, Kent, *UR-INE Trouble*, Vandalay Press, Scottsdale, 1997.

Jacoby, Tamar, Drug Testing in the Dock, *Newsweek Magazine*, Nov. 14, 1988. pg. 66.

Jarvis, Birney, State High Court Halts CHP Plan for Traffic checkpoints, *San Francisoc chronicle*, Dec. 20, 1986.

Jenkins, A.J., Keenan, R.M., Henningfield, J.E., and Cone, E. J. Pharmacokinestics and pharmocodynamics of smoking heroin. Journal of Analytical Toxicology 18:317-330, 1994.

Jones, A. B., H. N. Elsohly, E. S. Aragat, and M. A. ElSohly, Analysis of the Major Metabolite of Delta-9 Tetrahydrocannabinol in Urine. IV. A Comparison of Five Methods. *J. Analytical Toxicology*, 1984, v. 8, no. 6, pg. 249-251.

Jones, Donald W., D. Adams, P. Martel, and R. Rousseau, Drug Population in 1000 Geographically Distributed Urine Specimens, *J. Analytical Toxicology*, May/Jun. 1985, v. 9, pg. 125-130.

Joseph, R. E., Su, T, and E. J. Cone. In Vitro Binding Studies of Drugs Into Hair: Influence of Melanin and Lipids on Cocaine Binding to Causasoid and Africoid Hair. J. of Analytical Toxicology, 1996, vol. 20, pp 338-44.

Joseph, R., Dickerson, S., Willis, R., Frankenfield, D., Cone, E. J., and D. R. Smith. Interference by Nonsteroidal Anti-Inflammatory Drugs in EMIT and TDx Assays for Drugs of Abuse, 1995, vol. 19, pp. 13-7.

Kaye, Elizabeth, Drugless in L.A., *This World*, May 11, 1986, pg. 10.

Kerr, Peter, Anatomy of an Issue: Drugs, the Evidence, the Reaction, *The New York Times*, Nov. 17, 1986, pg. 1.

Kerr, Peter, Drug Tests Losing Most Court Cases, *The New York Times*, Dec. 11, 1986.

Kim, Hyum J., and Eugene Cerceo, Interference by NaCl With the EMIT Method of Analysis for Drugs of Abuse, *Clinical Chemistry*, 1976, v. 22, no. 11, pg. 1935.

Kirp, David L., Taking Uncivil Liberites: Mass Drug Testing, *Christian Science Magazine*, Mar. 25, 1986.

Klehs, Johan, Statement by Assemblyman Johan Klehs - Interim Hearings on Drug Testing, Assembly Bill 4242, Oct. 2, 1986.

Klein, Alfred, Employees Under the Influence - Outside the Law? *Personnel J.*, Sep. 1986, pg. 57-71.

Klein, Joe, The New Drug They Call Ecstsay, *This World*, Jun. 23, 1985, pg. 10-11.

Kopp, Quentin, San Francisco Drug-Test Law Impinges on Employers' Rights, *San Francisco Business Times*, Oct. 20, 1986, pg. 6.

Lacayo, Richard, Putting Them All to the Test, *Time*, Oct. 21, 1985, pg. 61.

Latimer, Dean, Drug Test Shocker: Alka Seltzer Scores as Dope! *High Times Magazine*, Sept. 1986, pg. 15.

Latimer, Dean, "Freedom Chemist" Admits Scam: "Melanin", *High Times*, Apr. 1987, pg. 20.

Latimer, Dean, Highwitness News: What To Do If You're Fired By A. Urine Test, *High Times Magazine*, Nov. 1986, pg. 14.

Latimer, Dean, Reliability of Drug Tests, *High Times Magazine*, Oct. 1986, pg. 56-59.

Law, B., P. A. Mason, A. C. Moffat, and L. J. King, A Novel 125-I Radioimmunoassay for the Analysis of Delta-9 Tetrahydrcannabinal and its Metabolites in Human Body Fluids, *J. Analytical Toxicology*, 1984, v. 8, no. 1, pg. 14-18.

Law, B., P. A. Mason, A. C. Moffat, and L. J. King, Confirmation of Cannabis Use by the Analysis of Delta-9 Tetrahydrocannibinol Metabolites in Blood and Urine by Combined HPLC and RIA, *J. Analytical Toxicology*, 1984, v. 8, no. 1, pg. 19-22.

Law, B., P. A. Mason, and A. C. Moffat, Forensic Aspects of the Metabolism and Excretion of Cannabinoids Following Oral Ingestion of Cannabis Resin, *J. Pharmaceutical Pharmacology*, 1984, v. 36, no. 5, pg. 289-294.

Leib, John, 30% of Major Businesses Testing for Drugs, *The Denver Post*, Mar. 23, 1986.

Lempinen, Edward W., and Tim Schriener, Bay Area Cuts Drug Use — But Still Leads the U.S., *San Francisco Chronicle*, 1986, pg. 1.

Less, Mura, Highwitness News: Piss Patrol Spotlight On: 3M, *High Times Magazine*, Sep. 1988, pg. 20.

Lewy, Robert, Preemployment Qualitative Urine Toxicology Screening, *J. Occupational Medicine*, Aug. 1983, v. 25, no. 8, pg. 579-580.

Lieger, James, Coping With Cocaine, The Atlantic, Jan. 1986, pg. 39-48.

Lora-Tamayo, C., Tena, T., and A. Rodriguez. High concentration of Ciprofloxacin in Urine Invalidates EMIT Results. J. of Analytical Toxicology, 1966, vol. 20, pp. 334.

Los Angeles Times Staff Writers, Competing Proposals to Fight Drugs, *San Francisco Chronicle*, Jul. 1, 1988.

Lurie, I. S., Problems in Using High Performance Liquid Chromatography for Drug Analysis, *J. Forensic Science*, 1984, v. 8, no. 6, pg. 149-251.

Macklin, Daphne, ACLU Case List, American Civil Liberities Union, California Legislative Office, Sacramento, CA, Dec. 3, 1986.

Maltby, Lewis L., Why Drug Testing is a Bad Idea, *Inc.*, Jun. 1987, pg. 152.

Manley, Marisa, Employment Lines, *Inc.*, Jun. 1988, pg. 132.

Marine, Craig, Hercules Drug Test in Court, *San Francisco Chronicle*, Oct. 12, 1986.

Martel, Patricia A., Donald W. Jones, and Robert J. Rousseau, Application of Toxi-Lab: A Broad Spectrum Drug Detection system in Emergency Toxicology, American Association for Clinical Chemistry, Aug. 1983, v. 2, no. 2, pg.1.

Martz, Larry, M. Miller, B. Cohn, G. Raine, and G. Carroll, Trying to say "No," *Newsweek*, Aug. 11, 1986, pg. 14.

Marx, Gary T., Drug Foes Aren't High on Civil Liberties, *The New York Times*, Feb. 24, 1986.

Mazzone, Lt. Col., Frank, Substance Abuse in the Workplace: The Securtiy Perspective, *Substance Abuse in the Workplace*, Haight-Ashbury Publications, San Francisco: April 1985, pg. 47-49.

McBurney, L. J., B. A. Bobbie, and L. A. Sepp, GC/Ms and EMIT Analysis for Delta 9-Tetrahydrocannabinol Metabolites in Plasma and Urine of Human Subjects,. *J. Analytical Toxicology*, Mar./Apr. 1986, v. 10, pg. 56-64.

McCarron, Margaret M., Phencyclidine Intoxication, *PharmChem Newsletter*, May/Jun. 1986, v. 15, no. 3, pg. 1-8.

McClellan, Keith, Work-Based Drug Programs, *Substance Abuse in the Workplace*, Haight-Ashbury Publications, San Francisco: April 1985, pg. 57-75.

McDougald, George S., U.S. Postal Service Notice, U. S. Postal Service, Jun. 26, 1986.

McKinney, Debbie, When it Comes to Drug Tests, How Accurate is Positive?, *Anchorage Daily News*, Oct. 6. 1986.

Mikkelsen, S. L., and K. O. Ash. Adulterants Causing False Negatives in Illicit Drug Testing. Clinical Chemistry, 1988, vol. 34, pp. 2333-6.

Miller, M.A. Laurence, Neuropsychological Assessment of Substance Abusers: Review and Recommendations, *J. Substance Abuse Treatment*, 1985, v. 2, pg. 5-17.

Miller, Ph.D., John G., Enzyme Immunoassay, *Lab 78: Lab Med. for Practicing Physicians*, Sep./Oct. 1978, pg. 45-49.

Milstein, Susan, State Court Limits Polygraph Use, *San Francisco Chronicle*, Jun. 26, 1986, pg. 6.

Miners, Ian A., Nick Nykodym, and Diane M. Samerdyke-Traband, Put Drug Detection to the Test, *Personnel J.*, Aug. 1987, Pg. 91.

Mither, Carol Lynn, High on the job, *Glamour*, Aug. 1986, pg. 252.

Montague, Mary W., Bosses Stike Back a Sample-Salting, *High Times Magazine*, Oct. 1986, pg. 15.

Morgan, John P., Urine Trouble — A Physician Looks at Testing, *Question Authority*, Feb. 1988. (Dr. Morgan is a professor at City University of New York).

Morgan, M.D., John P., Problems of Mass Urine Screening for Misused Drugs, *Substance Abuse in the Workplace*, Haigh Ashbury Publications, San Francisco: 1984, pg. 21.

Morganthau, Tom, and Mark Miller, The Drug Warrior, *Newsweek Magazine*, Apr. 10, 1989, pg. 20.

Morganthau, Tom, Mary Hagar, Mark Miller, Kim Willenson, Karen Springen, and Andrew Murr, A Question of Privacy, *Newsweek*, Sep, 29, 1986, pg, 18.

Murphy, Thomas A., Remarks by General Motors Corp. Chairman at the Assoc of Labor-Management Administrators and Consultants on Alcoholism, Inc., Detroit, MI, Oct. 5, 1979.

Neff, Craig, Steroids on Campus: The Boz Flunks Out, *Sports Illustrated*, 1988, pg. 20-25.

Nelson, M.B.A., Jack E., Drug Abusers on the Job, *Occupational Medicine*, June, 1981, v. 23, no. 6, pg. 4o3-408.

New York Times Staff Writers, No Drug Tests for Customs Agents, *San Francisco Chronicle*, Jan. 17, 1987.

Newcomb, Ph.D., Michael D. Ebrahim Maddahian, Ph.D., and P.M. Bentler, Ph.D., Risk Factors for Drug Use Among Adolescents: Concurrent and Longitudinal Analyses, AJPH, May 1986, v. 76, no. 5, pg. 525-531.

Nightbyrd, Jeffrey, *Conquering The Urine Tests: A Complete Guide To Success in Urine Testing,* Byrd Labratories, 225 Congress, Box 340, Austin, TX. 78701, 1986.

Nocella, C.P.P., Henry A., Strategic Planning by Security Personnel, *Substance Abuse in the Workplace,* Haight-Ashbury Publications, San Francisco: April 1985, pg. 43-36.

NORMAL, Urine Testing for Marijuana & Other Drugs, *Common Sense for America,* 1986, pg. 30-31.

O'Conner, Colleen, and Mark Miller, The Military Says "No," *Newsweek,* Nov. 10, 1986, pg. 26.

Oregon Marijuana Initiative, Drug Test Proposals Spark Debate, *The Marijuana Report,* May 1986, v. 5, no. 1.

Parker, E. Parker, J. Brody, and R. Schoenberg., Alcohol Use and Cognitive Loss Among Employed Men and Women, *AJPH,* 1983, v. 73, pg. 521-526.

Pauley, Jane, and Boyd Matson, Drugs in Sports: Striking Out? Today Show, Transcript, NBC-TV, Oct. 24, 1985.

Pear, Robert, Testing Plan Indicates Reagan's "Outrage" Over Drug Abuse, *New York Times,* November 18, 1987.

Peters, Tom, Tom Peters On Defense, Drugs, Education, *Bay Area Business,* pg. 23.

PharmChem Laboratories, Drug Panel (1000) and Methodology, PharmChem Product Brochure, PharmChem Laboratories, Inc., Menlo Park, CA.

PharmChem Laboratories, PharmChem Product Brochure, PharmChem Laboratories Inc., Menlo Park, CA.

Presnall, Lewis F., Folklore and Facts About Employees With Alcoholism, *J. Occupational Medicine,* 1967, v. 9, pg. 187-192.

Press, Aric, Gerald C. Lubenow, and Martin Kasindorf, Reality Versus Rhetoric, *Newsweek,* Sep. 8, 1986, pg. 60.

Product Literature, Abuscreen - Radioimmunoassay for Cannabinoids, Roche Dianostic Systems, New Jersey.

Product Literature, Abuscreen - Radioimmunoassay for Morphine, Roche Dianostic Systems, New Jersey.

Product Literature, KDI Quik Test, Brown Boxenbaum, Inc., New York, Dec. 4, 1987.

Product Literature, Luckey Laboratories, Inc., San Bernardino, CA, Bulletin no. S69.

Product Literature, Spot THC Without Instrumentation - Toxi-Lab Cannabinoid (THC) Screen, Analytical Systems, Kansas City, MO.

Quayle, Dan, American Productivity: The Devastating Effect of Alcoholism and Drug Abuse, *American Psychologist,* Apr. 1983, pg. 454.

Rajananda, V., N. K. Nair, and V. Navaratnam, An Evaluation of TLC Systems for Opiate Analysis, *Bulletin of Narcotics,* 1985, v. 37, no. 1, pg. 35-47.

Ray, L., Problems of Substance Abuse: Exploitation and Control, *Soc. Sci. Med,.* 1985, v. 20, no. 12, pg. 1225-1233.

Renauer, Albin, Drug Testing and Privacy Rights at Work, *Nolo News,* Summer 1988, pg. 10.

Rowan, Carl T., The Rush To Draconian Measures, *The Washington Post,* Sep. 14, 1986.

Rutkowski and Associates, *Employment Law Update,* Sep. 1986, v. 1, no. 1, pg. 1-8.

Sachs, Stephen H., Jack Swartz, and Gail Smith, Maryland Attorney General Letter, Office of the Attorney General, Oct. 22, 1986, pg. 1-30.

Safire, William, Frisking Each Other, *New York Times,* Mar. 14, 1986.

San Francisco City. Part II, Chapter VIII, Article 33A. San Francisco Municipal Code.

Sandlow, Marc, BART Sidetracks Drug Tests, *San Francisco Chronicle,* May 5, 1987.

Sax, Brian M., and William F. Adams, The Continuing Problem of Drug and Alcohol Use in the Workplace, Orrick, Herrington & Sutcliffe, Seventh Annual Seminar for Employers, San Francisco,

Schwarzhoff, R. H., and J. T. Cody. The Effect of Adulterating Agents on FPIA Analysis of Urine for Drugs of Abuse, J. of Analytical Toxicology, 1993, vol. 17, pp. 14-7.

Seymour, Senator John, Interim Hearings on Status of Drug Testing in the Workplace, California Legislature Sensate Select Committee on Substance Abuse. Oct. 25, 1988 in Sacramento, Oct. 26, 1988 in San Francisco.

Shafer, Jack, MDMA: Psychedelic Drug Faces Regulation, Psychology Today, May 1985, pg. 68.

Siegel, Ronald K., Animal Intoxication, This World, Apr. 6, 1986, pg. 9.

Siegel, Ronald K., Jungle Revelers, Omni, pg. 71.

Singleton, Jill, Worker Sues for $2 Million Over a Forced Blood Test, San Francisco Chronicle, Oct. 10, 1986, pg. 6.

Smith, David, Urine Testing in the Workplace: Standards of Practice and Evaluation of Results, Proceeds of the Institute for Addiction Studies, Oct. 3, 1986, Oakland, Ca.

Smith, David E., and Donald R. Wesson, Substance Abuse in Industry: Identification, Intervention, Treatment and Prevention, Substance Abuse in the Workplace, Haight-Ashbury Publications, San Francisco: 1984, pg. 5.

Smith, R. M., Arylhydroxy Metabolites of Cocaine in the Urine of Cocaine Users, J. Analytical Toxicology, 1984, v. 8, no. 1, pg. 35-37.

Staff Writer, 'Disease Concept' a Drug Debate Smoke Screen, The Journal, Jan. 1, 1985, pg. 9.

Staff Writer, Anti-Drug Smuggling Campaign Called Ineffective, San Francisco Chronicle, Jun. 9, 1989, Section A.

Staff Writer, Can You Pass the Job Test? Newsweek, May 5, 1986, pg. 46.

Staff Writer, First the Lie Detector, Then the Chemicals, Newsweek, Jan. 27, 1986.

Staff Writer, How People Fight Back, American Health, Jul./Aug. 1986.

Staff Writer, Probe of FAA's Laboratories, San Francisco Chronicle, Apr. 24, 1987.

Staff Writer, Ten Years of Legalization in Alaska, Common Sense for America, pg. 10-11.

Staff Writer, Texan is Selling Drug-Free Urine to Meet "Unanticipated Demand," The New York Times, Nov. 29, 1986.

Staff Writer, The High Court Weighs Drug Tests, Newsweek magazine, Apr. 3, 1989, pg. 8.

Staff Writer, Urine for Fun and Profit, Frontlines, Mother Jones, Apr. 1987, pg. 11.

Staff Writer, Urine Testing for Marijuana & Other Drugs, The Common Sense for America, pg. 30-31.

Staff Writers, Anti-Drug Bill Passed By Congress, San Francisco Chronicle, Oct. 18, 1986.

Staff Writers, Drug-Test Rules Belie Reagan's Assurances, San Francisco Chronicle, Nov. 28, 1986.

Staff Writers, The war on Drugs, The Coming Revolution, pg. 32.

Staff Writers, U.S. to Dye Toilet Water Blue in Testing Workers for Drugs, San Francisco Chronicle, Feb. 19, 1987, pg. 13.

Staff, Court Upholds Drug Tests for Job Applicants, San Francisco Chronicle, Nov. 18, 1989, pg. 9.

Staff, Drug Testing, The Office of Continuing Education, University of Texas, Jan. 22, 1987.

Staff, Employee Drug Screening Q & A, National Institute on Drug Abuse, U.S. Dept. of Health and Human Services, 1986, no. (ADM) 86-1442.

Staff, Fight Illegal Drugs; Don't Test Everybody, USA Today, 1986.

Staff, Instructions for U-R-Klean, Houston Enterprises, PO Box 27776, Tempe, Az. 85285-7776

Staff, Interdisciplinary Approaches to the Problem of Drug Abuse in the Workplace, National Institute on Drug Abuse, U.S. Dept. of Health and Human Services, 1986, no. (ADM) 86-1477.

Staff, The Test that Failed, *The Nation*, Jan. 4, 1986, V. 241, pg. 697.

Staff, Urine Tests Are Easily Faked, *Newsweek Magazine*, Jul. 31, 1989, pg. 5.

Stafford, D. T., H. S. Nichols, and W. H. Anderson, Efficiency of Capillary Column Gas Chromatography in Separating Lysergic Acid Diethylamide (LSD) and Lysergic Acid Methlypropylamide (LAMPA), *J. Forensic Science*, 1984, v. 29, no. 1, pg. 291-298.

Steele, Paul D., Labor Perceptions of Drug Use and Drug Programs in the Workplace, *J. Drug Issues*, Summer 1981, pg. 279-292.

Stroock, Anne, Random Drug Test Challenge Upheld, *San Francisco Chronicle*, 23, 1990.

Sutheimer, C. A., R. Yarborough, B. R. Hepler and I. Sunshine, Detection and Confirmation of Urinary Cannabinoids, *J. of Analytical Toxicology*, 1985, v. 9, no. 4, pg, 156-160.

Sutheimer, C. A., R. Yarborough, B. R. Hepler, and I. Sunshine, Detection and Confirmation of Urinary Cannabinoids, *J. Analytical Toxicology*, Jul./Aug. 1985, v. 9, pg. 156.

T. Mieczkowski, 1990. "The accuracy of self-reported drug use: An analysis of new data." In Drugs, Crime and the Criminal Justice System, ed. R. Weisheit, Cincinnati, Ohio, Anderson.

Takas, Marianne, They Want Your Body: Can Your Boss Test You for Drug Use?, *Vogue*, Apr. 1986, v. 176, pg. 156.

Talbot, G. Douglas, Essential Elements of a Model Employee Assistance Program, *Substance Abuse in the Workplace*, Haight-Ashbury Publications, San Francisco: April 1985, pg. 55-56.

Taylor, Jr., Stuart, Justices to Rule on Drug-Testing Plan, *New York Times*, Mar. 1, 1988.

Taylor, Michael, UC Won't Test Workers for Drugs, *San Francisco Chronicle*, Apr. 24, 1987.

Tessler, Ray, Judge Deals Blow to NCAA Drug Tests, *San Francisco Chronicle*, Aug. 11, 1988, pg. 1.

Thomas, Evan, America's Crusade: What is Behind the Latest War on Drugs, *Time*, Sep. 15, 1986, pg. 60.

Trice, Harrison M., and Mona Schonbrunn, A History of Job-Based Alcoholism Programs: 1900-1955, *J. Drug Issues*, Spring 1981, pg. 171-197.

Trice, Harrison M., and Paul M. Roman, *Spirits and Demons at Work: Alcohol and Other Drugs on the Job*, Cornell University Press, Ithaca, NY: 1978.

United States, The Bill of Rights, American Civil Liberties Union, Sacramento, CA.

Vereby, K., D, Jukofsky, and S. J. Mule, Evaluation of a New TLC Confirmation Technique for Positive EMIT Cannabinoid Urine Samples, *Res. Common. Substance Abuse*, 1985, v. 6, no. 1, pg. 1-9.

Verrey, Janice A., NBC News — Case Histories, NBC Network, Sep. 30, 1986, v. 1, no. 14, pg. 1-12.

Visclocky, Peter J., and Anne Marie O'Keefe, When Testing Violates the Constitution, *The Washington Post*, Sep. 14, 1986.

Vogl, Walter F., and Donna M. Bush. Medical Review Officer Manual for Federal Workplace Drug Testing Programs, Substance Abuse and Mental Health Services Administration (SAMHSA), CSAP Technical Report 15, DHHS Publication No (SMA) 97-3164, 1997.

Von Meyer, L., Detection of Cannabinoids in Blood and Urine by EMIT Confirmation by TLC, Z. Rechtsmed., 1985, v. 94, no. 3, pg. 219-225.

Vu Duc, T., EMIT Tests for Drugs of Abuse: Interference by Liquid Soap Preparations, *Clinical Chemistry*, 1985, v. 81, no. 4, pg. 658-659.

W. Baumgartner, V. Hill, and W. Blahd, 1989. "Hair analysis for drugs of abuse." Journal of Forensic Sciences 34, 6: 1433-53.

Walbrecher, David, Information on BreathScan, Prescott Technologies, Inc., Denver, Colorado, Dec. 5, 1986.

Waldholz, Michael, Drug Testing in the Workplace: Whose Rights Take Precedence?, *The Wall Street Journal*, November 11, 1986.

Wallbrecher, David, A Disposable Lifesaver, *Time*, Jul. 14, 1986, pg. 50.

Walsh, Dr. J. Michael, Drugs in the Workplace, PharmChem Product Literature.

Washington Post Staff Writer, What Compromise Drug-Test Program Would Do, *San Francisco Chronicle*, Jun. 5, 1987, pg. 15.

Washington Post Staff Writers Reagan Says None Exempt From Drugs, *San Francisco Chronicle*, Jul. 1, 1988, pg. A16.

Washington Post Syndicate. Drug Tests Nab 203 Federal Wrokers, *San Francisco Chronicle*, Mar. 8, 1989, pg. A-16.

Weir, Jeff, Bill Calls for Drug Testing of Worker, *Los Angeles Times*, Apr. 8, 1986.

Weiss, Philip, Watch Out: Urine Trouble, *Harper's Magazine*, June 1986, pg. 56.

Wessner, Laura, ABC News — Nightline Show #1386, Transcription, Journal Graphics, Inc., New York, Sep. 15, 1986, pg. 1-6.

White, Raymond S., The Let's Party Syndrome, *Street Pharmacologist*, Dec. 1982, v. V, no. 12, pg. 1.

Wicker, Tom, Civil Rights on Trial, *San Francisco Chronicle*, Mar. 14, 1986.

Wilde, James, Crashing on Cocaine, Time, Apr. 11. 1983, pg. 22.

Willette, Dr. Robert E., Formal Policy, Urinalysis Deters Drug Abuse in the Workplace, *PharmChem Newsletter*, Jul./Aug. 1984, v. 13, no. 4, pg. 4.

Willette, Robert E., Development of Assays for Drugs of Abuse, *Controlled Clinical Trials*, 1984, v. 5, pg. 466-471.

Williams, Lena, Reagan Drug Testing Plan to Start Despite Court Rulings Opposing It, *New York Times*, Nov. 29, 1986, pg. 1.

Wilson, Frederick, A Rapid Combined Drug-Screening System, Laboratory Management, Jun. 1984.

Wiltsee, Joe, Your Rights as an Employee, *Business Week Guide to Careers*, 1986, pg. 33.

X, Richard Weed vs. the Writer, *This World*, August 3, 1986, pg. 9.

# Index